Two Dads
and Three Girls

Searching for Sexual Identity, Falling in Love, and Building a Family through Surrogacy

A Memoir

Nick (Yu) He

to Sita,

Thank you for bringing

light to my life ♥

GIFT

Thank you so much for reading our journey of building a family of two dads and three girls with love and courage.

When we were on the surrogacy journey from 2015 to 2017, we always wanted to know how much a surrogacy journey really cost. Most agencies provided a generic range, which was helpful but not detailed enough. We tracked our complex journey, making a note of everything we spent money on, even a meal with the surrogate family or a gift.

In Part 2 of the book, we list lots of details of the surrogacy journey. We think it will be helpful for readers to understand the real costs that are attached to these events. That's why we created the surrogacy expense table to share with you.

To receive the gift, please go to www.2dads3girls.com and click "Gift" to claim yours!

For Mom and Dad, who show me
how to be a good parent.

For Bryan, who teaches me how
to love and be loved.

For Phoebe, Hanalei, and Chelsie,
who open a bigger world and
give more meaning to life.

CONTENT

3:30 a.m., Aug 2010, Vancouver 7

Part 1 - Two Dads 17

    Confused "Straight" Kid 18

    Transition to the West 40

    Meeting Bryan 62

    Couchsurfing in Europe 76

    Letter to Parents 97

    From Two Persons to US 112

Part 2 - Three Girls 130

    We Want to Have Kids 131

    Surrogacy 151

    Phoebe 170

    Becoming Dads 196

    Hanalei and Chelsie 224

    Two Dads and Three Girls 252

3:30 p.m., Dec. 2018, Seattle 268

Letter to Parents (给父母的信) 281

Acknowledgments 286

About the Author 289

Ask and Connect 290

"It is not the years of life you have but the life in those years that matters."

— A Chinese fortune cookie from Chinatown Seattle

3:30 A.M., AUG 2010, VANCOUVER

*I*t was 3:30 a.m., the Vancouver streets freezing and windy. I was moving my feet frantically. I tried to run, but stumbled, wiping the tears running to my chin. I was alone. There were not even ghosts around, only two people begging for money on the corner of Seymour Street. *I was more pathetic than they were*, I thought.

I went to PJ last night with Melek. Then we went to Odyssey. Both gay bars. It was my first time in a gay bar. When we walked into Odyssey, the whole two stories were shaking with Neon Trees' "Animal." The lyrics fit my mood very well. "Here we are again. I feel the chemicals kickin' in. It's gettin' heavier. I wanna run and hide… What are you waiting for… What are you waiting for… I won't sleep tonight."

I chucked down my third El Jimador tequila shot and jumped onto the dance floor. "I won't sleep tonight." I was singing at the top of my lungs. My feet were stamping on the floor and pushing me into the air. The harder I hit the floor, the higher I jumped. I loved the feeling of being free of gravity even just for one second. I was shaking my head, my body, and my spirit. My hands waved around, with my shoulders moving up and down like an animal. I tried to bend my knees and swing some dance moves I saw in the movie *Step Up 2*.

"Nice moves." A guy turned to me. With his red hair and beard and boyish face, he looked like Mitchell from *Modern Family*, especially with his waving hands.

"What?" I yelled.

"Nice moves!" He leaned his head closer to my ear. A breath of warm air flowed on my sweating neck, a brief tingling feeling. I could not see his face well with the disco lights flashing. But his breath tasted like alcohol. I danced even harder.

After Lady Gaga's "Telephone," I danced myself off the floor to take a break. The alcohol started wearing off. Melek brought me another shot of tequila. I downed it without salt or lime.

I grew up in a family where nobody drank or smoked; the number of beers I had had in my life could be counted on the fingers of my right hand. Now, I just kept pouring tequila down my throat. The strong fiery liquor sent me to another universe. It felt good. I felt good.

I grabbed a bottle of Blue Moon and started exploring Odyssey. The rapidly flashing lights. The blast of dance music. It was like a thunderstorm with the howling wind and sideways rain of lyrics making me want to break free and let go.

Melek and I went upstairs. It was full of bright red leather couches instead of the tall bar stools of the first floor. The music was less brain-piercing. I scanned the room quickly. Way fewer people than downstairs. We found a couch in the far corner and sat down.

"Okay?" Melek put his muscled arm around my shoulder and gave me a squeeze.

"I feel amazing! Thank you for bringing me here."

"Okay!" Melek smiled. I met Melek yesterday. He was from a Middle Eastern country that I could name neither in English nor Chinese. Short dark hair. Perfectly trimmed beard. His weathered skin sent out waves of warmth and safety. His words were few, but the deep voice added resonance.

After hearing my story of never having been to a gay bar, he brought me bar-hopping tonight. I was excited, thrilled, like a six-year-old boy waiting for Christmas. I wasn't using my brain, my traditional Chinese values, or my eighteen years of education to guide my behavior.

I was soaking up every second and every mixed alcohol and cologne smell. A guy sat down on our table. "Nice choice of beer." I turned my head at the strong Australian accent. He waved at me with his Blue Moon. With his completely shaved head, he looked like he had just come back from Afghanistan. His shirt was perfectly unbuttoned to reveal his chest, a little hairy and firm. The Gio Armani smell was familiar and not overpowering. "How are you, mate?"

"I am great! I feel wonderful! I feel amazing!" I couldn't hide my excitement. I finally felt that I was not different than everybody else. There was nothing to hide, nothing to be ashamed of.

Maybe it was his wild Australian accent, or his white teeth when he smiled. Our conversation progressed. His name was Zack. He loved traveling. Thailand, Malaysia, Singapore, Philippines... the mention of all those countries brought back wonderful memories. I had traveled almost the entirety of Southeast Asia when I was working in Shanghai. He talked about his job. He was in the technology industry as well.

He said he knew he was gay when he was seven years old. He told me he liked Asian guys, especially ones from America. As I was wondering whether I qualified since I had lived in America for only three years, he put his warm hand on the right side of my face and whispered, "I like you." My heart was in my throat.

He asked me to go back to his hotel with him. Five minutes away in a taxi, he added. I hesitated. I turned to Melek, who told me I was crazy.

My head was spinning with Neon Trees' "What are you waiting for? What are you waiting for? I won't sleep tonight." I told Zack to wait a second. I rushed downstairs and gulped another tequila.

A few minutes later, we were in a taxi on the way to his hotel. Zack kept talking about how wonderful and beautiful I was. He barely knew me. I had listened to his stories in the bar, but I wasn't making sense of anything. My logic had surrendered when I entered Odyssey. This was supposed to be a night to let go of who I was and explore who I should and could be.

Zack leaned into me and started kissing me. It was passionate. The taste of alcohol and the scent of his Gio Armani devoured me.

When we entered his hotel room, he turned down the lights and pushed me onto his bed. Jumping on top of me, he continued kissing and touching me. He was forceful. He ripped off my jacket and pants and threw them on the floor. What's going to happen? A light flashed through my mind. Am I going to have my first ever sex with this guy that I met barely an hour ago?

He moved up to my ear. "I want to fuck you so bad." The F-word that turned me on when watching porn now quenched my excitement. What was I doing here? I was still drowned in the five El Jimador tequila shots and two Blue Moons, but my last shred of conscience made me say no.

He pushed me down further, pressed his body on me. I struggled. He tried to pull my underwear down; I held on to it tightly. I said, "No." He didn't stop. My NOs were getting louder and louder. I writhed around and finally flipped him over. I grabbed my jacket and pants off the floor and charged out of his room.

The shots of tequila that led to so much laughter and fun and brought me to his room suddenly turned me into an emotional wreck. I was shaking. I couldn't stop sobbing.

Maybe it was from the alcohol wearing off, or the realization of the dangerous situation I was in, but my heart was pounding so fast, like I was running the hundred-meter race for my life. My heart was aching, as if a heart attack was ten seconds away. Was that even possible?

Age twenty-eight, I was still a virgin.

Where was my hotel? I started wandering. I always used Google Maps for guidance even from work to home. There could be new roads worth exploring, or the real-time traffic data could guide me home faster. But now, completely lost inside, I didn't bother to pull out my phone.

A cold wind blew my hair, pierced my body, made me shiver. *What am I doing here? What am I doing in this lonely city where I don't even know anybody?* I didn't know the answer, and I was too cowardly to search for it.

I thought about Melek, the only person I might call a friend. I should have listened to him. A friendship established two days ago was destroyed by me abandoning him. I thought about him telling me that he was homeless back in his country due to civil war. *Was that feeling similar to what I felt now? Lost? Scared? Didn't know where to go?*

There was a girl who took him from the street and married him. They had a boy who was twelve years old now. Then, his refugee application was approved by Canadian Immigration while being rejected by the U.S. and other Western European countries. He was reborn in Canada. Living in the free land, he also found out that he was gay. He started to date guys and experienced something not possible to him before.

"Did you know that you were gay back home?" I asked him.

"He he," Melek laughed. "I was barely surviving!" He paused. "But somehow I did feel different with guys back then. I always had some urge, or current, that ran through my body when I talked to guys. I knew there was more I wanted."

"Interesting." I always said that when I didn't know how to respond.

"I am openly gay now here in Vancouver, but I haven't told my son and his mom. They won't understand," Melek continued.

Listening to his story, I was amazed, stunned, and inspired. *Was this what my life was going to be? Was that why I moved to the United States? My education overseas was just a cover for a human survival instinct to find out who I was? Was that why I came to Vancouver – a place where I didn't know anybody – so that I could be myself, be gay?*

Thanks to my Chinese education, I never really needed to face my sexuality. In a system where parents and teachers cared mostly about test scores and rankings, I buried myself deep in my mind and heart and focused on what could get me glory – high-ranking scores and getting into a good college.

I grew up to be a "perfect" son and student. Never dated in middle school. Graduated as number one from my high school. Went to a top college in China. And found a great job upon graduation. I was used to not talking about my sexuality, let alone knowing myself well. I was just the perfect son and student that Mom, Dad, and my teachers wanted.

I continued the journey and became a "perfect" employee. I found great careers at SAP, McKinsey, and Microsoft, and gained more education at Duke University. I loved this game so much that I even wanted to print out all the logos of the schools that I went to and companies that I worked for and put them as stickers on my car. The naive me thought that the glorious names of the schools and companies could define me, shelter me, and save me from ever having to search for the real me.

I had no need, no reason to interrupt my quest to build the perfect resume and live a perfect life. No reason until the passage of time made the battle of my sexuality impossible to ignore.

The confidence I gained from my presentation at work was followed by tears and doubts about who I was at home. The happiness of talking and laughing with my friends during the day was replaced by the pleasure of turning on my computer to watch gay porn at night. I had barely had any real physical pleasure with anybody until the age of twenty-eight, and then the first time was with a guy in a bar pickup that almost ended in the worst situation ever.

Thinking of what just had happened made me shiver. I continued wandering the empty streets like a fly without a head.

"Stop lying! Yes, I am gay," I told myself one more time. I needed to say that aloud. The inner me, the true me, who pushed to come to Vancouver, was traumatized by what had just happened and was dead silent now. I didn't hear a word from him.

I needed my angry and desperate yelling voice. I wanted to call him back to give me the courage to continue the journey that I had started two days ago, to break through the shell that

I had created over the last twenty-eight years. It was a shell I was so comfortable in, that it would be easy to go back into it and be the person my family and friends knew well, or thought they knew well.

But what would my parents say? What would Mom say? No, no, Mom could not find out about this. Growing up in a culture where being gay is not an option, just like Melek, I could not let any of these "evil" things reach my parents. I was their proud son. I had followed the journey they set me on my entire life.

They could walk with their heads up back home because they had a son whom they were proud of. *If people knew I was gay, my parents would be laughed at by relatives, looked down upon by neighbors, and fired from the university they worked for.* The thoughts sent more shivers. I flipped up the collar of my jacket and wrapped my still shaking arms around myself.

I couldn't let my friends know either. Both in the U.S. and China, all my friends were straight. *What would they think? Would they think that I was a liar my entire life? Would they ever trust anything I said anymore?*

I couldn't let my roommates back in Seattle know. They were all straight guys. They would be disgusted by me. They would definitely move out. I needed their rent to pay my mortgage. I couldn't scare them away.

Maybe it was easier not to be gay. How I wished I was normal!

I thought about my ex-girlfriend, Meimei. How I wished it had worked out with her. But the feeling was not there. She was beautiful and one of the kindest people I had ever met, but I didn't have the same feeling as when I saw a handsome guy. The thought of holding a guy's hand gave me a feeling of happiness; the image of kissing a guy gave me electric excitement. Those feelings were not there with my ex-girlfriend.

But maybe I should just marry her, or any girl, and have kids. Life would be easier that way. Nothing and nobody needed to be changed but me.

As an immigrant my whole life, I had always been adapting and changing. I could definitely do it. *But should I?*

"Yes, I am gay," I confirmed to myself when I saw my hotel two blocks away. I needed a blanket to cover my face, my body, a place that I felt safe.

After I moved to Seattle and officially broke up with my ex-girlfriend a year ago, I watched lots of gay-themed movies. There were many sad ones where the main character committed suicide because of rejection from his family. But in some of them, people talked about being homosexual as a gift from God. It was something special, something to be proud of. *Should I?*

Maybe, for once, I should follow the "evil" thoughts and live the way that excited me? Maybe, for once, I should live for myself?

I trudged into my hotel room. I turned on all the lights and curled up on the floor next to the bed. It was 4:04 a.m. I was heading back home today. A three-hour drive. I knew I-5 very well but had no idea what was waiting for me ahead.

I was still sad, confused, hurt, and scared. I still didn't know what to do. But I was determined to summon a little courage to face my true self and look for a way out.

PART 1 - TWO DADS

Confused "Straight" Kid

"Not until we are lost do we begin to understand ourselves."

—Henry David Thoreau

"*D*e... Dee... De... Dee..." I struggled to open my eyes and stretched my right hand to reach for the source of the dream-piercing noise. It must be the black alarm on the nightstand.

"8:15 a.m. Damn!" Did I set an alarm last night? I couldn't remember. I had only passed out for a few hours. Half awake, I leaned against the bed and pulled myself off the floor. My body was exhausted. My heart still ached. My brain was dizzy but charged. I needed to go home.

I quickly packed up all my dirty clothes and bathroom bag. Everything easily fit into my backpack. I picked up the phone from the floor. Five missed calls. All from Mom. I did not have the energy or will to call her back. I left the room, grabbed a cup of coffee in the lobby, and went straight to the parking lot.

In my still-parked car, clutching the steering wheel, I tried to recall the night before. Everything was vivid yet blurry. *Odyssey, PJ. The handsome guys. Melek – did I say goodbye to him?* I searched for text history with him; nothing. "I am sorry about last night. I should have listened to you." I slipped a quick message to him, not expecting any response. *Zack, oh, thank God*

I escaped. That was scary. I didn't want to think about the scene in his hotel room.

But there was a silver lining. For the entire night, I felt accepted. Accepted for the part of me that I didn't even accept myself. This acceptance was a new feeling. In the past, I always had to fight for that.

As I was trying to gather the strength to drive back home, memories flooded back and intensified my mood.

Living in Seattle as a foreigner, I was an outsider. However, even before moving to the U.S., I had been a foreigner. I remembered the first time I moved with my parents when I was in fourth grade.

We had just moved from a small Tier 4 city in Hunan province to a Tier 1 city, Guangzhou, which is near Hong Kong, seven hundred miles from where we had been living. (Chinese city tiers are based on a combination of GDP, politics, and population.)

Everything was shinier and fancier in Guangzhou. They even had a shopping street that was called "No Night Street." The lights at night made the street brighter than in the daytime. People walked faster and held their heads higher. They spoke a local dialect of Cantonese. In the late 1980s and early 1990s, because of the economic influence of Hong Kong, Cantonese was the most popular language in China. Local people in Guangzhou created an exclusive circle for people who spoke their language. They always frowned at us when realizing that we didn't speak it.

The upscale and modern aspects did not make me like Guangzhou. I was terribly homesick. Hunan was where my grandparents and all my friends were. However, I was not given any time to deal with my sadness. A challenge was thrown in my face quickly.

Education was important to Mom. Before we unpacked all our belongings, contained in only three suitcases, Mom tried to enroll me in the elementary school that was three miles away from our home.

As part of the standard enrollment requirement, I took a test to see my ranking in the class that I was supposed to be joining. Two days later, we were sitting in the principal's office for the "welcome to school" meeting.

With a heavy wrinkled forehead and soul-killing eyes, the principal looked like Mr. Hancock from *Forrest Gump*.

"We cannot let your son continue fourth grade." He didn't waste time on any fluffy welcoming talk, but got to the point. "His test results are not good. He will make the whole class score look bad when we are compared to other schools."

"What?" Mom was puzzled and a little bit irritated. "That cannot be. He Yu was one of the top students in his class in Xiangtan..." It was a weird feeling to hear Mom using my full name.

"That could be the case. But this is Guangzhou. The education standard is higher here." He paused and turned his eyes to me for the first time. I was full of fear and shame and looked away. "He doesn't know any English. We start teaching English in the first grade here. Letting him go back to the third grade instead of the first is already a mercy."

My heart sank as the principal continued to talk. It was not his strong local accent that made me feel foreign; it was his tone, his content. It was the power he had to judge my ability and sentence me, to tell me that I was not good enough.

At this point, my voice joined the tears that had been swimming in my eyes for the last few minutes. "I hate this... I hate moving... I hate leaving my grandma, who has been raising me since I was a baby... I miss her... I miss my friends..."

The rest of the meeting was a blur. What stuck in my heart was the feeling of being rejected. What stuck in my mind was Mom's calming voice even when she was arguing. She never raised her voice, even when she had the upper hand.

On the way home, trying to cheer me up, Mom caught a little ladybug that was sitting on a leaf. She put the bug on her palm and extended her hand to me. "Such a beautiful bug. Do you notice that it looks so different than the ladybugs back in Hunan? It doesn't have the dots; it's an all-golden color."

Excited by this little creature, I stared at it. It was not round, more like an oval; it was flatter than a traditional red-dot ladybug; its head was also smaller, with eyes popping out more.

"You know why this ladybug has a golden color?"

I shook my head. "No... maybe... because... it is just different?" I murmured.

"Because it has pieces of the sun in it. It will shine even when the world around it is dark. It will light up the world. That is also you... you also have pieces of the sun in you. They will give you courage when all those around you are doubting you and losing faith in you."

A week later, I started my classes in fourth grade. I don't know what magic Mom used to get me in the class. It could have been her calm and persuasive voice, or her determination to have the best for her only son.

To prove myself, I poured every possible second into studying. From seven in the morning to ten at night, the only time I had a break was at lunch for twenty minutes and dinner for thirty.

I had always loved watching *Mickey Mouse* and *The Smurfs* on our 25-inch console TV, so to avoid having to battle the urge to watch TV, I cut the power cord of the TV with a pair of scissors while it was plugged in. Shorting the power cord not only sent the entire six-story building into darkness, but also made all the neighbors aware of my determination. Just what I needed!

Those golden ladybugs by the trail on the walk to school became my best friends for the remainder of elementary school. There were not as many of them as there were the normal red and black dot ladybugs, but I could always find one. They loved hiding underneath the leaves. I would carefully pick one up on the way home, put it on my palm, and talk to it about the new English words I learned that day, until it decided to fly away. The golden ladybugs gave me a little bit of courage in the new, big city.

* * *

THE THOUGHTS OF the golden ladybugs brought a smile. As the skyline of Vancouver disappeared in the rear-view mirror, I quickly took a sip of my second coffee from McDonald's drive-through. I wanted to call Mom back. She must be worried sick because I had not called her for six days. I wanted to talk to her about the golden ladybugs. But I didn't have the courage to pick up the phone. *What could I say?*

I hadn't thought about the golden ladybugs for so long, I had almost forgotten them. I buried them so deep in my heart, just like I hid my feelings during puberty, or the distant tingle of excitement when seeing or talking to a handsome guy.

Growing up in China, I never heard the word "homosexual." There was very little talk about sexuality of any kind. The sex education class was a joke. It was a forty-five-minute class consisting of reading a few paragraphs and looking through a giant chart that the teacher prepared. Yes, that's it – forty-five minutes of learning for the entire twelve years from elementary to high school.

Teachers and parents set the "no boyfriend/girlfriend" rule. They constantly reminded us of it. They shared the stories of so and so who started dating in middle school, fell behind in his studies, getting worse rankings in class every year, and didn't make it to college.

"Do you want to end up like so and so?" The scare tactic worked.

Mom believed in the same thing. No dating. No falling in love until college. She seldom mentioned it directly but told dating stories of other kids at the dinner table, stories that always had horrible endings.

I understood the stories were about others, but the message was for me. I kept quiet.

I was born in the first generation after the Open Door Policy, an economic policy initiated by Deng Xiaoping in 1978 to open up China to foreign businesses that wanted to invest in the country. And as an only child, I inherited many expectations. I was the person to fulfill my parents' hopes and make my family proud.

At the same time, China's huge population only allowed so many people to be successful. There were fifteen million babies born every year in China. Only one million would be lucky enough to go to college and get a decent job. Fourteen million, if lucky, would be able to escape their life in rural China and to go to work for the factories that made iPhones, Nike shoes, and Levi's.

Parents and teachers always mentioned that coming of age in China was a battle like "tens of thousands of soldiers going through a single-log bridge". We needed to beat everybody to win and have a better life.

That single-log bridge was the national college entrance exam.

It took place in June and lasted three to five days, depending on the major chosen for college. All the high school seniors sat in randomly assigned classrooms to take the exam. The entire country was shut down for those few days. Streets were closed, no cars allowed because the honking horns would distract students taking the exam.

The news was all about the exam as well. Students fainted from dehydration or lack of sleep. Strangers helped get students to the exam room when there was a summer storm that flooded the city streets.

Of course, the juiciest stories discussed the content of the exam. The exam questions would be reviewed daily by all the media outlets, and the "correct" answers would be reviewed as well. Students would compare their memories of their answers to the "correct" answers to see how high they might score, which would determine their class ranking in school, in the city, and in the province.

Those rankings and "correct" answers! They were all that mattered my entire student life.

For twelve years from elementary to high school, everything was about ranking. There were small exams every week, medium exams every month, mid-term exams, and final exams. To mimic the national college entrance exam, teachers would rank all the students within the class and also across the entire grade.

Our rankings would be posted on the wall outside of the classroom. The most nerve-wracking thing was to see the rankings at the end of a term. Top ten or bottom ten meant dramatically different attitude from parents. But no matter what, summer breaks and winter breaks were scheduled with studies, classes, and mock exams from morning until late at night.

Seeing my name higher in chemistry and lower in history than a friend's was not fun. Beating study buddies with whom I had been working so hard day and night eroded solidarity. But that was the only way to make myself feel worthy and my parents proud.

The prominence of the rankings told us that there is better and worse. To reach the goal, I needed to be better than others, even my friends. It was life in a jungle.

Twelve years of fierce competition formed how I thought. I was always secretly comparing myself to my peers and friends. I always need to be "better," even if "better" did not lead to happiness.

I also thought about all the "correct" answers I gave during those years. When it was math or chemistry, it was easier to have the correct answer. However, for subjects like Chinese and politics, it was so hard. "Why did the author write these sentences in 500 AD?" "What are the three key things that the Communist Party discussed in the annual meeting this year?"

There was absolutely no way to challenge those answers. My teachers could be very understanding, but they always stated, "That's what the exam designer wants us to say. Just say it so you can get a higher score."

Yes, to remember the "correct" answers. I always had a poor memory. And there were so many subjects and so many correct answers… I had already been leading a life of two dots and one line – 7:00 a.m. to 6:00 p.m. studying at school and 6:30 p.m. to 10:00 pm studying at home.

To make more time to memorize those answers, I decided to walk instead of ride a bike to school. This extended my journey to school from twenty minutes to fifty-five minutes. However, it gave me precious time to read, recite, and memorize.

Unfortunately, that practice ended one day when I rambled head-on into a streetlight pole while reciting… As my mom was trying to stop the bleeding after rushing to the scene, she decided that it was unsafe to let me continue walking to school.

Back then, there was *no option* to have a better future without giving the correct answers and being high in the rankings.

However, now, what was my correct answer? What were the questions I was trying to answer? Was the best question the one that I knew the correct answer to immediately, or the one that made me dig, think, and reflect?

Should I have driven up to Vancouver to throw myself into the gay bar scene? Unlike in fourth grade, I felt so accepted when I was talking and dancing with other guys in Odyssey last night. But with Zack, I felt violated. I almost lost my dignity. *Was that the correct thing to do?*

* * *

AFTER LAST NIGHT in Vancouver, I realized that somewhere deep in my heart, I always knew that I liked guys. I was always attracted to them. It was something that I had not articulated or explored before.

However, I didn't think I was born gay. I blamed the Chinese education system, blamed the pressure from parents and teachers. Most of all, I blamed what happened in middle school, a memory so painful that I had buried it for years.

In eighth grade, after a lot of hard work, I was finally admitted into a talent (gifted) class. This was the first ticket to a bright future – talent class in middle school meant a better high school, which would lead to a higher chance of a college education.

Students in the talent classes were naturally divided into two groups: the ones who were nerdy and worked hard to get there, and the cool kids with rich or politically powerful parents. I was definitely in the former group.

Two weeks after I was placed in the class, I had not talked to anybody. People were either desperately studying their asses off, or eagerly showing off their brand-new Nike Air Jordan shoes.

I was accustomed to moving into a new environment. But the cold faces and high pressure of studying made me go back to my old class during the ten-minute breaks between classes throughout the day. My new classmates noticed that and gave me the name of "Er Wu Zai." It meant "cheap traitor" in Cantonese.

The first time I heard my new name, my Cantonese was still not good; I didn't even know what it meant. I just kept smiling and turned my focus to the chemistry practice exercises I was working on. They laughed louder and harder.

Later that day, I learned the true meaning from friends in my old class. I wanted to cry, but I resisted as hard as possible. "Focus on studying. Let's see who will laugh in the end," I told myself all the time.

Around this time, I noticed a girl, Ting, in class. She had a slim body, long black hair, and big round eyes with long lashes. Having typical narrow Asian eyes, I was always attracted to big, beautiful eyes.

Two months after I had been admitted to the class, I was sweeping the classroom floor after everybody had left for the day. I enjoyed the quietness of the empty room. No peer pressure. No judgment. The only thing I communicated with was the countdown to the final exam sign hanging above the blackboard. "Eighty-seven days to go. I can do this!" I told myself. I was also taking the opportunity to recite the periodic table loudly. Yes, chemistry was my favorite subject!

Then Ting ran into the classroom. She was already out of our green-and-white-striped school uniform. Instead, she wore a silky white dress with a yellow jacket. "Oh my! She is so beautiful," I told myself.

Noticing me looking at her, she gave me a big smile. "I forgot my chemistry exercise workbook!"

"Eh." I nodded.

"You are good at chemistry, right? I saw you ranked in the top five in the class on the last chemistry exam."

"I love chemistry!" I couldn't believe that she noticed that. "I love to use two ordinary elements to make magic happen! Do you know adding pure potassium to water will create sparks and fire? So unbelievable!" I could not hide my passion.

She was smiling the whole time as I finished my declaration of love to chemistry. "Could you help me with my chemistry? I kinda suck at it..." She blushed a little bit.

"Of course!" I yelled.

We started our mentor-mentee relationship. We spent every possible moment after school together. Our mentoring also expanded from chemistry to math and biology. I tried to avoid history and Communist politics because I sucked at them too.

I was happy. I had finally found somebody in the new talent class. This must be what people called "boyfriend and girlfriend." This must be love.

My deskmate, Zhang, noticed all this. (In China, it is very common for two students to share a desk in the classroom.) He had grown up in a rich family. He always wore the latest Nike and Adidas shoes. He told me they cost $100. My mom was making $300 a month. I would never wear Nikes.

He did not study hard or well. His focus was on hanging out with his guy friends and dating all the beautiful girls in our class and other classes. We never really talked. Our communication was limited to his jokes about my thick glasses or the mountain of textbooks I had on my desk. I never had the courage, the time, or the witty repartee to respond to him.

It was a summer day. Communist politics class. I was bored to death. I felt a hand reaching over and groping my private area.

It was Zhang. He was using the big textbook and his shiny new pen box on the desk as cover.

He squeezed hard and whispered, "I see you and Ting always studying together. You know that she is my girlfriend, right?"

Stunned, heart beating fast, sweating, I didn't know what to do but nod furiously. I didn't want the teacher to see this.

I buried what happened that day. I tried to limit my time with Ting. I was a good student. I wanted a bright future and a good college education.

Less time with Ting didn't help. Every other day, Zhang's hand would reach under me. I was so scared of it, but in some way, I felt a weird excitement at his touch.

I started to have dreams and nightmares. In one of the dreams, in one second, Zhang was touching my private area in the classroom; in the next second, we were suddenly in a dark room, just him and me. He started kissing me. The feeling was so good, and I felt like surrendering entirely.

However, Zhang was not himself in my dream; he was a ghost in black, without any facial features, just a black shadow. I woke up in the middle of the dream sweating hard.

I had been scared of ghosts for my entire life. Even today, I need a light on in my bedroom to fall asleep. But in that dream, the black ghost made me feel good and gave me an excitement I had never experienced before.

It was like I was in hell and heaven at the same time. The kiss led to physical excitement and enjoyment. The kiss led to a dark future that I did not want to unfold. *Could my physical body be in heaven while my mind was in hell?*

I needed to put a stop to all this and focus on studying. I tried to ask more questions in class to draw the teacher's attention. But in a "stuffing the duck" education system, it is mostly the teacher talking. I did not get much chance to have eyes on my side of the classroom.

Mom heard from someone that I was spending lots of time with a girl. She kept subtly reminding me of the importance of no dating and focusing all my energy on school and studying. Yes, study hard, no dating, a great college, and a bright future. I reminded myself every day.

Without Ting, I was kicked back to just myself and studying. She tried to reach out to me several times, but I just walked away and didn't say anything. I was too weak to process what was happening in my body and mind. My heart also didn't have the courage nor the bandwidth to push myself even a little.

I have always blamed Zhang's hand as the biggest reason for me being gay. It was logical to my naive mind. The pleasure of Zhang's hand on my private area forced me to experience the touch of another guy and ironed a huge "gay" label on me for life.

* * *

I DID NOT have a girlfriend in high school. I decided to bury what had happened in my deepest memory and not think of it. Pandora's box is not supposed to be opened. I was pretty sure about that. Get into the best college, I told myself. I set that as my goal for my entire high school career.

I loved the traditional Chinese New Year's Spring Festival. Hanging a red couplet of wishful words on the front door kicked off the celebration and put everybody in a holiday mood. Everybody was happy, like when there is a day of full sunshine in a Seattle winter.

To adults, the best part is the celebration show on CCTV (China Central Television) on New Year's Eve. It is like the Super Bowl in America but organized by the government. Every single TV channel broadcasts the show from 8:00 p.m. to

12:00 a.m. that evening. People start guessing whether their favorite artist will be on the show months ahead.

My favorite was the fireworks. I had always been the one to buy fireworks and orchestrate a customized fireworks show for our family. I would hold the show on the empty playground in front of our six-story concrete apartment building. I used to get lost watching the colors of fireworks blossom in front of my eyes.

No time for that during the three years of high school – I had to study harder.

I put the holiday out of my mind. I had already devoted 358 days to study; those additional seven days of the Spring Festival celebration could be my edge. For three years in high school, during those seven days when everyone was relaxing and spending time with family, I chose to go to the empty school and sit in the empty classroom. The quietness of the classroom gave me peace of mind.

The unheated classroom and 35-degree (Fahrenheit) wind enabled me to focus even when I was sleepy. I tried to eat less because I knew that eating a lot made me dizzy. I started drinking Nestle instant coffee at 9:00 p.m. to have a final two hours of a clear mind for studying before bedtime at 11:00 p.m.

Three years later, in July 2000, in our cavernous school auditorium that could fit the entire school, standing in front of hundreds of my classmates and younger students, I shared my success and studying tips. Yes, I graduated number one from my school and got admitted to my parents' dream college, Shanghai Jiao Tong University, which had a hundred thousand applicants from my province and only admitted fifty-two.

The long, dark brown wooden benches in the auditorium were filled with students with eager eyes. Each of them was prepared with a pen and notebook to write down anything I said that could help them get into a top college the next year.

I was one of them last year. I had been trying to cross the "single-log bridge," but now I had successfully crossed it. The three spiderweb-wrapped spotlights focused on the letters on the blackboard that had been used too often to completely erase past writing. But the bright red "Welcome Yu He as Number One Graduate" was too bold and bright to miss.

The congratulations from so many strangers, the proud smiles of my parents and jealous looks of my classmates swamped me in happiness and pride. They also validated the road that my parents had set out for me. Follow that, and I would be happy.

* * *

THE FIRST TIME I heard the word *homosexual* was in college. Unlike in elementary and high school, college is all about freedom. My fellow students were all winners who had passed the "single-log bridge." We were far away from parents and could do whatever we wanted. That's what most students told themselves. I was excited about the big change, but I was lost inside. I was so used to being told what to do. But with the freedom, what now?

One day I was eating in the cafe reading the school newspaper. In the paper, there was a short article about two male students who engaged in inappropriate activities in school. "They were sick. They had diseases. They were homosexuals," the paper said.

The article gave me a shiver. I recalled my feelings when Zhang's hand was on me and the weird tingling feeling when I saw guys playing soccer. I quickly shut the thoughts down. "They are sick," I told myself.

I had some personal issues when I first went to college. After growing up with a single goal, to be admitted to college, while living a simple life of just studying every day, I was utterly lost two months into my freshman year. To make it worse, I had never lived away from my parents. I was terribly homesick. I missed Mom's delicious salty-fish eggplant, nightly coffee at 9:00 p.m. for the two-hour boost, and even the stories about other students failing because of dating.

I used to sleep like the dead. Even before the college entrance exam, I slept well. But I couldn't sleep now. Every day, the morning birds' singing interrupted the one to two hours of sleep I could get. One of my roommates also played a first-person shooter computer game, Counter-Strike, all night. The noise of fingers hitting the keyboard still haunts me today.

One to two hours of sleep every day, terrible homesickness, and the loss of my goal made me depressed. Every evening, when the sky darkened, I got scared. I worried about lying on the bed that would keep me awake the whole night. I yawned and cried at the same time.

I used a yellow pay phone to call Mom. To save money, I talked to her for less than three minutes a day. I washed my face with tears on the way back from the phone booth to the dorm. Those walks were like being dragged into a courtroom to be sentenced. But I did not commit any crime. Why did I need to pay the price?

Mom suggested I do more exercise to tire my body. I started running every night at 9:00 p.m. That did not help. I was thinking about suicide. I did not tell my mom, but she must have noticed something different. She found a psychiatrist at home whom she consulted on my behalf. She insisted I find one at school.

Instead of a psychiatrist, I met Bo, a true friend who saved me from my depression and suicidal thoughts.

Bo was my roommate. In my college, we were all assigned a bed in an eighty-square-foot room that was shared by four students. Bo's bed and desk were just opposite mine.

He was from the same hometown as me. He spoke the local dialect, Hunanese. I did not. My grandparents were migrants too. They moved to Hunan, where Chairman Mao grew up, to build a steel factory. In a place where there were no natural resources or a market for goods, raw stone was shipped in by train, while finished steel was transported to customers thousands of miles away.

My family was part of this little steel town that employed forty thousand people. My grandpa was one of the founding members. Our family was from the north of China, which had a completely different lifestyle and cuisine than Hunan province. Our family kept it that way. Even today, my ninety-three-year-old grandpa does not speak the local language nor eat the local spicy food.

In a new environment where we were all looking for friends, we looked past what separated us and clung to what was similar. The cultural differences between Bo and me did not become an obstacle to our friendship. Growing up in the same province, Hunan, was enough.

One night, a national holiday, when most students were home, I decided to stay at school to save money. Nothing to do, I was just lying on my bed in the dorm. Bo came in with a bag of yellow apples. "Do you want an apple?"

"I don't like apples. Each bite makes me feel like my teeth are falling out." I popped my head out of bed and looked at him. Carrying two giant bags of fruit, he must have just finished grocery shopping for the week.

"Try this one. This yellow kind is soft, not crisp." He grabbed one apple and extended his hand right next to my face.

I took it and had a bite. Wow. It was soft. It was sweet. It was different!

"What are you doing tonight?"

"Nothing yet... hoping to fall asleep, I guess."

"I am going to watch a movie. Do you want to come?"

"Sounds good." I jumped out of bed.

That was the beginning of our relationship.

Bo was almost a head shorter than me. He had a big, round head, so round that I thought a math professor designed it. He moved slowly and talked slowly but jumped like a rabbit when playing his favorite sport, basketball.

He always thought about others before himself. He listened to my fears and gave me a channel to vent. It was like finding a lifebuoy. I started pouring my thoughts, feelings, and emotions into him.

Watching a movie on the fifth floor of the library became our routine. The movie room was tucked back in the corner. The experience was called "two-person and one machine." It literally was two chairs in front of a TV. There were more than one hundred TVs in the room. Bo let me pick the movie every time. This was my first real exposure to Hollywood culture. I started liking Jim Carrey from *Dumb and Dumber* and learning more about Christmas tales from *The Grinch*.

My adventures with Bo expanded to traveling together. We jumped on random buses from our school in Ming Hang all the way to different parts of Shanghai. We loved taking photos in front of the skyscrapers in Lujiazui, where there was no nature but, instead, jaw-dropping designs of glass and concrete. It was not like the messy farmland China I grew up in – where people used fermented human feces to water vegetables planted on the sidewalk – but a perfectly designed garden with buildings.

Just when we were guessing how tall one of the buildings was, the people next to us started talking about how soon there would be another one even taller two blocks away. Shanghai, or the whole of China, was going through a phase of needing to have the tallest building, longest bridge, and largest airport in the world. That title made me feel good and proud, although it did not change any part of my daily life.

We were amazed at Yu Garden, which was a big tourist spot in central Shanghai. The classic temple-like wood buildings were a dramatic contrast to the skyscrapers in Lujiazui, which was only a couple of miles away.

There were so many vendors selling various art pieces: A tiny glass bottle with a beautiful and delicate Chinese painting on the inside, or a hundred versions of *fu* (*happiness* in Chinese) written on a goose egg. I was amazed that the country I grew up in had so much history and culture. If they put this in our history class in high school, I would have been much more interested, I told Bo.

Our adventures also extended to little towns near Shanghai. We sometimes boarded trains on Friday night to enjoy a weekend getaway. I wanted to see the world, see the Chinese garden that was shipped to New York for the World Expo in 1910, see the bamboo forest and heavenly West Lake in Hangzhou, and taste the beyond-description yuanxiao rice ball in Ningbo.

Those are some of my favorite memories of my college years, not only because I was seeing the world and living my life for the first time, but more importantly because Bo was traveling with me.

A friend once told me that it is not where you are going, but who you are traveling with that matters. It's so true. Those travel weekends gave me a way to explore a relationship with another human being. After the lack of soul-searching and relationship-building in high school, I was finally given a chance. The relationship with Bo gave my daily life a new purpose and lifted my depression.

As I was learning more about Bo, something magical happened. I started to hold his hand. We held hands watching movies, in classes, and sometimes wandering on the streets. I was always the first one to put out my hand, but he never rejected and always held my hand tightly. The two hands together represented the trust between two people, building a bridge between two hearts.

Was that love? I didn't ask myself that question. I was too busy enjoying the moment.

The happy time didn't last long. One day we were holding hands, walking on the way to the post office near the phone booth where I used to call Mom. Someone passing by pointed at us and yelled, "Faggot! Faggot! Faggot!"

Bo instantly pulled back his hand. My face turned red and my heart pounded. That familiar feeling: the feeling of shame and not being accepted.

After that day, Bo started keeping his distance from me. He made other close friends. We still spent time together, but our hand-holding happened less, and something was just different.

The stranger's yell of "faggot" and Bo's response knocked me back into depression. I kept thinking about the article in the school newspaper. I didn't want to be labeled that. I would put myself and my parents to shame.

I saw myself standing in front of hundreds of students, just as I did after graduating number one from my high school. However, instead of "Number One Graduate" on the blackboard, it was "Homosexual Criminal" written in blood just as they did it in the Tang Dynasty when the entire family was sentenced to death for one family member's sin.

However, this did crack an opening to the deep questions I had buried for so long: "What is homosexual?" "What is gay?" "Am I gay?"

TRANSITION TO THE WEST

"Knowing yourself is the beginning of all wisdom."

—**Aristotle**

"When I discover who I am, I'll be free."

—**Ralph Ellison,** *Invisible Man*

riving on I-5 south, still on the way from Vancouver to Seattle, I felt good to see all the familiar license plates starting with WA. Mount Rainier in the background also reminded me how beautiful the state I lived in was. The Mount Fuji of America. I wish to climb that mountain one day, I said to myself.

I was completely closeted in this country, the country I now called home. Canada felt more familiar. No miles, but kilometers. No Fahrenheit, but Celsius. Plus, the freedom of being gay. I could hang out with guys in the gay bars in Canada.

After the past two days, I was sure I was gay, and more importantly, I was ready to face the feeling and thoughts a little bit more. I had enjoyed the talking, holding hands with and kissing another guy. The physical excitement!

I had spent a night in Zack's hotel room. It was scary, but there was some truth to the experience. It was not even the first time I had been in a stranger's hotel room. The smell of Gio

Armani was somehow familiar. Oh, the shameful memory that I tried to bury for so long! It was pouring into my brain now.

* * *

2003, IN MY junior year in college, because my major was software engineering, we needed to use computers. There was a computer room at school, but it was super inconvenient, and the machine was really slow. Lots of my classmates started to buy laptops. They were expensive, but their portability made them convenient and cool. Whenever somebody got one, we would all gather around to admire.

Contemplating how to have one that I could call my own, I started subtly mentioning to my parents how my classmates' laptops helped during the coding class. Just like how my parents never directly asked me not to date in high school, I never directly asked them to buy a laptop for me. I just casually told them stories about my classmates.

Three months after my indirect and persistent marketing, they bought me a Founder laptop. It cost over $2,000, which represented two months of their combined salary.

My family did not have a lot of money, but Mom never made me feel poor. When I was in elementary school, she believed that eating fish helped the growth of a child's brain. The effectiveness depended on how fresh the fish was. However, live fish were costly. The price of a dead fish was normally less than half of the live ones.

Mom would stood in the fish booth of the outdoor local market, rain or shine, waiting for hours until one of those fish became tank-dead. Sometimes this did not happen for the entire afternoon. But when it did happen, she came home with the biggest smile and cooked the most delicious fish. She believed that she was making me smarter and giving me a better future.

Mom also taught me how to be generous, always giving instead of asking. "When a man achieves the Dao, his poultry and dogs rise to Heaven within him." Always citing the Chinese saying, Mom was a big believer that if she was in a better place, she needed to help other people enjoy the benefits too.

Every Spring Festival, we took a twenty-four-hour train ride to visit my grandparents and cousin's family in Hunan. Before the trip, Mom always took me to the Dollar Store in Guangzhou and asked me just to go crazy. Looking through all the toys for my cousin, housewares for my grandpa, and room decorations for my grandma, I never felt that we were poor.

The Founder laptop Mom and Dad bought me brought me a wave of admiration and jealousy from my classmates. I felt good about it. But more importantly, I could finally start to connect to the internet and a world full of knowledge. *Maybe there were answers to my questions?*

However, having a laptop in college did not mean that I was completely free on the internet. China had a big firewall that blocked most of the open-minded international websites, such as Google, Wikipedia, etc. All the colleges in China were in a special education network. Yes, we got the fastest internet speed compared to the rest of the country, but we were also tightly monitored.

I wanted to search "homosexual," "gay," and any related content. But I didn't want to do it on my laptop on the school network. I didn't want to be caught and expelled. Luckily, this was the blossoming time of internet cafes. Pretty much like

Starbucks today, there was an internet cafe on almost every corner.

While most of my classmates went to the cafes to play computer games like StarCraft, they were my secret spots to learn about homosexuality.

I was very picky about the computer and internet cafe. The computer needed to be in a dark corner. The seat needed to back up to a wall so that nobody could see my screen.

For my first search, I typed "homosexuality" into Baidu.com, which is the Chinese equivalent of Google. I was blown away. I was shocked. Hands shaking violently, heart pounding so hard.

"Homosexual is a disease."

"Homosexuality is a shame for the family and the society."

"Homosexuals need to be cured."

I soon learned the related word: AIDS. From all my reading, it seemed that AIDS was the ultimate disease, even taking the crown from cancer. It was incurable.

It was also the disease of homosexuals. Yes, homosexuality = AIDS.

Am I homosexual? Do I have AIDS? Am I alone? Where are the other gay people?

As I continued to search gay topics online, I soon found an oasis that kept me afloat. Although the government blocked most Western gay websites, somehow Gay.com was accessible.

Gay.com became my secret joy. I loved looking at half-naked hot guys' photos. I always needed to have multiple Internet Explorer windows open on the computer. Looking at those photos needed to be limited to two to three seconds. I had to instantly cover up the photos when people passed by.

There was a chat room on Gay.com where strangers around the world put their photos and profiles online. They wanted to talk and meet up. I did not have any photos, but I registered an account quickly and started engaging in conversations with other gays online.

I always kept the conversation short. My English was not good enough, but also, in my mind, "gay" was still the devil; it was a disease; it equaled AIDS, which was the ultimate terminal disease. If I had that, I would completely fail my parents.

Most of the conversations ended quickly. But one message string with a man named Tom kept going. He was from Vancouver, Canada. He told me that it was a beautiful city, the best in the world. He told me that there were big trees. Forests upon forests. Mountains over mountains. The ocean was so cold, but breathtaking.

He asked me when I knew I was gay. I said I was not gay. He asked me whether I had a boyfriend. I said no. I tried to avoid any questions related to being gay. He asked me to visit him. I said I couldn't. I had no idea how.

Three months later, he told me that he would be visiting Shanghai for Christmas. He wanted to meet up.

I was excited and nervous. I was finally going to meet a gay in person! But more importantly, he lived so far away! He was foreign. He would not impact my normal life! Nobody should know, and nobody would.

His hotel was on the Bund, the place where East met West. The handsome and classic Western buildings built in the 1900s were backed by small, dark, and dirty local residential buildings.

It was a two-hour bus ride from my school in Minhang to the Bund. Sitting in the last row of the bus, I was tapping the bar on the seat in front with my gloved right hand while my feet kept thudding on the floor. I was trying to push back the thoughts of the disbelieving faces and yelling from my school, my parents, and my friends that popped into my mind from time to time.

"What are you thinking?" I asked myself. This was the craziest thing I had ever done. A Chinese boy who had been told that his whole life was about studying hard, getting into a good college, securing a great job, and getting married, I felt like throwing everything away and tasting the apple from the Garden of Eden for once.

Buildings and trees were passing fast outside of the window; so was my planned future. I looked at the people sitting in front of me. The normally crowded bus was quite empty now because it was so late on a Saturday night.

Did they notice that I was shaking? What would these strangers say if they knew what I was going to do now? Trying to distract and calm myself, I put on my earphones and hit play on the Discman that I bought with savings from eating only white rice and Chinese pickles for two months in my sophomore year.

"Can't Lose What You Never Had" by Westlife was playing. I bought the CD for 75¢ on the street outside of my school. I had listened to their CD for two years nonstop.

Sometimes when I was studying in my dorm by myself, I imagined that Westlife was singing the songs in front of me, around me, and just for me, especially when they sang, "I lay my love on you." *Was Tom as handsome as the guys from Westlife, whose names I didn't even know?*

The bus arrived at Xujiahui. I jumped out of the car and ran to my next bus. I ran so fast that my heart felt like it was going to come out of my throat. I pushed my legs faster and faster. It was like if I slowed down, I might decide to go back to school and the life I was familiar with, the normal life that was suffocating me slowly.

I didn't think about what Tom and I would do. I had no idea. I had not even kissed anybody before. The most intimacy I had ever had with any human being, guy or girl, was holding hands with Bo, which got me labeled as "faggot" and laughed at. Turning up the volume, I pushed the thoughts away again. It was now or never. Now or never, I told myself.

Tom was almost half a head taller than me. His sandy-blond hair was perfectly combed and spiked up. With his pure blue eyes, he was like Ryan Gosling, but in his late thirties. He was wearing a blue North Face jacket with a white shirt underneath. He was a very sweet gentleman. He was waiting for me in his hotel lobby and gave me a big hug when he saw me. His wide arms completely surrounded me when he embraced me. I felt warm, comfortable, and safe.

I had no idea how he knew it was me. Maybe it was my scared and eager look; maybe it was the fake Nike brown jacket I told him I'd be wearing or my thin and tall build I described when he asked what I looked like. He smelled strongly of a fragrance. I never knew men also wore fragrances. He told me it was a cologne called Gio Armani. I loved it. It was new. It was foreign. It was fresh.

He asked me whether I was hungry and led me to a dessert shop not far away from the hotel. It was a frequent stop for Bo and me. We drifted around the city after some yuanxiao rice ball soup. I always enjoyed the soft, black sesame filling. Mom cooked it when I was a kid to cheer me up and always when I went back home from college.

Tom told me that I was as sweet as the yuanxiao. I didn't know how to answer but just smiled. He told me that back home he had an ex-wife and three kids. They all now knew he was gay. He still talked to his ex-wife and was friends with his kids. He went snowboarding with them every winter.

I was surprised. *How could you be friends with your kids? Or be friends with your parents, the ones who set rules and goals while providing support?* I didn't ask but just kept eating my yuanxiao.

On the way back to the hotel, Tom reached his right hand to my left. I pulled my hand away quickly. I didn't want other people to see this. I didn't want other people to call me "faggot" again.

He continued talking about his life back home as we walked into his room. This was my first time in a high-end Western hotel room. It was so clean, so simple, and so modern. The desk was made of dark rosewood with sophisticated but natural woodgrain, not like the black iron one I had in my dorm, or the plain wood bed that was covered with Mickey Mouse stickers at home. I sat on the chair. It was leather. It was bouncy.

"You can raise the chair up." Tom pulled a lever that was on the bottom of the chair. A sudden force shot me up a few inches. He looked up and smiled at my giggles from the excitement of the little roller coaster ride.

He leaned over and pushed his lips onto mine. It was more than lips. I tasted the sweetness from the yuanxiao. I tried to follow through and moved my tongue to meet his. *Was this how I should kiss another person?*

I surrendered all my thoughts, closed my eyes, and just followed Tom's lead. He lifted me up from the chair and pushed us to the bed. He undressed me and kissed every inch of my skin. He wanted to do more, but I said no. This was the first time I had been with a guy. Kissing and fooling around were enough for me.

"That's all right..." He sounded disappointed. He lay down right next to me. He touched my face with his right hand. "You are such a beautiful boy." His hand moved to my hand, and his fingers intertwined with mine. I squeezed my fingers a little bit. I always enjoyed holding another guy's hand, just not in public.

He continued to talk about his life in Vancouver. He talked about the first night he was with another guy when he was in college. He had tried to forget and married his ex-wife. He talked about the happy and fake life he tried to build up with his ex-wife and the happy and real life they created. He said their kids were what made him happy every day and provided a purpose for living.

I didn't ask any questions. I just stared into his beautiful blue eyes and listened. I brushed his hair. It was so soft. In this precious first experience with a guy, I wanted to absorb as much as possible. Sometime later, I fell asleep.

I woke up super early the next morning. Tom was still sleeping. I stood in front of the giant window that offered an amazing view of Lujiazui on the other side of the Yangzi River. This tiny corner of land hosts some of the tallest buildings in China and in the world.

In the Bund, it represents the old China, a history of being ruled by the West. In Lujiazui, it showcases the country's growing economic power, the new development, and the future. *Sometimes, you just need a bridge to cross the river from the old to the new*, I thought.

Tom woke up. He wanted to grab breakfast together. "It's Christmas. Let's spend the day together."

"I need to go. I still have school work to finish." I used the first excuse that came to mind.

"All right. Vancouver is hosting the winter Olympics 2010. Come visit me!" He grabbed something out of his suitcase. "Here is a postcard of Vancouver. Here is a two-dollar Canadian coin of a bear. Just keep them as a souvenir. Hope they will remind you to visit Vancouver in 2010."

"I will," I replied without thinking too much.

The memory of Tom and the night during the Christmas of 2003 rose from the deepest part of my brain. A lost memory. I had always heard of selective memory and never truly understood. Now I could see some part of me had sealed the memory with Tom tightly.

I had not thought about the exciting but shameful night for so long. *Was that why I went to Vancouver in the last couple of days?* Tears started running down my chin. I saw an exit on the freeway; I needed to stop the car. I found the first gas station I saw after the exit. It was a Shell. I jumped out of the car and ran into the restroom. Sitting on the toilet, I started crying aloud.

I thought I went to Vancouver because of the authentic Chinese food, the cheap Chinese massage that made me feel good, and because it was a hundred miles away from Seattle. It was a city where I did not know anybody. However, I had just realized that it was because of a forgotten promise I made back in 2003 to a stranger from Vancouver.

The night with Tom had crawled into some deep corner in my mind. It made the city of Vancouver a comfortable place in my heart. Subconsciously, Vancouver became a safe harbor for being gay, a city where the first gay person I had met lived. A city where I could come out and be friends with my ex-wife and my kids if I chose to go that way. It was like "Lujiazui" to me, and I-5 from Seattle was my bridge to the land of true self and freedom.

Calmed down, I moseyed back to my car. I saw a car with a sticker "HE>I" parked right behind mine. Growing up in a country where all religions were wiped out, I never believed in any higher power such as God, Buddha, or Allah. But considering what I just remembered, maybe there was a higher power that was leading me and connecting the pieces of my life.

* * *

JUST AS FAST as I ran to Tom's hotel, I ran to my bus to go back to school. Sitting on the bus, I started sobbing. The smell of Tom's cologne lingered. It was attached to my dark brown jacket now. The feeling of desire, comfort, and excitement was gone. I felt disgusted by the smell.

"What have I done?" I asked myself. I took the jacket off as fast as possible, threw it on the dirty floor of the bus and stepped on it.

Am I gay? Maybe I am... The thoughts scared me.

If my parents know, they won't talk to me anymore...

I am not a good student anymore. I am not a good kid anymore...

I will be expelled from school. My classmates, my childhood friends, my parents' neighbors will all laugh at me and look down on me and my family...

The world spun faster and faster. My breath became short. There were no tears anymore. All that left was fear.

Back in my dorm with my black iron bed and desk, as I was taking the third shower to try to get rid of the sinful cologne smell, another thought struck me: *I have been with a gay now. We had some intimate moments. Do I have AIDS? Oh, I may have AIDS now!*

The thought pushed me to another level of fear that I didn't know existed. Everything seemed to stop. Somebody had just hit a gong as hard as possible in my head. The cologne scent was the last thing I needed to worry about now.

I collapsed on the shower floor. The guy in the next stall must have heard the noise. "Are you all right?" I didn't respond. I always thought the communal shower floor was disgusting. But now it was the only thing that stopped me from continuing to fall into the abyss.

I lay my entire body down and let the shooting water from the shower head hit my face directly. I used to complain about the water pressure; we needed a faucet to spray water out instead of shooting directly. But now, the pressure of the water created pain on my face and pushed so much water into my nose that I almost choked.

I was not in Lujiazui anymore, not even in the Bund. I was pushed back thousands of years. Like a caveman who didn't know much about the scary world or what would happen to him, let alone have any chance of being in charge of his destiny, I only had a leaf or piece of rabbit skin to cover my private area and a terrified mind, waiting for my fate to be revealed.

I am going to die! I jumped out of the shower and didn't even dry my body. I threw the brown Nike jacket on and charged to the internet cafe that brought me to Tom. I frantically looked for any information related to AIDS on Baidu. We did not have sex, but we did have intimate moments. Information was limited. All I could find is, "Homosexuality is a disease. It is the devil. It is related to AIDS."

What will happen? Will I die? My thoughts started digging a hole that didn't have an end. I didn't have anybody to talk to. Bo was busy hanging out with his new best friends. I was too afraid to call Mom. I started limiting phone time with her. I used to call her every other day, but I couldn't anymore. I knew if I talked too much, I would lose control and start crying.

I joined the group of students that played computer games all night. They had upgraded their game from StarCraft to Warcraft. I gave up all my social and studying activities. I played day after day and night after night. Warcraft became the drug to numb my mind.

I did what I do best: bury my thoughts and feelings. I shoveled the fear of death together with the fear and curiosity of who I was and buried them deep in my heart.

Graduation came. My new job started. I was lucky to get a great job that made my parents proud again. I became a software engineer at SAP Labs China, a German company's research center in Shanghai.

Lots of people find excitement in entering a new phase in life. To me, there was no difference. I was walking on a sheet of ice and living an autopilot life. Nothing really excited me.

My high school Chinese teacher taught us a trick to feeling happy during those boring study days when nothing was exciting. "Stare at yourself in the mirror in the morning. Start moving your lips up and smiling. Even if you don't feel like it, smile for five minutes a day. You will be happy." As a good high school student, I practiced that whenever I felt down. It worked.

Now this trick was the only medicine to help pump me up in the morning. During the day, I went to work with the most optimistic attitude. I always laughed out loud and showed people that I was happy. I lived like there was no tomorrow. At night, after coming home, I played game after game until my hands hurt and my brain was dead. I played like there was no tomorrow, then crashed. I spent the next day the same way.

Another six months passed. I was still alive. Still obsessing about the symptoms of AIDS, I seemed all right. I was tired all the time because of the computer games and fake optimism. But there were no purplish spots on my skin, and I was not losing weight.

"AIDS is deadly for sure. Maybe I do not have AIDS," I thought. "This must be another chance that the higher power gave me," I told myself. I decided that I needed a normal life. I would bury all these feelings even deeper and never seek them again.

This was when I met Meimei. She was one year younger than me. She graduated from a rival college, Fudan University, right across town. As with Harvard and Yale, the friendship and rivalry between the two schools always made the graduates from the two universities frenemies.

She caught my eye the first day when she joined our team at work. She was a true lady. Her hair was long and black. Her eyes were big, sparkling, and full of stories. She always wore beautiful dresses. But the most shining part about her was her personality. She was very kind. Never freaking out. She had a voice that could calm a troubled mind.

I felt very comfortable with her. I always gave her the biggest smile and talked about my "dreams" that I made up from all my remaining courage and imagination.

To make it more perfect, she lived in the same community where I rented. There were nine eighteen-story apartment buildings. The faded yellow stucco exterior and leaking windows made the ten-year-old buildings look like they were from the 1940s.

Meimei was living with her parents, and their apartment was just two buildings away. We started walking to work together. We talked about food, fun places to visit in Shanghai, and troubles at work.

After work, like all the young couples, we went to the upscale Pizza Hut in People Square for our date. Oh, those luxury Pizza Huts that were known as first date places! It wasn't until I arrived in America that I realized that Pizza Hut didn't have the golden image it built in China and a girl would feel embarrassed if her first date was at a Pizza Hut.

Those are my favorite memories of living in Shanghai other than traveling with Bo in college. I finally had a girlfriend and a life. I was normal. I started cutting back my computer game playing at night. I resumed watching *Friends*, a show that I had liked since I was in high school. I loved watching how comfortable, easy, and fun life was in the show. *Maybe I could have something like that one day.*

I told Mom about Meimei. Mom was thrilled. We had not been in touch often during the year after my night with Tom. I always told her that I was busy. This news gave her hope of seeing me come back to the path that she and all Chinese parents want their children to be on. It made her see the next step in her son's journey – getting married to a beautiful and kind girl and starting a family.

However, I knew there was something missing. After a few months of dating, we had never kissed. I thought that would be the next step in our relationship after holding hands. But I never had the urge or courage to kiss her. I know she wanted it, but I couldn't lie to myself.

Attraction is supposed to occur between opposite sexes. For me, the attraction was just not there. Whenever I tried to execute the plan to kiss her in those perfect moments, a scream from a tiny me in the deepest part of my heart would jump right in front of it.

Mona from *Friends* told Ross that if a relationship was not moving forward, it was going back. Without moving forward, however, I was determined to make this relationship work. We didn't need to kiss. We didn't need to have any physical relationship. I loved her and she loved me. We would make this work. Somewhere in my heart, I knew this was my last chance to be normal, to make my parents proud, and to make society accept me.

At the same time, all my friends and colleagues knew that I had a girlfriend. That gave me relief from social pressure. I was not the weird single guy who never dated anymore. People stopped bugging me about who my girlfriend was or setting me up with their friends. All the gossip was not about me anymore. I was happy about that.

I decided to hang onto the relationship with Meimei for as long as possible.

* * *

QUITE LIKE NEW York City, Shanghai was the international hub of China. Most young people living in the city had big aspirations. With the thousands of years of emphasis on education, going abroad to study was one of the dreams.

My colleague George at SAP told me that having an MBA from a top school was a golden ticket to a great career and high-paying job. With an MBA from NYU, he was leading a product-design team in our company. He was always traveling to different countries and living a great life.

I also found out the software engineer job was not for me. I liked communicating with people more than talking to a computer all day. I liked listening to their problems and helping them brainstorm ways to make things better. Getting an MBA was a way out of the technical niche.

But deep inside, I knew there was something more. No matter how much I wanted to, I couldn't continue to seal the true me deep inside or pursue the relationship with Meimei any longer. I knew that there was no future, but the uneducated, selfish, and cowardly me could not find a way to face it.

The easiest way was to escape to a land on the other side of the Pacific Ocean. It was foreign; it was unknown; it was mysterious. Just like my own identity. The eight-thousand-mile distance might give me shelter from Meimei, from my parents, and from all the pressure of society.

People always talk about the "American Dream." That tagline could make my parents prouder while creating more distance between us. The time difference and high cost of phone calls would cut communication frequency and duration.

Maybe in America being gay was an option. There were so many *Friends* episodes talking about homosexuality. Ross's ex-wife was gay. People seemed to accept her. *Maybe I could explore myself more and listen to what was buried deep inside of me? Maybe I could kiss a guy other than Tom, a guy I liked? Maybe hold his hand on the street? Maybe I could have a boyfriend?*

After two years of preparation and application, in 2007, I packed my two suitcases and landed in Durham, North Carolina, to start my expensive MBA education at Duke University. To a land far from limitation and thousands of years of rules. To a place that was far from my parents, Meimei, and my friends. To a place where I could forget who I was and maybe look for what I could become.

Sitting on the American Airline flight from Shanghai to O'Hare, and then to Durham, I was excited. It was like Andy digging the last few feet of his secret tunnel in *The Shawshank Redemption*. I dreamt of standing in the rain, looking up in the sky, and laughing out loud; saying goodbye to my past and embracing a bright future with nothing but freedom.

However, coming to the US didn't give me the opportunity or freedom to face my identity at all. Just when I had Googled and found out what each letter of "LGBT" in the LGBT club stood for, I was buried by my reality. I was so focused on escaping that I did not realize what I had signed up for.

The two-year education meant a student loan debt of $150K with 11 percent interest. I couldn't afford not to find a job. No job meant not being able to stay in America. Day one in my MBA program, the professor asked us to work on our resumes. Write it and rewrite it until you can recite every single word and tell every story like one from Jack Welch's *Winning*.

To make it worse, the Great Recession hit right after my first year. Most companies were laying off and even shutting down completely, not to mention hiring international students who needed visas and had a long way to go to learn to live and work in American culture.

I also didn't have much experience. The average student's work experience was seven years; I barely had three. This short work history made my resume weak compared to my classmates'. I thought I was past competing with my classmates. Who knew that I had thrown myself into an even more brutal competition?

I was repeating my twelve years of Chinese education life, just in a foreign land and a different time. I rented a room in a townhouse that was owned by my American classmate, Craig. In a two-story cedar building with three bedrooms, my room sat on the ground floor. It was the smallest and cheapest, and also came with the extra "bonus" of a washer and dryer in my closet. In order to have peaceful sleep, I set up a laundry time sheet for my roommates.

With a busy schedule, I couldn't enjoy Mom's cooking anymore but frequently stopped to have KFC fried chicken and pork steak at Waffle House. My commute to school evolved from a bike to my 2001 white Ford Focus, with the driver-side door completely smashed in. It only cost me $3,000. That's what I could afford at the time.

I did enjoy exploring American life and culture with Craig. I knew that I was 100 percent made in China, but I was not going to just hang out with my Chinese classmates. Otherwise, why had I bothered to come to the US to study?

That rule made me enjoy *Scrubs*, Craig's favorite show; go crazy at the '80s or white parties; and learn how much Americans were into sports. I painted my face white and blue and stood with thousands of fellow Dukies at Cameron Stadium to cheer for our beloved Blue Devils. The stamping on the floor, the jumping in the air, and the shouting of "Let's go, Duke!" transported me into another space where, briefly, there was no pressure to succeed at school, find a job, or explore myself.

My favorite moment was when Craig talked about how much he "hated" Michael Phelps. In his senior year in high school, Craig was supposed to win the Wisconsin state championship of freestyle swimming. However, a freshman, Michael Phelps, came out of nowhere and crashed his dream. I could not believe Craig was on Phelps's level. I felt so proud to call Craig my roommate.

However, my brief interaction with American culture was suffocated by all the pressure of getting a job. During the interview season, when people were receiving many invitations, I was the one driving home sad every day. Tears and the voice of Delilah on the radio were the only things accompanying me from the school library to home late at night or in the early mornings.

I knew my GPA (great point average) was important. That's what lots of companies look for when they screen resumes. So I studied really hard and was the last person to leave the library most nights.

I knew my English was not good enough. Who wanted to hire somebody who had problems pronouncing "th" and "s," who mixed up *he*, *she*, and *it* all the time, who did not change tenses, and who always said "I am/do" instead of "I was/did"?

I set my alarm for 5:00 a.m., drove to the famous Duke Forest, and found a corner where nobody could hear me but squirrels and deer. I pulled out the practice material and started reading aloud to improve my English. Later in the interview season, I also read my resumes, stories, and my answers to potential interview questions.

I read so much and so loud, I lost my voice a few times. I made a commitment to email/call five alumni a day. I needed to sell myself. I squeezed any opportunity possible to find a job, rather than find myself as I had thought I would.

Fortunately, my hard work paid off. I was invited to an interview with Microsoft, my dream company. In an early afternoon in September 2008, after my interviews at Microsoft, I received a phone call from the recruiter that I was offered two, not just one, jobs! I could even choose which one I liked more. Maybe because I wanted to have more control of my life, I chose the one with the job title of Product Planner.

Driving on the 520 Floating Bridge from Microsoft's headquarter in Redmond to Seattle, I saw the snow-capped mountains of the Olympic National Park in the distance. Over the mountain, the Pacific Ocean separated my old apartment in China from my soon-to-be new home in Seattle.

Maybe I could live in a house that I called my own? Like what I saw in Hollywood movies? I thought about the proud faces of Mom and Dad and visualized the laughs, the raised eyebrows, and the prideful voices when they told their friends that their only son worked for the biggest technology company in the world and in the company's headquarters in America.

The 520 Floating Bridge was not as grand as the one that connects the Bund with Lujiazui, but it could be leading to my new life. A life where I finally might be able to dig deeper into who I was, explore my sexuality, and face my true self.

The sunshine lifted the fog on Lake Washington. I felt I was in heaven. I was finally in the Pacific Northwest, the place that Tom mentioned has mountain over mountain, forest upon forest, and a breathtaking ocean.

* * *

"TAKE EXIT 182 on I-5 to Interstate 405 on the right." Google Maps' navigation brought my thoughts back to the road from Vancouver to Seattle. It had been two years since I got the good news from Microsoft. I had made this city my home. I hiked all the trails that I could find to see the big fir trees and the cove by the oceans.

Thanks to the Great Recession, real estate was like a hot potato that nobody wanted to touch. Housing prices were at rock bottom. I bought a four-bedroom house with FHA's 3.5 percent down payment option. I rented out three bedrooms to people I found on Craigslist to help me to pay the mortgage.

But was that all I wanted in America? What was I escaping from? What was I searching for?

I thought about the same-sex family photos that my colleagues put on their desks at Microsoft, and guys holding hands on the street in Capitol Hill in Seattle. Being gay was not only an option, but also could be normal.

Those scenes gave me an urge to dig deeper inside to seek answers to the questions that I had not had a chance to face until the past few days in Vancouver.

Looking outside the window in front, I saw Mount Rainier, so grand and magnificent. It was 120 miles away, but it looked like it was just in front of my face. It was like my sexuality, which I needed to face now. There was no doubt I was gay. I should just stop lying and start living.

Ring, ring, ring... It was Mom on the phone again. I wanted to answer the call. I wanted to hear her comforting voice and tell her everything that had happened in Vancouver. I wanted to share all the memories I had of growing up. I wanted her to hear my side of the story. But I was still too tired from all the tequila and too scared to answer the phone. *I'm almost home. Let me just keep driving.*

MEETING BRYAN

"At the center of your being, you have the answer; you know who you are, and you know what you want."

—Lao Tzu

"*I* need to meet more gays," I told myself after coming back from Vancouver.

Unlike the controlled Chinese internet, the internet in the U.S. was open and available. I soon found out that Craigslist was not only for renting a room or buying my 2001 Ford Focus; it was also used to meet people and hook up.

The game on Craigslist was easy. Post half-naked (sometimes fully naked) photos of me with an introduction and get ready to exchange photos with the other person. I found some good guys there. A grocery store owner in Green Lake, a Microsoft executive assistant in West Lake, and a government employee in downtown Seattle.

However, I realized that the expectation for the meetings was different for most of them than for me. They wanted sex, no talk, get it done and leave. I wanted to know the other person. I *needed* to know the other person who was also gay. I craved hearing their stories. I had so many questions...

"When did they know they were gay?"

"Did they tell their family and friends?"

"Are they scared?"

"Do they think they were born gay or turned gay?"

I also wanted to hold hands and kiss. I wanted to enjoy the intimacy between two guys. I still believed sex should be saved for the guy whom I really loved.

Every night after work, instead of playing Warcraft or talking to my roommates, I locked myself in my bedroom and started looking through posts on Craigslist. There was an entirely new world there with new words that I had never seen: DDF – drug and disease free; M4m – man looking for man; top, bottom, or versatile. *Which one was I?* I had no idea.

I kept my posts short and simple. "Asian. Male. 150 lbs. 5'11". New. Discreet. DDF. Looking for somebody who is in a similar boat." I didn't have much hope since I thought most people on Craigslist were experienced. I was a little surprised at the number of replies I received.

One of them was Shane. His reply was as short as my post. But his photo caught my eye. No naked body or dick pic. He was standing in an ancient building in Naples, Italy, his email said. I could not see his facial features well, but he was fit. I decided to meet him that night.

I could not host because I was not out to my roommates yet, so I went to his place. It was in South Lake Union, right by Whole Foods. SLU was where the headquarters of Amazon was. The condo building he lived in was as fancy as it could be. I buzzed the number he gave me. "Come up," he said on the intercom.

Shane was still wearing his business casual clothes when I showed up at his door. He was my height. The tight pants showed his big thigh muscles. The blue shirt fit perfectly to his wide shoulders. He looked like an Armani model. He had short, curly dark hair, a high-bridged pointed nose, and big, deep, dark eyes.

"Give me one minute. Let me finish my Connector booking for tomorrow." He turned around and weaved back to the dining room area and his computer. *He works for Microsoft*, I thought. The Connector is the Microsoft shuttle that brings employees to work.

I took a glance at his home. His unit on the tenth floor had one wall that was completely glass and a perfect view of the Space Needle. His furniture looked like it was all from DIVA, the premium Italian furniture store in Seattle.

As I was still soaking up the atmosphere, Shane grabbed me from behind and started kissing my neck. It was passionate but also soft. I turned around and pushed my lips on his.

He pushed us to the bedroom, picked me up, and threw me onto his bed. He jumped on the bed and continued to devour me. We were rubbing our bodies against each other's. Our moaning got louder and louder until we both masturbated and came.

Lying on the bed with Shane next to me, I felt satisfied but hollow inside. My body was pleased but emotions drained.

"Do you work for Microsoft?" I tried to start a conversation.

"Yes," he muttered.

"Which department?"

"Enterprise." He kept his answers short just like his email. "I need to get up early to catch my Connector ride."

"OK...Sounds good." I dressed and left his fancy condo.

Five days later, I got an email from him. "It was hot last time. Want to meet up again?" I was a little bit surprised. The physical intimacy was pleasant, but I didn't feel hot at all. I didn't feel any connection to light the inner fire that made me feel hot.

"Can we talk more this time?"

"Sure," he replied.

Lying on his bed that night, I started to ask all kinds of questions. "Where are you from?"

"Toronto."

"When did you know you were gay?" Silence.

"Do your parents know?"

"No."

"Where did you study?"

"Harvard."

"What do you do at Microsoft?"

"Executive assistant."

All the answers to my questions were one or two words. I knew he didn't want to say more. He turned to me and started kissing me.

I tried to push my lips away. "Could we talk more?"

"No." He was firm.

Five minutes later, I left his condo. As I was walking out, he told me that for what I was looking for: Match.com was a better choice.

* * *

I WAS A doer. I created a Match.com profile that night after coming back from Shane's apartment. Oh man, there were so many questions to introduce myself. I didn't even know there were so many sides to me. This was more complicated than my business school application.

The website also asked for photos to show different parts of my life. I didn't have many photos of myself. The close-up photo they asked for didn't exist. I was very insecure about my looks. I never liked them. I always thought I got the worst features from my parents: a big face, flat nose, jug ears, and small eyes.

My parents were electronic engineering professors in a local college; they never cared about their looks and never dressed up or anything. There was no need for me to either. For three hundred days of the year, I had to wear the school uniform.

My wardrobe shopping was once a year during the Chinese New Year. Mom normally gave me $20 and asked me to buy some clothes for myself. Having no idea what to buy, I went to Giordano, similar to Old Navy in the US, and picked the first T-shirt and jacket I saw.

Determined to finish creating a profile that night, I cut and cropped some photos that had me in them and posted them on Match.com. After the three photos uploaded, I started to browse through others' profiles. Looking at those photos, reading through those descriptions, I was blown away. *Who said a perfect guy was impossible? They all lived on Match.com!*

Beautiful faces, fit bodies, killer smiles; love traveling, reading, sports; strong sense of humor, also loved helping people and always donating time to charity... and would love to meet guys that were similar...

There were just so many perfect guys. I needed to send them messages and get to know them. It was easy. It was math, and I was good at that. One out of five – worst-case scenario, one out of ten – perfect guys would likely respond to me. *I would soon get to know them, their stories, their families. We would go on dates in Capitol Hill. We would hold hands or even kiss on the street. We would be proud of being gay.* My imagination carried me away.

I sent twenty-four messages that night. I crafted a customized message for each man, finding similarity between us. Simon said he liked traveling, so I talked about my experiences in Israel and Egypt. Peter mentioned he was a foodie, so I asked him whether he had been to Facing East in Bellevue. John was proud of his job and was career-driven, so I laid out my plan to climb the corporate ladder at Microsoft.

I went to sleep that night with a big smile in my heart. There was a sense of belonging and so much hope. I woke up the next morning with the greatest eagerness. Jumping out of bed, I went straight to my computer to check on replies.

None. None. None.

Maybe people didn't respond that fast. They all had amazing lives. It must take time to reply. I comforted myself. A week later, still nothing. People all said gays were the most handsome and fun people. Maybe I was not good-looking enough. Maybe my humor was not enough. Growing up in China, humor was never part of my life.

I was sad and disappointed, but I was not letting this stop me. I went back to Craigslist. This was when I noticed Bryan.

* * *

JUST LIKE ALL the Craigslist hookups, I didn't know his name at first. He posted a photo. Fully clothed! He had beautiful eyes and dark curly hair. He was standing in front of some big trees. The big fir trees that Tom mentioned. He had a smile that was welcoming and genuine. I liked him. I sent him an email with my fully clothed photo.

We decided to meet that night at 9:00 p.m. He lived in Mill Creek, a golf course town located directly north of Seattle. It was by I-5 and on the way to Vancouver. I hadn't noticed the town when I was driving back and forth to Vancouver.

Parking my car on the street, I grabbed the six-pack of Blue Moon I'd bought. I'd never brought beer to meet a guy before. I wasn't sure why I did it this time. As I knocked gently on the red door a couple of times, my heart was pounding fast. I was excited but also worried this would turn into another hookup that I was not into.

Opening the door, Bryan welcomed me with a big smile. He was a little bit shorter than me. He had big eyes and long, curly eyelashes that almost touched his eyebrows. The eyelashes flipped up and down as he breathed.

I took off my shoes before walking into the living room, just like what I grew up doing, which was required by Mom. Old habits die hard. The wood floor was a little bit cold on my feet.

Bryan invited me to sit down on the couch in the center of the room. It was so comfortable. I was sinking in but was also completely supported by the cushion. The sage cushion looked like suede, but my skin didn't feel cold when touching it. *This was the kind of couch where I could take a great afternoon nap*, I thought.

I scanned the room quickly. It was an older one-story house, maybe built in the 1970s, but everything seemed modestly updated. Bryan turned down the light a little and joined me on the couch. A fire was crackling in the fireplace by the window that overlooked the big yard, bathing the dark room in its flickering light. The smell of burning wood made the air dense, but also made me feel refreshed. It was like we were camping in the forest.

"How are you doing?" His voice was casual and manly.

"Good. How is your day going?" I handed him a Blue Moon, nervous and excited.

"I am good. Had a busy day today. After getting off work, I went to paint this house in Queen Anne..." He took a sip of the beer and continued to talk about his day.

I was a little bit surprised. That's like me when I first moved to the U.S. I always gave detailed answers about how my day was going when people asked me, "How are you?" Then one day, my classmate Scott told me that the question was just a conversation opener. No real answer was needed. Just a simple, "I'm fine," would do.

Ever since then, I tried to restrain myself from sharing my day when asked how I was. And right now, Bryan was going through the ups and downs of his day in detail. This was amazing. "I love houses in Queen Anne! They have so much character!" I replied.

We talked and talked. I found out that Bryan was born in Los Angeles and moved to Seattle when he was two years old because his dad got a job at Boeing. He knew he was gay when he was five years old. I barely remembered anything from that age. But Bryan told me that he had special feelings for other boys then.

I learned that he loved Barbie dolls when he was a boy but never had the courage to play with one openly. He was also not openly gay. None of his family or friends knew.

I talked about my struggle with sexual identity growing up in China. I talked about traveling around the world in my first job after college. I talked about what brought me to the U.S. and to Seattle. I talked about my gay bar experience in Vancouver. I told him that none of my family knew either.

We must have talked for hours. His words, his openness, his smile connected to some part of me that had never been reached before. I felt something different than in previous meetups. It was like I had known Bryan for a long time.

As he continued talking, an urge to touch him, embrace him, and taste him pushed me closer to him. I put my hands behind his head, pulled him in, and started kissing him. He kissed me back passionately. His lips were so soft. I felt like melting into his kiss. The stubble on his shaved face was rough on my skin and sent tingles through my body. I wanted to devour him and be devoured by him.

I woke up the next morning so tired, but also so refreshed and excited. At age twenty-eight, I was not a virgin anymore.

For the entire day, my body was telling me that it needed rest, but my spirits were so high. I loved the connection with Bryan. He listened, and he talked. He genuinely seemed to want to know me and share his stories with me. I was so glad I hadn't settled for a hookup before.

We continued seeing each other over the following days. I took him to a Korean restaurant. He was scared by the little mummy-like dried fish with heads that were served as an appetizer. He took me to Zeeks Pizza to have his favorite pepperoni and olive pizza. We rode in his 1990 Toyota 4Runner. It was so rusted and tough.

He wore a pair of foldable pilot sunglasses when he was driving. The sunglasses brought out his facial features really well. Very long nose, large forehead topped by curly brown hair. A clean-shaven face but shaded beard area. It was a man's face. Parking the car in a random parking lot, we made out for hours. After that, we adventured to Capitol Hill and held hands, skipping on the street. I thought about holding hands with Bo and was amazed at how far I'd come.

* * *

I ALSO INTRODUCED Bryan to JD, who had become my most loyal friend in the past few years. Right before leaving Durham, I decided to adopt a dog. I always found guys with a dog very attractive. A man and his dog. The loneliness, the companion, and the wildness.

JD was from a shelter forty minutes away from Durham. I found him online. He looked like a typical husky with a black body, dark face, and two white eyebrows. But he was a mixed breed, maybe Labrador, the shelter told me.

His hair was shorter and shinier than that of a purebred husky. Fully grown now, he only weighs fifty-five pounds. His eyes first caught mine. He has a look of, "I am scared, but I am strong." I guess that's who I was at the time.

The people in the shelter picked a name, Dakota, for him. Since I loved Star Wars and sometimes fancied that I was a Jedi master, I called him Jedi Dakota. JD for short, which was also the main character from *Scrubs*, the show that I picked up from my roommate Craig at Duke.

Raising JD gave me a new meaning in life. I had never loved like this before. Abandoned by his previous owner when he was four months old, he was completely dependent on me to provide him food, comfort, and love. He became a new channel for my urge to love.

In Seattle, JD and I spent a lot of time in Marymoor, which was said to be the second biggest dog park in the world. The thirty-plus-acre playground is Disneyland for humankind's most loyal friend. There are rivers, an extensive grassland, a forest, endless trails, and open meeting areas. I made a commitment to take JD there at least twice a week.

I asked Bryan to go to Marymoor with JD and me. Bryan was not thrilled. He told me that when he was a kid, his parent's giant malamute dog, Buddy, once put Bryan's entire little head in his mouth and left a mark. Ever since then, Bryan was scared of dogs. Trying to deal with JD one on one was one thing; going to a park that was full of dogs was another.

Every relationship has problems to solve. I would make Bryan love JD one day, I told myself.

* * *

AS WE SPENT more time together and I got more and more into Bryan, I realized that he was dating another guy, Juan. Bryan told me that he met him before meeting me. I knew that we had only been dating for a few days, but knowing that there was another guy made my heart sink.

I thought there was a special connection between us. Now I wondered whether Bryan felt the same connection with Juan. *Did he talk to Juan for hours? Did he kiss Juan with the same passion with which he kissed me?*

After he told me about Juan, Bryan was very clear about his open relationship status. He did not believe in exclusive relationships or marriage. His mom left him when he was eighteen. She got into drugs and abandoned the entire family.

She lived in a trailer with her drug-addict boyfriend, parking the trailer on her husband, Bill's, street. One year later, she and Bill got a divorce. Her settlement was $100 K, and she spent it all in one year. Everybody in Bryan's family had severed their relationship with her except Bryan. He was still contacting her and giving her money for groceries or gas.

This was like the Hollywood dramas I watched on television. I couldn't comprehend how all this had impacted Bryan's heart and belief in family and marriage. *He must have buried his emotions and pain about his mom deep. Maybe like how I buried who I was?*

While I was willing to understand where Bryan was coming from, I also knew what I wanted – an exclusive relationship. Growing up in a traditional Chinese family, the term *open relationship* was never in my vocabulary. My parents fought a lot, but they always made up and moved on. My mom talked a lot about how marriage was work – important, worthwhile work. That's the kind of relationship I wanted.

I had that talk with Bryan on our fourth date. I told him that I liked him and didn't want him to see Juan or other guys anymore. Bryan told me that he loved spending time with me. He said that I brought something more than other guys he had dated before. He saw something special in me and about us. He had already told Juan about me. If this continued going well, he could see a future just with me.

* * *

A FEW MONTHS ago, when I was struggling with my sexual identity, I had booked a backpacking trip to Europe for this summer. Traveling had profoundly changed my life, even more than the Chinese education system had.

I was fortunate to travel extensively internationally in my first job at SAP after graduation from college. I was in charge of teaching the latest technology to SAP partners, and I visited different countries almost every other week. My trip always comprised a three- to five-day presentation followed by a couple of days of sightseeing.

Spending time with people in Malaysia, Egypt, and Israel made me question why there was no religion where I grew up. I asked myself what I believed in but couldn't find an answer.

Watching the flag-raising ceremony competition at the border of Pakistan and India gave me an awareness of intercountry politics that I had no interest in before.

Being immersed in the diverse and free culture of the Western world in Australia, France, and the USA made me doubt that the boxed life planned by my parents and Chinese society might be the only reality.

Those thoughts from traveling brought me to where I was today. I wanted to throw myself out into the world again, to let the universe help me learn more about myself.

When I was in business school, my friends and I couch surfed forty-six states in the United States. We used the Couchsurfing platform to find local people who wanted to provide a couch, a bed, or sometimes a room for us. Couchsurfing hosts were not doing this for money; instead, they were looking for human connection and communication. They wanted to learn about others' stories and share their own.

I had some of my favorite travel memories from those couch-surfing experiences. We slept in a doghouse with two golden retrievers in Texas; we stayed in a luxury bedroom that was remodeled by HGTV in Cleveland; we rode horses in the snow at Miss Oregon's family farm.

Seeing the diverse spectrum of my hosts' lives kept me motivated and humble. The happiness that my hosts were after was quite the opposite of what my business school goals were – career and money.

As I was actively searching for Couchsurfing hosts for my first stop in Frankfurt, I stumbled upon a host that was a gay couple. That sparked lots of ideas and feelings. *How cool would it be if I made most of my stays on the trip with gay hosts! There was so much I could learn from them.*

I typed "gay" into the keyword field on the search menu. Ta-da! There were so many hosts who were openly gay. I was thrilled and booked the rest of my trip this way, except for in Amsterdam where I was going to meet my best friend Ally, to have my first ever coming out and to travel with her for a few days.

While I was excited about my trip, I didn't want to leave. Bryan and I had only had five dates, but I knew I was falling for him. Our talks, his shaved chin, the passionate kisses, my first sex, his troubled family past, and his openness, even telling me the other boys he was seeing.

I felt a spark; I wanted a future, and I believed we could have one. He told me that he felt the same way. I knew if I stayed and spent more time with him, our relationship could move to the next stage. He might let Juan go soon. Now, with my trip, he would have more time to spend with Juan. They might develop stronger feelings for each other.

But I couldn't think too much now, I told myself. I was really excited about the trip, especially because I was going to stay mostly with gay hosts. *How much I could learn about them, about sexuality, and about myself!*

At our last dinner before I left, I told Bryan how much he meant to me and how much I wanted to be with him exclusively. Surprisingly, or not surprisingly, he told me that he was falling for me too. He said that was not an emotion he had before for other guys. He didn't know where this was leading but wished me a great trip and said we could talk about it after I came back.

COUCHSURFING IN EUROPE

"One's destination is never a place, but a new way of seeing things."

—Henry Miller

"See you in eighteen days (sad face)." After sending the message to Bryan, I turned off the phone.

I didn't want to leave. The last four weeks meeting guys in Vancouver and in Seattle had been an amazing journey. It was the first time I felt free, not only physically but mentally and emotionally. I finally reached out to the area of me that I never dared to explore.

"Life is about experience," I told myself. Not all of the meetings with guys turned out well, but I did have some physical pleasure and also learned. At least I knew all the acronyms on Craigslist's Men Meeting Men section now. That was a new language skill, just not for my resume.

More importantly, I met Bryan. I felt a connection. I could not get him out of my mind. It was different from the feeling with my ex-girlfriend; it was different from the feeling with my best friend Bo.

It was like there was a chain that connected my heart to Bryan. Every move of his would pull the chain and yank on my heart. It hurt a little bit, sometimes a lot, depending on what he was doing. My thoughts were full of him all the time. *This must be love.*

I felt vulnerable and scared. I knew Bryan was in an open relationship. When I wasn't home, he would definitely spend time with Juan, as he had said. Every time I thought about it, my heart ached. I just needed the next eighteen-day fully scheduled journey to push away the thoughts and heartache that were killing me inside.

Traveling was not about where I was going, but who I was traveling with. I believed that the gay families I was going to stay with would give me new perspectives on gayness, a topic that I hid from for twenty-eight years and was so eager to learn more about now.

I also decided to come out to my best friend Ally when I met her in Amsterdam. The thought was so uplifting and scary. But, hey, my life would not be normal and planned by my parents and society anymore. The whole journey in front of me, just like this trip, would be new, exciting, scary, and unpredictable.

* * *

MY FIRST STOP was Frankfurt. I stayed with Hermann and Gerhard. They were in their fifties and lived in a suburb of Frankfurt not far from the airport.

Gerhard was the person whom I was talking to and the one who orchestrated the couch-surfing logistics for their family. He picked me up from the airport in his little yellow VW Beetle that was older but well kept. *How much more German could that be?* I thought as I got in the car.

"Hermann is still at work. How was your flight?" Gerhard turned to me and gave a smile as he clicked on the left blinker.

I took a good look at him. White beard, short hair, and a wrinkled face made him looked like a Santa Claus who had just finished a brutal fishing trip in Alaska. His smile was so warm and welcoming, and it was followed with little low-voice chuckles, like the engine rumbling of his Beetle.

"I am good." I returned a big smile as big as the happy mouth on Amazon's logo.

"So, you mentioned you're gay?"

"Yes, I am gay, but very new." I felt both nervous and relieved to say that for the first time, to anybody. I thought maybe it was because Gerhard was still a stranger, which made it easier for me to come clean to him at our first meeting.

"I will show you gay culture in Frankfurt," Gerhard promised, letting out a big laugh.

The landscape changed quickly. The modern Frankfurt airport was soon replaced by trees, rivers, and low residential buildings. In ten minutes, we arrived at a little town.

I stepped out of the car. The street was not wide and was lined with two-story stone houses. I loved the design of the houses, unquestionably German, just like all the houses in Leavenworth, a German tourist town outside of Seattle. The roofs were red clay, and there were brick decorations and patterns on the walls and around the windows. The flower beds underneath each window were full of little yellow, red, and purple flowers.

"This is our house." Gerhard pointed at a white building made of stones, maybe hundreds of years old. I needed to soak up all the culture and history, I told myself.

Gerhard showed me the guest room, which was in a structure like a tool shed, in the garden, and invited me to drink some fresh herbal tea he made. Gerhard was very open. He shared every single piece of information about his life with me. He and Hermann had been together for more than twenty years. They were married.

Gerhard said, "Most of my straight friends are divorced, but we are still together..." It was so true. In this heartless world, true love was rarely found, no matter straight or gay. I was jealous and admired them at the same time. I hoped that one day I could find my love in life. I hoped it was Bryan.

However, what shocked me was that although they loved each other so much, they also actively looked for other men to have sex with. Gerhard had a couple of friends with whom he had regular sex at least monthly. They were each all right with their partner in life having sex with other people.

"Hermann having sex with another man is like him playing golf with his friends... I have no problem with that..." Gerhard told me. "Well, frankly speaking, it took me a while to really accept this... I don't mean about the sex; I mean the emotional attachment. Hermann is the one who likes the people he fucks, and I worried that he would fall in love with one of the other people that he has sex with."

"Interesting..." I didn't know what to say. And this time I was really speechless.

Gerhard continued, "But I then realized that love and having sex are totally different things... Now we both have sex partners and also look for people to have sex with together. We love each other very much and will stay forever."

I didn't imagine my first stay would provide such direct talk about sex. The sexual content of our first conversation was more than I had had in my entire life. Gerhard referred to the sex-driven open relationship (SDOR) as a gay style and said that I was still thinking in a straight way – date, date, more date, and finally sex...

Maybe what Gerhard said was accurate about how most gays lived, maybe it wasn't. To me, there was one thing for sure:

I couldn't suck somebody's dick without liking him, and I couldn't have sex without emotional attachment.

That's why after so many attempted hookups, I had only had sex with Bryan. I liked the physical intimacy with another guy, but at the same time, I wanted to be exclusive with someone, someone special. This was important to me. I wanted the emotional connection. I was and wanted to continue to be a responsible and committed person.

We continued our conversation into the night with a delicious dinner in a nearby restaurant that served *schweinshaxe* (roasted pork knuckle) per my request. When I went to bed, I couldn't stop thinking. *Is Bryan living the SDOR lifestyle that Gerhard was talking about? Maybe he and I are really different?*

The next day, Hermann's niece visited. Gerhard took me to the local grocery store and loaded up on freshly baked bread and cured meat. Sitting in their sunny garden, staring at the blossoming pink and yellow flowers, we had a long and relaxing lunch.

I thought my life in Seattle was slow! I finally understood what it meant to take it easy and enjoy. I wanted to do this with Bryan. Beautiful places, relaxing meals. I started fantasizing about what it would be like.

Hermann invited us to go geocaching right after lunch. People who participated in the game had hidden a "treasure" in a secret place in the neighborhood. They then wrote a little plot and posted a clue to the geocaching website.

We went to the website, found a plot that was interesting to us, and then followed the clue to find the hidden treasure. The treasure was not usually anything expensive. However, it was always something special that showcased the creativity and intelligence of the preparer. This was the best way to explore the area where Gerhard and Hermann lived. We walked the entire afternoon through different villages, abandoned buildings, and forests.

We talked about different cultures, politics, and life. I couldn't believe Germans paid almost 50 percent tax on income! To make it crazier, they were happy about it! I was surprised by how much they hated Google because they believed the company was invading their privacy. Coming from China where the entire internet is controlled by the government, I thought Google was the best thing in the world.

I learned that Germans really care about education and spent a lot of time (and tax money) making sure their kids learn well. I learned that they love delicious food and have all kinds of secret recipes for different dishes. I learned that they love family gatherings and try to have one at least once a week. *How different we are while at the same time so similar!*

I called Bryan that evening. He had not returned my text messages in twelve hours. I got worried, and my heart started hurting physically. He picked up the phone immediately. He was excited to hear my voice. "How are you, babe?"

"I am good. Just miss you so much."

"I miss you too."

I started sharing what I learned from Hermann and Gerhard, about the geocaching stone art we found, and about the delicious schweinshaxe I ate. I tried to steer the conversation away from the free sex lifestyle they were leading. That was the last thing I want to share with Bryan.

Then Bryan said, "Guess what? I ran into Juan driving on the street today. What are the chances?"

My heart sank. It hurt more, but somehow I could not feel it clearly. I didn't want to ask what happened next. I told Bryan I missed him and hung up the phone.

On the third day, to keep his promise, Gerhard took me to all the gay culture spots in Frankfurt. I needed to go to the bathroom. Gerhard told me that there was a gay hookup bathroom we should check out. It was a public bathroom in the densest part of the city. It was just one giant room with long urinals on the floor on three sides. I covered my nose because of the strong urine smell.

I pulled down my pants and tried to pee, but I suddenly realized that the two people next to me were getting closer. They put their heads in front of me and stared at my private area.

All my urge to pee was gone. I was still pushing, but when one guy's hand reached out, I instantly pulled my pants up and ran outside. This was too much and too crazy for me. Having only seen scenes like this in pornos, I could not believe that this was reality!

Gerhard took me to a gay bathhouse that evening. He told me this was not a place to take a shower but to have sex with another guy or sometimes in a group. I didn't want to go inside. It was like putting all the horny guys on Craigslist in a giant room together. I knew how that would end up, and I knew what I would do. I had tried so many times.

Maybe it was to be polite, or maybe it was because I was still hurt from what Bryan told me the previous night, but I followed Gerhard in. At the check-in counter, we got a key for a personal locker, a bathrobe, and a condom. "Having safe sex is the most important thing," Gerhard told me with a serious face.

The bathhouse was very dark inside, with only a few depressing red lights. There were so many rooms that I lost count. "They're for sex," Gerhard told me. "There aren't many guys here today. I'm going to look around." He disappeared in the red-lit darkness.

I wandered around a little bit and found a sauna room. There was nobody inside. Perfect! I needed some hot steam to help me relax from the jet lag, the fatigue of traveling, and thinking of Bryan.

After ten minutes or so, I felt a little light-headed. I went out to the center of the bathhouse, where there was a bar area. I ordered a cappuccino and a bottle of water.

As I was sipping my drinks in my underwear, a guy walked toward me. He wore only underwear as well. He looked like an Abercrombie model – short hair and extremely fit body with his six-pack clearly defined.

As I was checking him out, he looked deep into my eyes and pushed his tongue into my mouth. I didn't push him away. Maybe I was thinking of Bryan and what could happen between him and Juan, and I wanted this to be my revenge.

He asked me to go back to his hotel with him. I said yes. It was a small economy hotel by the airport. The bed was twin size. But everything was so clean and simple. It was like a little IKEA showroom. We talked more during the taxi ride and in his hotel room. I learned that his name was Stefan. He was from Bamberg, Germany, and was en route to a two-week vacation in Mexico. He told me how much he loved warm weather.

I told him about my journey of coming out during the last couple of months. I told him about Bryan and how deeply in love I felt. Maybe because we were out of the bathhouse, or because it was clear I did not want sex with strangers, we didn't do anything. Lying on his twin bed, we just held each other's hands and fell asleep.

The next morning, Stefan went directly to the airport. I took a taxi and went back to Gerhard and Hermann's home.

The last few days passed quickly. I was introduced to a world that I could never have imagined, and I was shocked by how free sex was in my hosts' life. I was happy for the life they were living, but I was even more certain that it was not for me. I wanted a committed and exclusive relationship with a guy.

Saying goodbye to Gerhard and Hermann, I jumped on the train to Munich.

* * *

OTTO WAS MY host in Munich. He was straight, but he had a life that was more unorthodox than a gay life in China. When he was eighteen years old, his girlfriend and he decided they never wanted kids. He had a vasectomy.

He owned properties around the world and even islands in the United States, but when we went out for lunch, he stole a knife because he liked the carving on it. *Why not just ask to buy it?* I wanted to ask, but stopped myself.

He was a true foodie and would drive his Ferrari to towns in surrounding countries, such as Salzburg in Austria, for dinner at least once a week.

"*Carpe diem.*" He told me that was his life motto. When I learned that term from *Dead Poets Society*, I was still in China. I couldn't understand it at all. In a country where everybody was raised like ants or bees, following precise orders and always saving for the future, I couldn't imagine a life focused on thinking about right now. *Only the moment right in front of me, instead of the future?* That reminded me of Bryan somehow.

That's how Otto had been living, and he was making the most of it. "Be happy for this moment. This moment is your life." What Omar Khayyam said truly was the way Otto was living.

He loved meeting different people and had multiple houses in Munich to host different couch surfers. When he hosted people, he tried to cherish every second of the experience by showing the best of his culture and learning about the other.

He took me to a big park nearby for a stroll. There were so many tall trees. They were not like all the newly planted trees in communities and parks across China, where the focus was all on the future. The trees here in the park carried history. The trees were also wider, with more leaves, so different from the fir trees in the Pacific Northwest, and equally magnificent. "Is that what the famous Black Forest looks like?" I asked myself.

There was a group of white swans swimming in the lake, so elegantly and peacefully. The park had a sense of ego and narcissism, as did the way Otto talked and moved.

A large group of people were doing exercises in the park. "That's like in parks in China!" I yelled. "Old people in China do group exercises every day in the park!"

"It is different here," Otto said. "They receive tax credits when they join exercise programs like this. I bet you guys don't have that in America. The healthcare industry will never allow Congress to pass a bill like this in America."

I just nodded my head. He knew more about America than I did as a new immigrant.

I didn't mention anything about being gay. Maybe it was shame, or maybe it was the sense that Otto wouldn't understand, but I still wasn't ready to talk about my sexuality with another human being who was not gay. Otto openly shared all his relationships, but also had a German-gentlemanly way of not asking too much about my personal story.

At night after everything settled down, however, I faced the elephant in the room of my sexuality. To make it worse, I started missing Bryan so much. I texted him every day. When he didn't respond immediately, I thought he must be spending time with Juan. *Maybe he would choose him instead of me?* That thought made me sad.

Carpe diem during the day, but at night, all I could think about was my past and future. *I am gay. Who am I kidding? But how can I tell my parents or my best friends Joe, Echo, Ally? I have lied to them for my entire life. I am going to meet Ally in two days. I am going to tell her everything.* I started debating with myself. The thought of telling them made it hard to breathe. I didn't want to think further.

* * *

AFTER SAYING GOODBYE to Otto, I started my journey to Ghent, Belgium. I was going to meet with Tang and Noah.

On the train from Munich to Ghent, I opened my computer and examined their profile in detail. They were a gay couple. Tang was from Singapore, but he had lived in Belgium for over nine years. Noah was from Ghent and was a police officer. They had been together for quite a while and were deeply in love with each other.

Since I was only staying one night at their place, I needed to make the most of it. As soon as I met Tang, I felt the similarity and connection. It was not just our looks – dark skin, short black hair, Asian eyes, skinny body – but also where we were in life.

86

He was just five years older than me. He was an Asian in a relationship with a white guy. He lived in another country in a Western culture where he was a minority. Most importantly, he and Noah were in an exclusive relationship. While I respected Gerhard and Hermann's lifestyle, it didn't align with what I wanted my life to be. Everything about having sex with others while being committed to each other contradicted my values.

We went to a restaurant called Amadeus Gent 1 right by their house to have all-you-can-eat ribs. With more than one thousand reviews and a score of more than four out of five on Google, the ribs did not disappoint. Tang and Noah invited some of their friends too, a straight couple.

Sitting there, devouring all the ribs, I loved how normal everything was. Tang and Noah didn't hide their affection toward each other. They addressed each other as "honey" and "babe." Noah casually wiped away a drop of BBQ sauce on Tang's right cheek. Tang reached out to hold Noah's hand when they were talking about their first date.

What a simple, plain, boring, and less dramatic relationship Tang and Noah had! I loved their life! I was jealous! *Would I have one like this with Bryan?*

I summoned all my courage and sent a long text to Bryan. I told him I loved him. I told him I wanted a relationship like what Tang and Noah had. I told him I was okay with him being still undecided. I believed we would be together in the end. Yes, I told him I loved him again.

Done sending the text, I turned off my phone. I didn't want to wait for his response. The delay in his response only made me worried and jealous.

The next morning, there were five text messages from Bryan. The last one said, "Give me some time. I love you too."

* * *

I WAS GOING to meet Ally in Amsterdam. I was so excited and scared. Ally was my best friend in high school. We studied together at school and set up studying goals and raced each other to finish.

Every day, after the tiresome studying at school, we rode back home together on our bikes. Her home was further from school than mine. I enjoyed saying goodbye to her and challenged her on the evening study goal while watching her cycle away.

She was a little bit overweight, while I was skinny as hell. Our classmates called her "Meatball" and me "Chopstick." We were never bothered by it.

Ally was more than a friend; she was an inspiration. She had the most illuminating smile, the most confident voice, and the most courageous attitude.

Ally always loudly announced her goal in front of the entire class. She declared she wanted to be the best in Chinese. The next quarter, she was picked by the Chinese teacher to be her teaching assistant, and she always ranked at the top in the class exams. The quarter after that, she announced her love for chemistry class, and the same thing happened.

I was fascinated. With all my parents' love and protection, I was born and grew up in fear. I always worried that if I said I wanted something, I wouldn't get it. I always expected the worst, and said so, to protect my fragile heart and ego.

Inspired by Ally, I decided no matter what she wanted to do, I wanted that too. Ally bought a certain study book for chemistry, and I bought one the next day. Ally set a goal to finish thirty reading comprehension exercises in a week, and I pushed some items off of my agenda and added those reading comprehension exercises to my list.

Later, she told me she was going to get her MBA in Boston. That, combined with the thoughts of running away from my lies to my ex-girlfriend, made me decide to follow her to the U.S. I landed in Durham in North Carolina, but not too far from her. I drove up to visit her in the bone-chilling Boston winter. We wandered to Maine to taste lobster and ski.

She was like a sister to me. If there were anybody I should be open to first, it would be Ally. I decided to tell her I was gay.

I arrived at her apartment in the north of the city. It was smaller than I expected, and what I got was a sleeping bag on the floor. I wasn't bothered; I was so excited and scared to see her. I was going to spend five days with her. These would be precious moments. I needed to come clean to her from day one.

I booked a reservation at a restaurant called De Kas, which was highly recommended by my colleague at Microsoft. The restaurant was in a giant glass building in the middle of Frankendael Park. It was a fixed menu with the chef deciding what to offer based on supply. All the vegetables served were grown in the garden in the back. All the meat was from animals that were locally raised. The restaurant was so upscale and beautiful. Ally was excited. She was happy that I booked such a nice place.

My brain was overflowing with the thought of telling Ally that I was gay. Sweat was rushing out parts of my body that I didn't know *could* sweat. Different scenarios jumped into my mind like flashcards.

I should make it personal and start with my childhood story...

No, no, I should talk about the gay couples I met first. Starting with travel is always good...

Bryan, I should definitely start with Bryan. We said, "I love you," to each other already, even thought it was through text...

Sipping red wine, Ally was excited to see me. She was also thrilled about living in another country and pursuing a shiny career in the investment banking industry. Her smile, her confidence, and her courage...

Raising my glass in a trembling hand, I choked the wine down. I hated drinking. Drinking was not a tradition in my family, but now, just like the night in Vancouver, I needed alcohol to be as courageous as Ally.

"I need to tell you something." Tears started rolling down my cheeks. "It is about me. I don't know how to start. Please just bear with me."

In the next sixty minutes, I dug through everything I could about my past. I talked about my "girlfriend" from middle school, my parents asking me never to date, my loving relationship with Bo in college, and Bryan. I told her that I loved him, that he was in an open relationship and still seeing another guy. I told her about how much that hurt me, how much I wanted a committed and exclusive relationship. I talked about the trip, the gay couples that I had met and the dramatically different gay lives that they were living. I told her that I didn't know what my life would be going forward. I didn't think my eyes would ever be dry again. I was so scared, but I just wanted to be true to myself and her.

She listened. She nodded. She looked at me with the softest eyes. She reached out her hands. She cried with me. She gave me a chance to say who I was for the first time.

She told me that she was surprised, but she totally understood. She said she was glad to meet the true me, and she would help me in whatever way she could throughout the journey. She praised my courage. I told her that I stole it from her.

At the end, we joked about what these two crying Chinese meatballs and chopsticks were doing in an upscale restaurant in Amsterdam. We had a good laugh.

Since I was so nervous preparing, actually debating rather than preparing, for the conversation with Ally, I had not planned anything for the next few days. Ally, by contrast, had planned a whole schedule for our time together.

Our first stop was Italy. Ally planned a great hiking journey for us in La Spezia, a group of five fishing villages. Each of them was unique, but they shared the same charm, peace, and love.

After sixteen hours and three different train rides, we checked into a small hotel that was run by the locals. It was my first time not staying at somebody's house on this journey. "It's fine," I told myself. "I will have more self-exploration with Ally."

The hiking trails were along the cliffs of the Ligurian Sea. Like the grand Great Wall in China or the completely man-made stone garden in Suzhou, the trails here were built with mostly hand-carved stone. Stepping on each one was like stepping on a part of Italian history.

I had imagined a sandy beach when Ally told me the location was by the Mediterranean; however, the coast was marked by giant rocks like little mountains emerging from the water. On the mountain itself, there were two- to three-story houses, pink, yellow, red, green, all colors, seemingly springing directly out of the cliffs. *Where were their foundations? How did people build them?*

The water of the Ligurian sea was a deep, shimmering blue. Some fishing boats were lingering in the bay. A cluster of young, shirtless guys was sitting on a giant rock in the water. One dived into the water headfirst. His friends gave a couple of loud cheers. They all had darker skin. *Must be local boys*, I thought.

The sun was hot and intense. Lots of hikers had their shirts off to enjoy a full sunbath. *Why not?* I took off my shirt too and exposed my Seattle skin to the hot Italian sun. This was my first time hiking half naked. I was on a journey of trying new things, I told myself. Carpe diem.

There was little shade on the hike. All that survived here was cactus, aloe, and some short bushes with small, white, waxy leaves. Occasionally, there was a bigger tree giving shelter from the intense sunshine. That's where lots of people were resting and having a water break.

Wherever we looked, there was love graffiti. There were "J loves N" heart carvings on trees, red and white painted names on rocks, and a wall of love locks put up by people from around the world. They were either there to assert their commitment to each other on the wall or to make a wish to have that one day with somebody.

Ally urged me to put up one myself since love was what I was going after right now. I told myself I would bring Bryan here one day and we would put a lock on the chain wall together.

We left Italy the next morning and headed to Ally's friend's wedding in Switzerland. I loved traveling in Europe. No matter where we were going, there was a train to take us there. The train was pretty basic and old. It reminded me of the trains I took when I was a kid in China. It was just much cleaner and better maintained, like all the centuries-old buildings.

The tickets were expensive, at least to me. Each train ride cost more than a hundred dollars. Thanks to Ally's recommendation, I bought a package that allowed me to take unlimited train rides for ten days over a three-week period. This helped a lot since we needed to take four other trains to get to the little town where the wedding would take place.

The wedding was in Utzenstorf, Switzerland, where the groom was from. The bride was from China. Her parents couldn't be there for the wedding due to health reasons. Ally was dedicated to providing as much support as she could. Whatever Ally decided to do, I would follow. It had been like that for the past fourteen years.

The wedding reception was in a castle called Landshut, which was first built in the twelfth century and then rebuilt in the 1670s. There was a rose garden, the clearest river in the world that I could not help but jump into, beautiful sunny weather, an old wooden hanging bridge, and a charming castle in the middle. There was nothing more romantic than this.

Since the bride's family couldn't make it, the groom's family made an effort to make the wedding as Chinese as possible. There was so much lucky red everywhere. All the tables were decorated with Chinese art pieces. The candies for guests were wrapped in traditional Chinese double-happiness paper boxes.

In the evening, each of the guests was handed a white candle in the shape of a lotus, which symbolizes the purity of love in traditional Chinese culture. The candle was so delicate, I needed to hold it with two hands. We also received a loose hard paper lotus petal. The host of the ceremony asked us to write our wishes for the newlyweds on the paper lotus petal, put it on the lotus-shaped candle, light the candle, and then put it in the stream in front of the castle.

We then each lit a Chinese lantern and walked with our little lotus candle floating in the water to the junction where the stream met the river. At the junction, the newlyweds had a net to catch all the candles. They picked out the paper petals and put them in a box.

The host told us that the newlyweds would take one flower petal out a year from now on. The then husband and wife would read the wish together and live up to the wish for a year. Since there were one hundred guests, that new tradition would last them more than a lifetime.

"May love and courage make you happy together forever," I wrote on my paper. I thought the wish was for them. But on some level, it was a promise I made to myself.

I was still thinking about Bryan all the time. I missed him deeply. Although we texted "I love you" to each other, not being able to see him and knowing he still was in an open relationship filled me with dread.

Ally told me that I was falling for the feeling of falling in love but was not really in love with Bryan. I barely knew Bryan. She said I was like a twenty-eight-year-old teenager who had tasted love for the first time. I was dazzled by the emotional and physical excitement and connection with another human being and was fantasizing a future with Bryan because I believed it was the only one possible.

"How many people end up with their first love?" Ally asked me. I didn't answer. I thought she was completely right. But at the same time, I knew there was something special about Bryan, about my feeling toward him, and about us.

People always talked about love at first sight. I never believed in that, and I didn't think that was the deal with Bryan and me. We were definitely physically attracted to each other, but for us, it was more like the perfect match of two troubled souls.

One was hurt by his family tragedy, from his mom tearing apart what is supposed to be the strongest trust and love in life – between a child and his mom.

One was hiding from the truth of his sexuality in a culture and society where being gay was not an option.

Both were eager to have a chance in life, to be healed, just to be normal, to be loved, to have what life should offer. The suffering that had happened in two families, two countries, and two cultures created a bond that was about more than just sex.

At the wedding, the groom's mom shared some good thoughts. "We cannot change our past, which has been defined already. Similarly, we can only plan our future, but cannot determine that. Love is not about grasping another person, or a static image; it is a process and motion. Love is about exploring the other person, deeper and deeper, until we reach the bottom of each other and we still want to be with the person, for good or bad."

Listening to what was said, I started sobbing. Her words were like sunshine melting the snow and ice that had covered my heart for so long. Looking back at my journey of self-exploration, I couldn't believe that I came out to myself already. I also had found Bryan, whom I wanted to call my boyfriend and build a life with. We might have different ideas for now, but nothing was insolvable as long as we both wanted to try. I wanted to learn more about Bryan, the good and the bad, and to love him forever.

Leaving Ally was as tough as I imagined. When I was exploring myself in what felt like a new life, emotions tumbling free, Ally's company was my anchor. She was not just an ear to talk to and a shoulder to lean on. She understood me. She knew the way I grew up and the struggles I had in school. The moments with Ally were precious ones that I didn't want to end.

Ally was the person I had modeled myself after for so long. Now I needed to go on a personal journey to find love, something way more complicated and delicate than reading a textbook or applying to a school.

It was also time to go back to Seattle. In the past two and a half weeks, I had learned so much about myself. It didn't magically change me into a confident gay who was proud of my sexual identity. But I did come out to my best friend and learn to let my emotions out. At least I was "one best friend out" gay! I needed to hold this little victory close.

I was also eager to see Bryan. I missed his passionate kisses, touching his soft curly hair, and lying with him to listen to a random album I picked out from his extensive vinyl collection.

On the other hand, I was nervous about facing other things. *Work must have been piled up. Should I tell my roommates that I was gay? Should I tell my colleagues? I had not talked to Mom for three weeks. What should I say when she asked about the trip to Europe?*

LETTER TO PARENTS

"Only by speaking out can we create lasting change. And that change begins with coming out."

—DaShanne Stokes

"I've got a surprise for you. Come straight to my place." As I turned on my phone when my British Airway flight landed in Seattle Tacoma International Airport, a message from Bryan popped up. The message excited me. I couldn't wait to see him. *What surprise had he prepared for me?* Jumping into a taxi, I headed straight to his house in Mill Creek.

Bryan had cooked a delicious sockeye salmon dinner for me. He said this was the most Pacific Northwest way to welcome his loved one. With the delicious food and wine, I shared my eye-opening experience with Gerhard and Hermann but was clear that I didn't want that kind of relationship. I talked about Tang and Noah and told him that I hoped we could be like them. I talked about Ally and the journey of my first coming out experience. Bryan listened closely and nodded along the way.

I was too afraid to ask what happened between him and Juan, but Bryan brought it up himself. He did meet Juan when I was gone. He didn't go into detail, but he said he told Juan about us.

He gave me more history about him and Juan. They had met a few weeks before I entered Bryan's life. He enjoyed going camping, boating, or just hanging out with Juan. But with me, he felt that there was something different.

He told me that I showed him a different life. He loved my world-traveling experience, my Chinese culture, my education, my courage, my not perfect English, my need to calculate every math sum in my mind even in a grocery store line, my need to turn on the blinker to park in my own driveway, and the speed with which I devoured a peach. He decided to call me "Peach." I felt surprised and excited at what Bryan said. This was more than I was expecting. I was special to him, just like how I felt about him. I decided to call him "Mango," his favorite fruit.

I told Bryan that the feeling was mutual. He showed me how to live in the moment. The contentment with what he had, not what he could have. I loved when he sang his heart out for Whitney's "I Will Always Love You" in karaoke, something we had done before I left. He was so amazing, and everybody clapped. I told him that I was his biggest fan.

I told him that he had a work ethic second to none. I was so impressed that he got up at 3:30 a.m. every day and headed to Safeway, the grocery store where he had worked since he was eighteen, but he still gave it his best and offered the biggest smile every day.

I told him that I loved the way he kissed and the way we made love. I loved to cuddle with him and fall asleep in his arms.

We talked and talked like that day was the end of the world and we needed each other to hear all we had to say. We wanted our lives to merge. We wanted to wake up every day with the other sleeping right next to us on the bed. We wanted to text each other, "When are you coming home today?" instead of, "Do you want to hang out?" We want to go grocery shopping and plan our weekly dinners together.

The next day, I packed some clothes and necessary items into two boxes and moved in with Bryan.

Living under the same roof created a space for our love to blossom. We cooked each other our own favorite foods and watched each other's favorite shows at night. Bryan challenged me to jog with him in the morning, at 3:00 a.m., before he went to work.

Our world suddenly expanded to more than two individuals' lives added together. The love infused and magnified all the pieces of our lives. I found out the biggest advantage of being in a gay relationship – saving on clothes. Since Bryan and I were similar in size, we started sharing T-shirts, underwear, and socks.

* * *

MONTHS WENT BY fast as we enjoyed our newfound gay couple relationship. The yellow and red leaves on the trees in October soon fell and lay dead on the ground in January. A problem came up: my parents' annual visit from China to their dearest son in the US during the Chinese Spring Festival in February.

After coming out to Ally, I didn't tell anybody else about being gay. I didn't have any reason to. I was madly in love, and why bother giving myself a difficult job?

If I ranked the difficulties of coming out audiences, parents were definitely at the top of the list. Having traditional Chinese parents who had given direction to their only son for his entire life made coming out a mission-impossible job.

Did my parents even know what gay was? I wasn't ready, and I really didn't want to tell them that their son, whom they were so proud of, was gay. This would become the shame of the community. *What would happen to my parents' jobs at the school? Would this give them heart attacks? Would this break our relationship? Would they disown me as their son?*

On the other hand, I felt an urge to talk to Mom. Growing up, Mom was the one by my side all the time. I was Mommy's boy. I shared all my struggles with study and work with her. I just tried not to mention anything about relationships. The only thing I mentioned was my "ex-girlfriend," with the purpose of shutting down any questions about girlfriends and hopes for marriage.

However, my relationship with Bryan and my newfound identity was the only thing on my mind now. I tried to avoid calling Mom. When she called me, I always found some excuse. "I need to finish an important project at work." "I am going to the gym now." "Work is so much, I am so tired. I need to sleep."

Mom definitely noticed the change. But she didn't know what to do about it. I was pushing us into a territory that she had never experienced.

While I was overjoyed with Bryan and the feeling of falling in love, thoughts of Mom snuck in from time to time. I had just brushed the thoughts off before, but now, I needed to face them.

"They are coming in three weeks. They will see that I am living with you. What should I do?"

"Tell them." Sitting in front of the computer in the living room and browsing through classic cars, Bryan didn't even think much. "They will still love you..." The 50 percent German in Bryan made his answer straightforward and simple.

"You haven't even come out to your parents yet, how do you know? Besides, my parents are from CHINA! Gay is the devil, is a disease, is AIDS!" I was frustrated and raised my voice.

"Tell them not to come then." Still staring at the computer screen, Bryan replied fast and in a monotone. He never overthinks.

"How can I? They have been visiting me every year! Could you give a more useful recommendation?"

This became our first argument as a couple. I irresponsibly dumped the "unsolvable" problem on Bryan's shoulders and was mad at him for not being able to provide the good solution that I couldn't come up with.

"Write them a letter then." Bryan turned his head at me and realized that I was really upset. He was not easily angered and was always the calm one when I freaked out.

"Yes, a letter! I will send them a letter so I don't have to tell them face-to-face or over the phone. They can also decide what to do." My face lit up and my voice turned cheerful.

Still scared about the outcome, I poured my heart out in a letter. I didn't have much time since their plane was leaving in three weeks. Luckily, writing this letter turned out to be very easy. It was like lifting the cover of a steaming pot that had been boiling for so long. Once the cover was off, all the thoughts and emotions just came out.

The next day, sitting at the dining room table, I yelled at Bryan, "I am ready to send it."

"Wait. Let me change this..." I murmured to myself.

"I am ready to send it!" Thirty minutes later, the draft was still there in my Gmail. I needed somebody to push me to click the Send button.

"Maybe I shouldn't send it. There must be another way..."

"What's the worst that could happen?" Bryan walked to me with a cup of coffee he had just made.

"They could disown me as their kid. Or they could have heart attacks. Dad has a heart problem already and needs to use a heart monitor from time to time..." I was using all the excuses I could find and sharing all my worst nightmares.

"Do you want me to help you send it?" Bryan said.

"Yes, there is a reason I am with you! I love you." I squeezed out a nervous smile.

Ten seconds later, the thousand words of my true self were on the way across the Pacific Ocean to land it in Mom's inbox.

Letter to Parents (original Chinese version in the appendix)

Mom and Dad,

Hope you are doing well. I heard that we have finally installed a heating system at home in Hunan. Hopefully, the grandparents can have a warm winter now. I still remember when I was a kid, living in Hunan, I was always sitting right next to the briquette stove to keep myself warm. I loved getting snow from outside and putting it on the stove. The sizzling sound of snow melting and the strong smell of water mixing with hot iron are still like yesterday to me.

Mom always said that I was a person who only shared good news and never bad. I felt that way too. I grew up in a family where everybody made it a priority to share the happiness with people we love while hiding all the pain and suffering to deal with individually.

I always thought that I was a good and well-behaved kid. When I was little, Mom said studying was important, so I studied so hard, gave up everything I liked doing, and threw myself into the endless cycle of studying-testing-studying-testing. The only fun moment I had was riding my bike to DaoNeiJia, the local grocery store, to buy mandarin-orange-flavor jelly snacks. The simple joy helped the boring studying days pass. Looking back at the way I grew up, I really appreciated the decision to study hard when I was a kid. I realize the education I have received has given me a platform wider and more resourceful than what some of my friends have. When I was traveling around the world and visiting new countries, I knew the positive impact you have made on my life.

But the boring studying life also made me naive and immature in lots of ways. When I was in middle school, I thought I liked a girl in my class a lot. We were studying together every day and called each other Mentor-Mentee. All the pressure from studying didn't give me enough time or courage to tell her I liked her. I knew that if I dabbled my feet in a loving relationship, I would open Pandora's box and ruin my whole life.

I think the restriction of not expressing my love changed me slowly. I'm not sure why, but I felt ease and comfort in dealing with boys. There was no pressure or guilt. I slowly found that I was attracted to guys. It was a magical feeling that I could not describe. But I felt so thrilled, excited, and happy toward guys.

As you know, I met my first girlfriend, Meimei, after college. I didn't know what love was but did know that finding a girlfriend who loved me was the right thing to do. We had some happy times together. But I clearly knew that I didn't love her. I grew up in the period of China when the Open Policy created lots of conflict between traditional Chinese values and freedom of thought from the Western world. The Chinese society I was living in was having a perfect storm of chasing after money and an outdated value system. Most of the time, whatever others said was the right thing, became the right thing for me to do too. It has been my rule for life for so long.

But is that it?

I never had the courage to face the word "homosexual." It was a word representing crime, shame, and something that was unforgivable. However, living in America for the last few years made me aware of the other side of the story.

When I was interning at McKinsey & Company, I met a male colleague. He had worked at McKinsey for many years. He and his boyfriend went to get their MBA degrees at Harvard and MIT respectively. At Duke, there were lots of programs to support LGBTs, females, and African Americans. In America, the society that supports gays is called PRIDE. It means pride in Chinese. At Microsoft, there are groups for LGBT people. Even the benefits cover a gay husband or wife. After I learned the other side of the story, I found out that there was nothing to be afraid of. This also gave me an opportunity to really ask myself, do I like boys or girls? What kind of life do I want to have?

I have a boyfriend now. His name is Bryan. We have known each other for a few months now. He is my first boyfriend. I hope you can meet him when you come to Seattle.

I know that this must be a shock to you. You always talked to me about girlfriends, marriage, grandkids. I didn't want to hurt you with this email. I just want you to see the real me. Only sharing the good news and never the bad one tradition – I want it to stop here.

What is life about? I think it is to make yourself happy and make the ones we love and who love us happy. Mom and Dad, you are the most important people in my life. I want joy and happiness in your life. At the same time, I could not compromise and sacrifice my own happiness to create a fake world where everybody seems happy. I went through so much confusion, struggle, and pain before I came out to myself as gay, but now, I am clear-minded and happy. The real successful people are those who can face themselves, face the reality, who can squeeze lemonade out of a lemon and taste it with a big smile. I want to be like that.

In the past few months, I have told my story to my best friend Ally. She gave me unlimited support. This made me feel very happy. However, the age, culture, and education difference made telling you this my biggest worry. I know you grew up in a traditional Chinese culture and you might not accept the news. But I am also very hopeful. As you learn more about American culture, you may find that this is not a shameful thing and not against moral standards. Instead, this is a journey to find my true self, to find happiness and my true value. I am still the same me. Being gay doesn't change who I am and who I was.

I don't have any requests of you. I just hope that you won't share the news with the grandparents yet. They are getting old and may not want a surprise like this. I also hope that you will not share this with Aunty Yanzi. She lives with the grandparents. Slippery mouth may happen. I understand that you need a venue to vent and it is impossible for you to talk to your colleagues and friends about this. I talked to my cousin Adam about this. In his last quarter at Penn State, he did some training in this area. He is more than happy to talk to you about this.

Of course, I, your son, am always here if you want to talk. If you need time, I understand. I just want to let you know that I love you forever.

Tongtong
Jan. 5, 2011

* * *

ONE DAY PASSED, no response. Two days, three days, five days. Still no response. My worry and fear were getting worse. I had not given them a heart attack; otherwise, I would have received a phone call from Aunt Yanzi in Hunan. It must be the other outcome; they did not accept me.

I started to pour myself into reading. I needed to find courage somewhere.

"You must do everything that frightens you, JR. Everything. I'm not talking about risking your life, but everything else. Think about fear, decide right now how you're going to deal with fear, because fear is going to be the great issue of your life, I promise you. Fear will be the fuel for all your success, and the root cause of all your failures, and the underlying dilemma in every story you tell yourself about yourself. And the only chance you'll have against fear? Follow it. Steer by it. Don't think of fear as the villain. Think of fear as your guide, your pathfinder – your Natty Bumppo." What Natty said to JR in *The Tender Bar* seemed meant for me. I needed to stay strong. That's it.

Day seven, I got a reply from Mom. It was an email, as businesslike as the email I sent, not a phone call like what I usually got. "We are still coming. See you soon. Love, Mom." She kept it short.

I didn't have time to overthink. My parents were coming in less than two weeks. Bryan and I discussed whether we should both be at the airport to pick them up. We agreed that the best way was to have me meet them first and then decide the best meeting with Bryan.

Waiting at the international arrival gate at SeaTac airport, I started to get worried. I used to be so excited when my parents visited me. Their visits made this foreign land a temporary home. The delicious odor of Mom's cooking always filled my entire house. My American roommates normally commented, "What the fuck is the smell?" I always smirked and proudly said, "It is Chinese chive pancake. Do you want to try one?"

This time, all I had was anxiety and fear. The same airport, familiar arrival hall; it seemed that nothing had changed, but the letter I sent had pushed all of us into a new universe without a compass. *What would my parents say to me?* The thoughts of my parents suddenly seemed not homey but foreign.

Dragging the two giant suitcases, Mom and Dad walked slowly out of the gate. They looked shorter and thinner. The last time I saw them was one year ago. They had aged way more than a year. The extra wrinkles, cloudy forehead, and slightly messy and whiter hair must be the contribution of my letter. Mom always kept her hair well combed.

We hugged gently. I was too scared to look them in the eyes. They seemed to feel the same.

The traffic on I-5 was horrible. Inside the car, it was dead silent. "I don't live at home anymore," I murmured. "I have moved in with Bryan."

Mom started crying. She didn't say anything. In the back mirror, I saw that Dad's eyes were closed. The wrinkles were all raising up.

My tears couldn't be held in anymore. "I will drop you off at home." Wiping my tears, I continued, "My roommates Ye and Jake still live there. You met them last year."

Moving their giant luggage to their room, which was my bedroom, I said, "I am leaving. I still need to feed JD. You guys relax a little bit. Jet lag must be horrible..." I really didn't know what to say. The most comfortable and safe place used to be with them, but now I felt everything was alien and wrong. I just wanted to escape.

"You don't live here now, why we came here then?" Mom couldn't hold it in anymore. She cried out. I had never seen Mom so sad in my life. This was even worse than the time when Grandpa had a stroke and needed brain surgery when I was eight years old. She washed her face with tears every day at that time but was not this heartbroken and helpless.

"JD, even JD is not here anymore. We brought so much food from China. Two suitcases of food..." Mom opened the blue canvas suitcase; packs of snacks flew out over the edge. The smelly tofu snacks, sweet and spicy bamboo treats... Somehow I had lost interest in all those childhood favorites.

I didn't know what to say. I had not comforted Mom before. I didn't know how. I was always the one being taken care of.

Walking from the corner of the bed to Mom, Dad mumbled, "We will be okay. Just go."

Back at Bryan's house, I was devastated. I couldn't stop crying. Bryan was very understanding; he patted me and held me in his arms. I told him that I felt I was the worst son my parents could have.

I talked about Mom fighting for me when we moved to Guangzhou. My mom made me fall in love with the golden ladybugs and made me believe that I had pieces of sun in my body. I talked about the countless nights that Mom studied with me to help me prepare for exams. I talked about endless phone calls in college when my Mom tried to help my depression.

The more I relived memories of my parents, the more I felt ashamed of myself – not about being gay, but about how I made my parents feel.

Most of their colleagues and friends were spending the upcoming Chinese New Year with their son-in-law, daughter-in-law, and even grandkids. My parents were going to meet a white guy who was the boyfriend of their only son.

After so many years of raising me, now I was returning them this? They infused all their hope into me, and I left them with a shameful, devil, laughable homosexual son.

But I also knew that there was more to it than that. For the first time, I felt like I was truly living. If I wasn't living in the way I was supposed to, why live at all?

The distance between Mom and I was growing. Admittedly the letter created even more distance, but I felt like the worst had happened. The distance wouldn't expand anymore. I just needed to find the way back to Mom's heart. At the same time, Bryan reminded me that maybe they also needed some space.

The next morning, I was standing in front of the mirror "smiling" to myself. I tried to make it last for five minutes as my high school Chinese teacher said. The magic didn't work that day. Moving like one of the walking dead, I was on autopilot most of the day.

That evening, I brought Bryan to meet my parents. As Mom always did, she cooked a table of my favorite dishes from China. Those dishes were among my favorite memories in life. But at the black compressed-board IKEA dining room table, we just sat there silently. Most of the dishes were barely touched. There was no conversation. It was not just that they didn't want to talk; they also couldn't communicate. My parents didn't speak English. Bryan didn't know a single word of Chinese, other than *xiexie* (thank you).

In the next few days, we repeated the same routine. Bryan and I dropped by to eat Mom's dinner. Silent. We went back to Bryan's house and left Mom and Dad at my house. I wasn't sure what to do other than just wait. It was like waiting for a sentence, or probably the last direction that my parents would give me as their son.

Ten days later, Mom told me they wanted to go home. They asked me to change their flight to leave two weeks early. In the past, they had always found excuses to stay longer; now, they just wanted to leave. *Had they given up on me?* I was lost.

At SeaTac Airport, I helped them check in. The two huge suitcases were so light and empty now. They used to buy a lot of stuff to bring back to China for my grandparents and their friends. This time, they were bringing back only disappointment, anger, and sadness.

"I don't want to come here anymore." Mom turned to me as I was sending them to the security check. She kept crying. Her eyes were red from daily washing with tears.

I never thought I would face a choice between my parents and myself. One was the source of unconditional love for the last twenty-nine years; the other was the true self that I had just accepted after twenty-nine years of hiding and struggling.

Turning to Mom, I went on my knees. "Do you remember the golden ladybug, Mom?"

Mom was a little bit surprised.

I continued to cry, "You told me that I was unique and had pieces of sun in my body. I finally found the pieces, Mom... they were not like what you and I were imagining, but I want to protect them and let them shine..."

Mom started crying aloud. She walked to me, gave me a strong hug, turned around, and disappeared behind the security check.

I dropped my forehead to the ground. This was the only thing I thought I could do to pay respect to my parents and to thank them for raising me.

FROM TWO PERSONS TO US

"Love, like everything else in life, should be a discovery, an adventure, and like most adventures, you don't know you're having one until you're right in the middle of it."

—E.A. Bucchianeri, *Brushstrokes of a Gadfly*

*I*t had been a week since Mom and Dad boarded the airplane. The only communication I got was a simple, "We are home," when they landed in Guangzhou.

Unlike Hollywood dramas, the goodbye in SeaTac did not suddenly fix everything. They didn't yell at me, nor did they tell me everything would be all right.

I was a problem solver, but I tried not to think too much about my parents. The problem was too big for me to handle. It was also as Bryan said, "You cannot control what your parents feel and think. Just give them some space."

That's the spirit Bryan had lived for his entire life. Let other people be. Never push anything on others. Bryan didn't have a planned and dramatic coming out event to his dad, Bill.

Living across the street from us, Bill met me first before confirming with Bryan that he was gay. Bryan was his father's son. Bill didn't bother to ask Bryan anything more, but just accepted who he was and the entire situation. *How lucky was Bryan*, I thought to myself!

On the other hand, I loved my new life. Although I had not come out to my friends yet, coming home to see Bryan every night and truly being myself with nothing to hide made me feel free. I had not lived like this, without burden and pressure, ever.

Ah, the feeling of first being in love! We spent every possible moment together. Going to movies, trying out new restaurants, doing fun activities, and just holding each other's hand and being couch potatoes. Bryan showed me the side of American culture that was beyond *Friends, Scrubs,* and Westlife. Yes, for so long, I thought Westlife was an American band; only later when I started writing this book did I find out they were Irish.

Bryan was a big fan of classic American cars. Whenever he spotted one on the road, his voice went higher as he yelled with excitement, "Look, a 1969 Eldorado! So beautiful!"

"How do you know it is 1969?"

"I just know!"

He was right. Bryan could spend hours with his dad, Bill, talking about cars from different years. Their engine, their body design, their interior options, even the light bulbs they used.

Bryan was also a proud owner of a 1970 Cadillac Coupe DeVille. He bought it in 1996 for $500. Red at that time, it was completely trashed, inside and out. Bryan sanded the entire body, inch by inch, until she was ready to be painted classic black. He told me that it was his best investment. I loved the look on his face when he talked about cars. The passion and excitement were so irresistible.

Once in a band himself, Bryan not only sang well, but he also loved going to concerts. He was very proud that he had been to the band Chicago's concert eleven times. That was more than all the concerts I had been to. Before meeting Bryan, the

Jimmy Eat World concert in Philadelphia was the only one in my book. Now Bryan filled out our calendar with small shows from the likes of Tower of Power to big performances like Prince, Stevie Wonder, and Paul McCartney.

My musical taste was slowly evolving. I still loved cheesy music by Train and Taylor Swift, but I also gained a new fondness for music with lots of instruments, such as horn and saxophone, and also amazing voices like Whitney Houston's.

Our learning about each other did not stop at what we did together but included our pasts and where we were from. I was surprised to learn that Bryan used to weigh more than 240 pounds. He grew up as a chubby boy. He got a trainer from 24 Hour Fitness in Lynnwood and lost eighty pounds in less than one year.

Having the genes of my skinny father, I never understood the challenge of being overweight, but I could imagine the work Bryan must have faced to reach his 160-pound-body of today.

My surprisingly favorite part of our relationship was meeting Bryan's family at holiday gatherings. I was fascinated at all of the complicated blood relationships among his siblings. One half brother and sister from the same dad, two brothers from the same mom and dad. Everybody got along very well.

They also appreciated my presence at their family gatherings. Just like to his Dad, Bryan didn't announce his sexuality openly to his siblings but just brought me to the party. Everybody was interested in me and my past, just like I was curious about their stories.

"I like the international aspect you bring to the family," Bill told me one day. Trying to hide my blushing face, I didn't know what to say. I didn't expect this compliment from the guy who had worked his whole life with machines and had skin on his hands as rough as sandpaper. The unconditional acceptance from Bill and his family made me feel whole. Suddenly, the number of my family members tripled.

My biggest challenge in the relationship, or at least I thought at the time, was Bryan's fear of dogs. After a few months of living together, I finally made Bryan go to Marymoor with JD and me. At night, however, he still asked me to leave JD in my car. Bryan was still unready to accept JD in his life entirely. I was not happy about the situation, but I did not want to protest when I was so madly in love with him.

However, Bryan was also nice enough to make a comfortable bed in the back of my SUV for JD. Every night before going to bed, he also took on the duty of checking on JD to make sure he was set for the night. Slowly, Bryan was warming up to JD. But when I casually mentioned I missed having JD's furry body on our bed at night, he told me he would never accept having JD sleep with us.

I always thought it was hard to change somebody. However, in a few weeks, he surprised me with a dog house he built for JD in the backyard. JD finally graduated from staying in the car overnight to his own house.

Bryan also started to have more one-on-one time with JD, taking him running, touching his neck, and playing catch. I was thrilled about this change. JD must have been too. When we came home together, sometimes he ran straight to Bryan instead of me. That made me a little bit jealous, but I was happy.

Bryan's complete surrender to JD followed in a couple of months. Once I needed to travel to Chicago for work for a week. Bryan was tasked with taking care of JD. When I came back, I saw all the dog hairs on our bed. Yes, Bryan finally had JD sleeping on our bed.

* * *

I AM A planner. That is not only my official job title at Microsoft, but it is also what I do in my personal life. However, Bryan was the complete opposite. He was truly living a carpe diem life. This was what attracted us to each other before, but now it created friction as we started merging our lives.

I sometimes talked about our future – what we could do, where we would live, how many dogs we would have. Bryan always got a little bit annoyed and became totally silent.

Occasionally, when my mind went on eighty-mile-an-hour free flow, I also talked about marriage. It was not even legal at the time, but talking about it gave me a goal, which was what I was used to.

The only thing about the future that excited Bryan was moving to a sunny place like Hawaii. Hawaii was a destination any Washingtonian could dream of to get away from the clouds and rain.

To Bryan, it was more. Bryan told me that he fell in love with a guy from Hawaii even before meeting Juan. He visited the guy in Hawaii, and when he was back in Seattle, he was ready to move to Hawaii for him. But one day that guy just cut off contact with him. He tried to call and message. After tons of unreturned outreach, he was devastated.

It took him a while to recover from that. But that brief love made Hawaii a special place in his heart. He loved the warm weather, the ocean, and the gay-friendly atmosphere. *Maybe Hawaii to him is like Vancouver to me.*

Bryan didn't believe in marriage. He had just overcome his fear and committed to our exclusive relationship. It might be impossible for him to believe in marriage for a long time or forever.

His mom's sudden departure from his life created too much damage and shattered his trust in any stability in life. Nothing was in control. Nobody was dependable. Everything could disappear in just one day.

The divorces of his other family members and friends solidified his belief that marriage was not natural and always ended up hurting people.

In his senior year at the University of Washington, Bryan decided that he didn't want to study anymore. He quit school when he was four classes away from getting a degree in business administration. It wasn't that he had a big goal in life to chase like Bill Gates and Mark Zuckerberg; it is just that he preferred to play drums in his band and enjoy life rather than waste time studying something he might never use. He had worked for Safeway since and started a painting job that his brother Greg introduced him to.

Learning about all this gave me lots of empathy for Bryan's past, but also some worry about our future.

It was also at this time I realized Bryan was an alcoholic. The interlock breathalyzer device in his truck (the result of a DUI) never clicked in my mind. I asked him once what it was and was amazed to learn that there were devices like this to ensure driving safety in the United States, while seat belts were still optional in lots of cities in China.

I was never a drinker; nobody in my family was. What I learned from all the Hollywood movies was that drinking was cool; it was the way to be social. When I was getting my MBA at Duke, very rare tequila shots were my way of showing that I was a fun and cool person.

During my gay bar exploration, the shots did give me lots of courage and freedom to explore my sexuality. I felt fearless and worry-free. I forgot the limits and values that restrained me before and started yelling, laughing, and having fun. I was never really me, but also nothing more.

Bryan, on the other hand, was a prisoner of alcohol who was looking for a way out. Growing up in a family of drinkers, it was abnormal for him not to drink every day. Only later did I realize that when we first met, he was just finishing his home-stay program after his second DUI within two years. That six-pack of Blue Moon I brought...

When Bryan was sober, he could be very serious, especially in public. He cared a lot about what other people thought. He tried to refrain from kissing me in public at all and always talked to me like we were just two straight friends.

However, when he was drunk, he was very affectionate. Even when we were in a crowd, he would hold my hand, look into my eyes, and tell me how much he loved me and wanted me for his entire life.

I liked that side of him. There was an old Chinese saying, "Alcohol makes a person speak the truth." While I worried about our future, Bryan's drunk talk softened me and gave me hope.

Sometimes he blacked out after drinking. That was a totally different level of being drunk. He would be in autopilot mode – no logic and no rules. He washed all the clean dishes once. He peed on a random street in Capitol Hill once. He devoured a one-gallon container of ice cream once. Those were just some fun memories that I recorded on video and shared with him the next morning. We got some good laughs.

But one time, we were hanging out in a gay bar in Honolulu. Things went crazy after lots of tequila shots for both Bryan and me. I saw Bryan making out with another guy.

Anger. Anger. Anger. Never had my heart ached that much. A little drunk myself, I hit Bryan on his face and then his chest.

He turned up his head and cried, "Hey, what's that for?"

I was speechless. I ripped the bracelet he bought me to show his love for me and threw it away in the bar.

He then smiled and shrieked, "I love you, Nicky!" He forgot how hard I hit him. My knuckles hurt from the punch. I hit him again.

I dragged both of us back to our room at Moana Surfrider in Waikiki. This was supposed to be our first vacation together, in a place that we might call home in the future. But now, all I had was pain and anger. I was crying the whole way, while he was half asleep. From time to time, he looked at me. "What happened? Don't cry. I love you, Nicky."

I didn't feel any love. I didn't know how I fell asleep; maybe I didn't. I just remember crying the whole night.

The next day, hungover, Bryan kept apologizing and promising that he wouldn't hurt me again. I didn't even have the energy to respond. My heart was shut down. I barely had time to lick the wound, not to mention forgive him.

We didn't speak to each other for the remaining two days of our vacation. He tried to talk to me, but I avoided conversation.

On the red-eye flight back to Seattle, I had a weird dream. Bryan and I were living happily in a small cabin on the north shore of Oahu. I came home after playing with JD in the ocean, and Bryan cooked the most delicious seared tuna steak. I woke up in the middle of the dream and looked at Bryan, who was asleep next to me. I felt hopeless. *Dreams were always the opposite of real life. Maybe it was time to move on.*

The next day, on my way to work, Bryan stopped me at the door. "Do you want to break up?" he asked. I didn't say anything.

He continued, "I am terribly sorry for what had happened. I understand that you may not want to be with me anymore. But I am always here for you." I left without answering.

"Do I want to break up with Bryan?" I asked myself as I drove to work. "No, I don't. I love him. I don't want to give up something beautiful for a mistake that I was also responsible for. I was the one that kept handing him the drinks. I was the one who flirted with other guys first. I need to talk to Bryan."

Bryan and I had a long talk that night. It was less about making out with another guy. That had hurt me. It was definitely wrong. But it was more about what caused it that scared me.

I was pushed to face the reality – what an alcoholic was and what it meant to be in a relationship with one. Growing up, *alcoholic* was not in my vocabulary. I understood people could get drunk and do crazy and stupid things. But I never imagined I would be dealing with this problem.

I was shocked to learn that alcoholism was a disease. When Bryan picked up the first drink, some switch in his brain was turned on. He couldn't stop. He would find any way to get himself another drink.

He told me that his drinking was not because of anger or worry. It happened on any normal day when everything seemed fine until he picked up the first drink. That's how he got his last DUI. One second he was in a gay bar in Capitol Hill having fun; a couple of hours later, he was asleep on the road hitting the car in front of him. *How scary was it to be in that situation, not only for Bryan but for his family and now for me?* I didn't want that happen to him again.

Bryan told me that he would start to go to treatment and also AA meetings. Understanding Bryan's struggle with alcohol made me less angry about what had happened. It gave me a purpose to work with him and to build our life together.

Our relationship started with the six-pack of Blue Moon I brought to his house. At that time, I used alcohol as a way to be free, but we needed to get alcohol out of our lives if we wanted this relationship to work.

We decided that instead of thinking about not drinking, we should focus on the good things in life. Just like the book *The Secret* mentioned, if we were constantly thinking about not having debt, what we would get is debt. Instead, we should think about how to make more money and have more income. We may not combat evil directly, but we could have our angel strong and bright enough to create abundant light to fill our life.

To celebrate our one-year anniversary, we moved to a beachfront apartment in Juanita Bay on Lake Washington. Taking JD to swim in the lake and chasing ducks became our daily routine. We also had introduced our true selves to our individual friends and also met each other's friends.

Having moved my entire life, I deeply understood the power of traveling and the impact of creating new perspectives and experiences in life. To celebrate Bryan's birthday, we went to Cancun. Maybe it was the sun, maybe it was the ocean that is way warmer than the North Pacific, maybe it was the spells from the Mayan ruins, but we forgot the pain of the last tropical place and really enjoyed each other's company.

We tried to find even more opportunities to travel together. When I visited Duke for recruiting for Microsoft, Bryan flew over after the event. We went to Orlando and Miami and then drove the more than one hundred miles of State Route 1 until we reached Key West. We even went to Sunset Key and swam with schools of fish in the untouched ocean. We swore that we would look forward and continue to put more pins on our travel map and build more happy memories together.

Traveling is not about where you are going, but who you go there with. Sometimes it was about giving each other a little bit of courage to jump out of a waterfall or to swim into the azure water cave in Secret Falls, Jamaica. Sometimes it was about lying on the beach in Isla Mujeres, not even touching each other, but knowing that the person you love was right next to you. Sometimes it was about sitting on the couch at home, putting memory pieces together of all the turns in the drive to Hana or counting the number of flavors of Poke we could get at Food Lion near Hanalei.

* * *

SEEING ALL THE positive changes traveling had made in our life, we decided to invite my parents on a trip with us. Thanks to the Chinese education system, I never had a chance to travel with them extensively when I was young. *Maybe traveling with them could help fix our relationship?*

If I wanted to show them the unexplored spaces in their hearts, I needed to show them the unvisited places on our planet earth.

I crafted an invitation letter to my parents. I talked about the struggles that Bryan and I had and how traveling and focusing on good things in life really helped us. I talked about how this was my first real relationship and it was not easy. I talked about alcoholism, relapse, treatment, and also the breathalyzer device in the car. I talked about how free I was and how much love I had. I talked about how, for the first time, I saw a future in front of me, a future that I could choose, not decided by other people or a system.

More importantly, I talked about how much I wanted them to be part of my and our life. I begged them never to give up on me. I told them that I knew they wanted to know the real me. I told them they just needed to have a little bit of courage. I asked them to travel with us, to Yellowstone, to witness the wilderness, to be amazed by the natural colors and be wowed by the raw power of the earth that created us all.

Two weeks later, I got an email back. Bryan and I were thrilled! They were in! They planned to visit the next April. It had been over a year since I had seen them, the longest ever. I missed them terribly and was so excited about the trip.

We wanted this trip to be as close to nature as possible. Bryan had taken me camping on Camano Island several times. When he was growing up, his family used to go to Camano Island State Park to camp. Less than eighty miles north of Seattle, there were campsites with breathtaking ocean views, and sites hiding in the fir trees that created a world of only the sky and us, surrounded by nature. At this park were the few happy memories of growing up with his family that Bryan cherished.

We decided to camp for the entire trip. We would keep that as a surprise for my parents. We didn't want Mom and Dad to think about social rules, what they thought life should be coming from a steel factory town. We wanted them to taste nature and be devoured by nature. We wanted them to see what life could be.

America was built on cars; I learned that when I was in China. What could be more American than taking a road trip? We rented a red Chrysler minivan. A six-seater with tons of space was perfect for four adults and one dog. We took our time to enjoy the road trip with Mom and Dad.

We drove through McDonald's for our favorite: a #5 Sausage Egg Cheese McGriddle with a small coffee with two creams and two sugars. We stopped at small towns on the way to learn the local history and read about Lewis and Clark's journey west. Bryan was thrilled to be our guide for American History and Culture 101.

When we reached our campground in Yellowstone, Bryan worked with Dad to teach him how to set up a tent and showed Mom how to start a fire so we could roast some corn on the cob. They could barely speak each other's language, but using hand gestures with "Yi, yi, ya, ya..." it actually worked.

Most campgrounds in Yellowstone were at high altitude, at least six thousand feet above sea level. We could feel it when we breathed. To get more oxygen into our lungs, we needed to breathe harder and deeper. Surrounding us was nothing but mountains, trees, and the occasional sound from some hidden animal. There were so many signs reading "Be Bear Aware. Food Storage Required," which reminded us that we were not the strongest creatures in the world.

The trees were mostly pine with some familiar fir trees that reminded me of campgrounds on Camano Island. There were lots of dead and fallen trees on the ground too. Nobody touched them if they were not blocking any road. It was like paying respect to the forest and Mother Nature. Just let it be.

I thought about what Henry David Thoreau once wrote: "I went to the woods because I wished to live deliberately, to front only the essential facts of life, and see if I could not learn what it had to teach, and not, when I came to die, discover that I had not lived." I took a deep breath and wanted to take in the essential facts of life from the forest. *Maybe Mom and Dad would feel the same way.*

A lot of great campgrounds in Yellowstone didn't allow reservations and were on a first come, first served basis. In the morning, we always got up early to rush to the next campground. When we spotted a "great but not sure whether there is a better one" campsite, Mom would get out of the car to take the first empty spot while we circled around the campground to see whether there was a better one. Most of the time, the one we picked first was the best.

After settling down, Dad used what he learned from Bryan to set up the tent while Mom started getting the food ready. After lunch, we sat down by the fire that Bryan started. Nothing to do but just stare at the dancing flame. It was peaceful and magical.

A squirrel came to visit us. She was smaller and a little redder than the ones in Seattle. Mom gave the squirrel a Cheeto that she was snacking on. The little one came closer and asked for more. "Stop, Xiaoping (my mom's name), she will get constipated!" Bryan said. I translated it for Mom and Dad. We all had a good laugh.

During the day, we drove around the park to visit all the sightseeing spots. Just like all the Chinese tourists, Mom and Dad took so many photos of Old Faithful that showcased the power of nature and the big colorful hot spring that expanded our definition of color.

From time to time on our drive, we stopped when somebody spotted an animal. "A bear!" "A moose with giant antlers." "A huge number of bison!" We talked in Chinese and English. It didn't matter. The excitement made everybody happy.

On the way to Grand Teton National Park, which was our next stop, we spotted a dark hilly area not far away. "Let's go to see what it is," Dad said. Bryan drove us there. As we were climbing up, the whole world became an ocean of burnt trees. They were black, leafless, and lifeless.

We stopped the car. There was a sign. We understood that this was caused by a natural fire. A small trail led us to the top of the hill. Mom always had high blood pressure. I put my arms under her and walked slowly with her on the trail.

On top of the hill, looking to the north, there was nothing but dead trees. Countless. Dead quiet. There were no animals. No humans other than us. No other plants. We were all holding our breaths and letting air in and out very slowly. We didn't want to disturb the tragic scene.

"Tongtong, before, I would have thought a view like this is hell." Mom turned to me with eyes full of tears. I could hear her breathing. "After I went back to Guangzhou from our last trip [visiting us], I was in hell..." She started sobbing. Bryan and Dad decided to walk back to the car and gave us some privacy.

"I cried every night after work. I didn't have anybody to talk to. You are the hope for our family. You are the number one graduate from your high school. You are in America to pursue a great life. You are our family pride. My friends and colleagues asked me how my trip to the U.S. was. I just lied and told them everything was fine." Mom wiped her eyes.

She continued, "I didn't know what would happen. The judgment from others. I worried I would lose my job. One day, helplessly, I watched a video about a young guy in Taiwan coming out to his parents. The story ended tragically with the boy jumping out of the building he lived in."

She started crying aloud now. "How much pain he must have gone through. How much pain you must have been through...I don't want you to kill yourself."

I turned to Mom, and my eyes met hers. "I would never do something like that!" I couldn't stop my tears.

"I've had so much fun on this trip getting to know you better and getting to know Bryan. I am so happy to see the life you are living and being a part of it. Maybe it was me who needed to change. Just like what you said, maybe it was me who needed to have a little bit of courage and let go of what others would say. I am really proud of you..."

Trying to control my tears and voice, I muttered, "Remember, Mom, you said that I am like the golden ladybugs. I have pieces of the sun in me. Even when it is dark around, I will light up my heart..."

The camping plan in Grand Teton was ruined by a hail storm. Who knew that in May, there was hail! We were lucky enough to book the last room available in the Teton Lodge. Just like what *The Alchemist* said, sometimes in life when you really want something, the whole world comes to help you.

The next day, it was so sunny with no clouds in the sky. We learned that there was a photo of Grand Teton hanging in the White House. Amazed by the greatness of the mountain, we decided to kayak on Jackson Lake to get closer and be devoured by Mother Nature.

It was Mom and Dad's first kayaking experience. We got two double kayaks. Bryan and Dad were in one, with Mom and I in the other.

Paddling away from the shore, looking at the mountains, hearing the birds tweeting, our spirits were lifted. "Let's race to the island there." Bryan pointed at a piece of land a few hundred yards away.

"Let's do it!" I yelled with excitement.

I thought I had the natural advantage – I could talk with Mom in Chinese. Since Mom and Dad had not paddled before, communication would be key. How wrong I was! As I was still talking to Mom about the right way to hold the paddle, Dad and Bryan had already paddled way ahead of us. Their paddling was not exactly synchronized; Dad's hold on the paddle was too low, but it worked. *Sometimes you just need to start paddling*, I thought.

"Let's go, Mom! Just paddle! Follow me, left, right, left, right..."

PART 2 - THREE GIRLS

WE WANT TO HAVE KIDS

"There's only one place I want to go, and it's to all the places I've never been."

—Nikki Rowe

I am an immigrant. I was an immigrant. I always lived in a mindset that I was worse than others. When I moved to Guangzhou in fourth grade, I didn't speak the local dialect and I was way behind in my studies. When I moved to Shanghai for college, people there dressed better and had an international view that I had never experienced. When I moved to the United States, it was even more apparent: I was an "alien" on my visa.

It was not just about my legal status. When I first arrived in this country, I worried about my speech. When people heard my accent, the mix-up of "th" and "s," they knew I was not from here. The feeling of being an outsider, not accepted, kept me in fear.

When I moved to Duke, as a Culture 101 tip, my professor advised me to avoid politics during conversations with strangers. I could not have talked about it even if I wanted to; I knew nothing about the two major parties, their platforms, or even the names of the leaders other than the presidents. However, when I turned on the TV or went to CNN.com, politics were everywhere.

Not knowing anything about it always gave me a feeling of not belonging. Election season was the worst. All the "I voted" stickers that friends posted on Facebook reminded me that I was a second-class citizen. Wait, I wasn't even a citizen at all. Just like I didn't have any influence on China when I lived there, I didn't have a say about the future of the country I now lived in, the one I chose to build my life in.

Later I learned that although I am an American citizen now, my Asian look always labels me an outsider. Once I was on a train from California to Seattle, and a lady sitting next to me started chatting with me. After I told her that I was going home to Seattle, she insisted on asking me seriously, "Where are you truly from?"

The immigrant mindset always triggers fear and alarm. But it also gives me the strength to "always give it a try," enables me to have the humility of "I could be better," and empowers me with the knowledge that "other people have their own battles to fight."

When I started working at Microsoft, I worried every day about being laid off. It was 2009, and the economy was still tumbling. Microsoft was actively laying off people as part of its reorganization effort to make the company leaner and more efficient. Luckily, the company was helping me apply for a green card that would give me permanent resident status. However, the process usually took five to seven years.

If I lost my job, I would need to leave the country *immediately*. That was the thought that ran through my mind every day. I always tried to shut it down and live in the moment. Carpe diem, I told myself. Don't worry about things I have no control over.

In 2013, after five years of waiting, I finally got the email from my immigration attorney at Microsoft that I was eligible to become a permanent resident. The thought of shedding my "alien" status and not having to go through the extremely long line at SeaTac after an international trip excited me. It was the end of a long sentence and offered me the freedom and stability I had desired from the first day my feet touched the soil of America.

In the same year, the US Supreme Court ruled that same-sex marriage was legal! The news was everywhere, especially in Seattle. I tossed out the idea of getting married to Bryan. Knowing his ironclad opinion about marriage, I was not expecting his quick "let's do it" enthusiasm.

Did something change? Did he heal from all the broken marriages in life? Bryan told me that my parents showed him a side of marriage that he had not seen before. It was not perfect, but both parties worked hard to make it last.

We lived a frugal life and definitely did not want to spend much on a wedding. Saving the money to travel was more ideal for us. We decided to get married at the courthouse.

It was August 15, 2013, a surprisingly rainy day in the dry Seattle summer. It was just Bryan and me, with my parents and two best friends.

Bryan and I vowed in front of Judge Jorge that we would love each other forever no matter what. Those words and thoughts were what we already knew and had promised each other, but it still moved us when we said it aloud, in front of a judge and in a courthouse. Bryan later told me that I was shaking the whole time.

After the ceremony, we rented a little electric boat on Lake Union to celebrate. Halfway through our ride, we parked at

Ivar's and grabbed some typical Seattle fish and chips. As we enjoyed our food on our ride back to the harbor, the sun peeked out of the clouds. The reflection on the lake almost blinded us.

It was simple; it was sweet; it was cheap. It cost $265 for the entire wedding, including the fish and chips from Ivar's! Even today, Bryan and I are still very proud of that!

After I came out to my parents, I set up a rule of "coming out." Only do it in person and when it is necessary. It is not who I am that I need to be proud of, it is what I have done. I don't need to put a big sticker on my head saying that I am gay. I only do it when the time is right and I have a reason.

I decided to share the good news of our marriage with most of my friends and then teammates and manager at Microsoft. Not surprisingly, they were more than supportive. Getting married to Bryan made me even closer to everybody at work.

After hearing the great news, my immigration lawyer also told me that I had another option to apply for a green card – through the marriage. The time it took would be the same as my current journey through Microsoft.

Options! I always did not have that luxury in life. I was thrilled! I decided to use our marriage to give me permanent resident status. It was celebrating our love. It was like being a rebel and fighting the system with love. I hoped to use love to cure my fearful immigration mindset.

Ever since coming to the US in 2007, I had dreamed of this moment. I thought it would be something huge, dramatic, that would make my life completely different. But just like nothing changed immediately after I sent the coming-out letter to my parents, life didn't change after I got my green card a few months later.

However, it did provide a sense of freedom and stability as I expected. Maybe after so many years of living under a system of studying and focusing on crossing a single-log bridge, I could finally choose what I wanted to do?

Ally once said that she wanted to be a Starbucks barista. I made that my goal too. Maybe it was the time to make that happen? I always wanted to travel around the world. I was lucky enough to travel to thirty-five countries already. Maybe it was the time for Bryan and me to take that number to eighty, or maybe a hundred?

With our newfound freedom, what could Bryan and I do to make our lives amazing and exciting? *What could I do?*

* * *

BRYAN AND I had made significant progress in building a life together. After Bryan's complete surrender to and falling in love with JD, we decided to get another dog to keep JD company.

Unlike my adoption journey in North Carolina, where there were so many choices, in Seattle there was a short supply of shelter dogs. We went back and forth to the Seattle Humane Society every other day to find a sibling for JD. However, we always came back with disappointed faces and, "Sorry, JD. Maybe next time."

After so many days, the people working at the shelter must have felt bad for us. One day after we looked through all the available dogs, they told us they just received a dog that didn't have shots yet. It was found on the street near SeaTac. "Do you want to meet him?"

"Of course!" We were thrilled!

Let's be honest. It was not love at first sight. Jack had all-yellow, short hair, with a charcoal-black nose, just like the dog from *Old Yeller*, but maybe a pound smaller. Jack looked like he was scared and hated the world all the time.

We hesitated a little. But at three years old, the same as JD, he was not a puppy anymore, which meant less work for us. In the initial meetup walk, JD also did well with Jack. We decided to give it a try.

When I first adopted JD, I wanted to be a good father for him. Barely knowing how to take care of myself, I started reading lots of books about raising dogs. One book that really touched me and still makes me cry today is *Merle's Door*.

It was about a man named Jon who adopted a dog that had an IQ and EQ beyond the ordinary dog's. Jon raised Merle to be an independent thinker. My favorite episode was when Jon and Merle went skiing. While Jon chose one way to go downhill and asked Merle to follow him, Merle, as independent as he could be, chose a completely different path downhill. It took Jon four hours to find Merle.

"That sounds amazing! An independent thinker! That's what JD needs to be!" I told myself. How naive was I? How wrong could I be? JD was not only gaining weight every day with his growing paws, but also his ambition and curiosity grew exponentially.

I kept my promise to spent time with JD at Marymoor every week. JD, however, never kept himself on the right side of the park. There were fences along the Sammamish River set up to protect salmon and wildlife, such as ducks and geese. Whenever I opened the car door, JD would jump out and head straight to the fence. He always looked back at me before launching the jump to the other side. His "I am scared but I am strong" look was still the same. He had just added the taste and pride of an "independent thinker."

He was the one that broke all the rules and jumped all the fences. The fence to a leash-only bird-watching trail? Jumped. The fence to the mud ditch? Jumped and rolled in. After he jumped to the other side, he always disappeared for quite a while. Calling his name was no help other than getting attention from other dog owners. *They must be thinking how terrible and irresponsible I am as a dog owner.* To defend my position, I had prepared a whole speech about how I trained JD to be a free thinker. Luckily, I have never needed to use it.

JD was a free thinker, thanks to *Merle's Door*, and we soon learned that Jack was a crazy thinker. Whenever we opened the car door after pulling into the driveway, Jack would jump out of the car and disappear. We normally spent at least thirty minutes going through the neighborhood to find him in somebody's yard eating dirt and poop.

As a beta in the family, Jack followed whatever alpha JD did. JD loved working on big bones. Jack also started loving it. Apparently, he loved it too much and split his right big tooth in half to the root. We removed the entire tooth at the vet. We also learned that Jack didn't have a sense of pain.

Jack could sense something in certain people and would charge toward them. This significantly limited our time playing in Marymoor. That meant that JD also couldn't go to the park. "Shared suffering is one way to build a relationship. This will make you and Jack the best brothers of all time!" I comforted JD whenever he gave me the look that it was time to go to the park.

Jack's charging toward people led to bad consequences sometimes. Once, he saw somebody walking a hundred yards away. He ripped off the leash, jumped off a wall that was twenty feet high, and landed with his chin on the concrete sidewalk. Blood and more blood is what I remember.

To make matters worse, we couldn't discipline Jack. When we raised our voices even a little bit, he would put his ears down, tail between his back legs, and slip into the bathtub. *How did he know to hide in a bathtub when he was scared? Maybe he was abused before?*

I was losing hope in raising Jack. He created more trouble than I could or wanted to handle. I missed the days going to Marymoor with JD. Bryan, on the other hand, made it clear that giving up on Jack was not an option.

* * *

BRYAN AND I also stumbled onto something we love to do together – real estate. Still deep in my $150K student loan payment, investing was the last thing on my mind.

That changed when Bryan showed me a house on Zillow one day.

It was right by Northgate Mall, a big shopping mall in north Seattle. The house was owned by Bank of America, and from the photo, it looked like a haunted house. The yellow exterior paint was chipped on both the south and west sides of the building. The grass on the 5,000-square-foot yard was as high as our waist.

Not having a real estate agent, we called the listing agent directly and asked him to show us the house. We met there at 7:00 p.m. After peeling off layers of spiderwebs from the front porch, we entered the 1920s house. A strong smell rushed into my nose. I almost threw up. It was like vomit and sewage had a baby. "Maybe some dead rats," Bryan said casually.

No power. No heat. We looked through the house with our flashlight. Upstairs was a three-bedroom house, while the downstairs basement had been converted into a two-bedroom mother-in-law sometime in the eighties.

"All the big items seem all right; the only things needed are cosmetic updates," Bryan added. "Floor, paint, kitchen...The house just needs some love."

Bryan's dad, Bill, was a machinist. He worked as the main engineer for a vendor for Boeing. Bill could design and make anything with his giant machines, which occupied his entire two-car garage. Just like his dad, Bryan was handy. He remodeled his 1979 Rambler from the updated kitchen counter to the refinished bathroom, from the new hardwood floor to the freshly painted wall. The remodel potential of the house in Northgate aroused Bryan's interest.

What excited me was the financial perspective. Although my career was going in a great direction at Microsoft thanks to my amazing manager, I saw how fragile and cold an American company could be. When it was layoff season, after HR delivered the notice in the morning, you needed to pack up to leave in the afternoon. This was so different from what we had in China and what my parents had – a job for life.

I needed a more diverse income stream to hedge the risk from my still promising career. Real estate seemed to be a low-maintenance and passive way to achieve that. The first house I bought when I arrived in Seattle started to turn a profit after I moved out and rented out all four bedrooms.

We decided to give it a try. The price tag was $200K. It had been on the market for over ninety days. The Great Recession had made everybody scared of buying houses.

We put in an offer for $170K. It wasn't just that we knew the market value very well, but also that we couldn't afford any more at that time. Bryan was living a perfect American consumer life – making $45K a year, spending every single dollar, and saving $0 in the bank. Being a Chinese immigrant, although deeply in debt to Sallie Mae and Citibank, the insecurity mindset made me save up just enough to pay the 20 percent down required to purchase the house.

This was the beginning of our new life. Bryan was handy; he could fix anything. I was good at math, duh! I could make sure the return on investment would be worthwhile.

We closed on the house smoothly and moved into the downstairs two-bedroom mother-in-law apartment while Bryan worked on the remodeling every day after his Safeway shift ended at 3:00 p.m.

In the evening, we ate either ramen noodles or Chinese takeout in the middle of the 1920s grand living room that had a beautiful San Francisco-style bay window facing the busy Northgate Way. We plowed through the room full of paint cans, broken door handles, and old cabinet pieces, and enjoyed our delicious dinner with the fresh paint smell. We didn't mind too much. We were more focused on getting the remodel done and renting it out.

A few months later, we finished remodeling and rented the upstairs out for $1,800. Our mortgage was only $900. This made us $900 a month while we were living there for free. We were thrilled about this stumbled-upon and hard-worked-for accomplishment.

We decided to repeat the success. All our free time was switched from finding good restaurants to eat in and fun movies to watch, to finding great houses to invest in.

Growing up in Seattle, Bryan understood the good areas, the bad areas, and the potential up-and-coming areas. We started living out of boxes and moved every six months to a year to a new house, remodeled, rented it out, and moved to the next one.

Investing in different houses not only let me explore the neighborhoods in Seattle that I had never heard of, but also taught me more about American history and culture.

We bought a triplex in Central District, which was Seattle's segregation area in the 1960s. Built in 1901, the 4,200-square-foot mansion was owned by a Russian jeweler who owned a shop on 1st Avenue in downtown Seattle in the 1910s. A once upscale neighborhood became the scar of segregation and then turned into a rundown triplex in the 1980s.

Walking inside the living room with its eleven-foot ceiling, touching the heavily textured and once luxurious wall, and seeing all the modern townhouses being built through the original single-glass window, I saw my own journey of migrating to America, from a country where my race comprised more than 90 percent of the population and I was never bothered by the thought of race, to being reminded every day through the media that I was a minority here.

* * *

LIFE WAS BUSY, especially when there was something that excited both Bryan and me. However, as the number of houses we owned grew, I felt that there was something missing.

Since I grew up in modern China, ruled by the Communist Party, there was no religion in my vocabulary. The Cultural Revolution had wiped out all the belief systems. But I always wondered whether there was somebody up there, some higher power that guided us and led our journey in the world.

Those thoughts were never sorted out until I read *The Alchemist*. The book made me listen to my heart, the winds from the world, and the signals from the environment.

Now living in a free country, married to Bryan, I had more breathing room for my memories, and they started coming back, especially memories of childhood.

Before moving to Guangzhou, I was a five-year-old who spent every single moment with my best friend Lei who lived two houses down. He and I loved catching dragonflies by the little lake, the water of which was used to irrigate the vegetables we ate every day, and building sandcastles in the Sand Ball game that my grandparents loved playing. But my favorite game was playing Mommy and Daddy.

We normally tied my yellow blanket to the dark brown strings under the hollow bed frame made of coconut leaves. That became our home. The frame was at the right height for us to sit comfortably underneath it. We used some little square chairs to divide the tent into different "rooms." Not having any baby dolls, I brought my favorite stuffed animals, a Nemo-like fish called Fishy, and a fuzzy bunny called Jumpy.

Lei and I took turns being Mommy and Daddy. He cooked in the kitchen, which was the room right by the edge of the bed, while I took the kids, Fishy and Jumpy, to play on top of the bed, which was our playground. When he finished cooking, he yelled, "Dinner time!" with a high-pitched mommy voice. I then rushed the kids back to the tent. Washing hands was the number one thing to do, I always told Fishy and Jumpy. We then "devoured" the delicious meal that was made of the leaves of dozens of plants from the balcony.

That was the strongest memory I had of wanting kids. Studying and hiding from my sexuality never gave me a chance for my thoughts to wander in that direction. After puberty – after I started suspecting I liked guys – it was much too scary to think about.

It wasn't until I got JD that I had the feeling of being a parent again. He was not only my young Jedi and best friend, but he was also my son. His entire life depended on me since the day I brought him back from the shelter. The peeing on the carpet, the chewing on pair after pair of roommate Jenny's shoes, the doggy walk even on the coldest night.

Raising him created a sense of responsibility that I had never had before. I wanted him to grow well and healthy; I wanted him to be happy. I cut my game-playing time to take him to the dog park, and I left parties early because he needed a walk and to be fed.

I found out that his happy tail-wagging and face-licking created a level of happiness for me that I had not experienced before. It was simpler but stronger, and it lasted longer.

Those memories and feelings gave me thoughts of having a baby. I was finally living in a country where becoming a parent was possible no matter who I loved. I wanted to bring the relationship with Bryan to the next level. I wanted to be a good son and give my parents what they wanted – to be grandparents. Thinking about all the shame and regret I had, I also wanted to create a generation that could live without those stereotypes, with love and courage.

I talked to Bryan about the idea. Just like his enthusiasm for our marriage, he surprised me by saying that it was a great idea! He was on board! He told me that he wanted to be a parent and thought this would bring our life to the next level.

From the experience with Jack, I knew Bryan would be a much better father than I could ever dream of being.

* * *

NOW WE WERE talking about having babies! What were our options? It was not like we could just do it and make it happen overnight...

When I was in China, we had the impression that American people didn't care about family but only focused on individual needs. My experience at Microsoft was quite the opposite. It seemed that kids were all anyone talked about other than work. My teammates could skip a review meeting with our vice president just because he had booked a Disneyland vacation with his kids or could leave work immediately when the daycare called saying that her child was not feeling well.

In China, however, all the emphasis was on your career. Just like studying was the priority for students, an adult could sacrifice bringing up his/her child for a job. People left their babies at home with grandparents and traveled thousands of miles to Tier 1 cities to work. They only saw their kids once a year if they were lucky.

American people prioritized their family, and there were different ways to build a family too. My colleague Kim had adopted her daughter a couple of years ago from a family in Eastern Washington. She was experienced and recommended I go to the Microsoft Adoption Exhibit and attend some of the Microsoft Adoption Club meetings.

I went to all those meetings and exhibits that showcased dozens of adoption-related agencies and organizations. I learned a lot.

It seemed that the decision process was a list of multiple choices. Open or closed adoption? Domestic or international adoption? Must be newborn or all right with older babies? Yes or no with foster to adoption? I was supposed to be excited about multiple choice because that was part of all the exams that I had taken. I was really good at exams, but something didn't feel right with the choices I was given here.

While we were still learning and digesting all the info, Bryan told me that he really wanted a Chinese baby. "Chinese babies are just so cute! We should get one from China directly! I heard that there are so many abandoned babies there!" Growing up in an all-white family, Bryan always liked people from other races. The guy Bryan dated before me was Mexican, and all the boys that he had been with were Asian, Latino, or Black.

I, on the other hand, always wanted a baby of a different race than Chinese. It seemed that all other races had bigger eyes, longer eyelashes, and longer noses, all the features I dreamed of having.

Before we had a chance to persuade each other of what our baby's racial composition should be, the Chinese government solved our problem – adoption was not an option for gays in China. Some people lied on their application and said they were single men. Bryan and I were very uncomfortable with that approach. Done with our own lies about sexuality, how could we start our kid's life with a giant lie?

I told my mom and dad about the idea of having a baby. They were thrilled. I knew that deep inside they were still not 100 percent comfortable with me being gay. They had not talked to any of their friends about Bryan and me yet. All the family photos Dad shared on his social network app WeChat were carefully selected to make sure Bryan was not in them.

Bryan told me he completely understood where this was coming from and didn't take it personally. Having a baby in our family would definitely distract Mom and Dad from thinking about my sexuality and would give them a new purpose in life – to be the best grandparents ever!

Since Mom and Dad had gone back to China after our Yellowstone trip, we had resumed our every other day phone call. One day, I mentioned to Mom Bryan's preference for having Chinese babies and the restriction of the Chinese government on gay adoption. I told her that we were still thinking and were leaning toward "open adoption" because that seemed to be a popular thing that everybody was talking about.

Two days later, Mom called me excited! "Guess what? Your dad and I have an appointment with a local adoption agency in Guangzhou. We will go visit them! We will just say we want a baby! We can then do the adoption with you when we visit you in the U.S.!" Mom was so proud of their genius idea.

I was speechless. As crazy as the idea sounded, I was moved by her love for me and the determination to help Bryan and me create a family.

The excitement did not last long. Four hours later, Mom told me that they were disqualified for adoption because they already had me and the Only Child Policy forestalled more kids for them. All the limits, all the rules that constrained my whole life before, still haunted me even after moving to the U.S.

Bryan and I decided to do a domestic open adoption. It was not only cheaper but also seemed the most gay-friendly way. We picked one of the highest-rated agencies in Seattle and attended their first meeting.

Sitting in a circle with ten other eager parents to be, we shared our stories and learned lots of useful information. But the more we learned about the process, the less excited we were about it.

After putting the application on our dining room table at home, we didn't touch it for a few months. We were dragging our feet. There was something not clicking in our minds or hearts.

After applying, we needed to wait for a year or several years to potentially have pregnant mothers review our application and decide to give us their baby. A newborn baby was hard to come by. There was a very high chance that we would only start to build a relationship and take care of the baby when he or she was a couple of years old.

Even if it was a newborn as we preferred, the mothers who gave up their babies at birth were under a lot of stress and living a lot of drama. We heard horror stories of what women do when they're young and don't want the baby. There could be drugs and alcohol involved. These were all rumors from friends and the internet, but they scared us.

Besides, what if the birth parents came back years later to look for the baby, or worse, our son or daughter wanted to look for the birth parents because she or he couldn't find any resemblance to Bryan and me?

Also, even if we said we didn't care, blood mattered to us. We wouldn't have the happy moments of seeing ourselves in the baby, or our harmless joke, telling the child, "You got Daddy's small eyes and big ugly nose."

But there were no other options, or so we thought.

"Why not try surrogacy?" We had heard of that, but not thought about it at all until our friend Corrine asked us when she visited from the East Coast.

Without thinking too much, I asked, "Isn't it very expensive?"

"So, sell one of your houses and do it. Don't get me wrong, I love and respect people who adopt, but having your own blood-related baby is different. You won't regret it in twenty years," Corrine insisted, looking at her own son devouring the Thai basil fried rice in front of him.

"We'll see..." We then redirected the subject quickly because we thought there was no way we were going down the path of surrogacy.

* * *

THE PROCRASTINATION OF filling out the adoption application was colliding with our urge to take the next step of our life – having a child. The more we waited, the more uneasy we felt about adoption.

We wanted the entire fatherhood experience, from the pregnancy and kick in the belly, to the birth, the sleepless nights for the first few months, walking them to the first day at school, and crying like babies when they left for college.

We recalled what Corrine said and pushed us toward and realized the power of limitation and constraint that we put upon ourselves. Once we decided surrogacy was not an option, we had tunnel vision and didn't think twice about it.

Somehow, the little one inside of me, the one who urged me to go to internet cafes when I was in college to search for "gay," pushed me to search surrogacy online.

My daily job is to do research, synthesize information, and create proposals. The more I Googled about surrogacy, the more I was amazed by it. It became closer and seemed reachable. I soon created a table to compare surrogacy and adoption.

Items	Adoption	Surrogacy
Duration	1-3 years	1-3 years
Cost	$20-30K	$80-150K
Control of who we will receive	Almost no. The more criteria, the longer to wait	Yes, we can pick egg donor and do DNA testing
Age of the baby	Depends	At birth
Biological related	No	Yes
Complexity	Less	More
Time needed from us	Less	More

After we listed everything, surrogacy seemed to be a better choice. The downsides were time and money. We would need to be heavily involved in the process to create our new family member. *Wasn't that what we wanted?*

The cost would be extremely high. Thank God that our real estate investments were taking off. Bryan and I had accumulated a handful of properties that provided a great cash flow in addition to our salaries.

Amazon's amazing growth also put Seattle on the map for real estate investors worldwide. The investors always said that the top two richest people in the world, Bill Gates and Jeff Bezos, both lived in the Seattle area. Catering to the increasing need, Bryan and I both became agents and started helping other investors from around the world repeat what we did for ourselves and find great investment properties in the Seattle area.

Additionally, we always lived very frugally. We did spend only $265 on our wedding! With more ramen noodles, we could make surrogacy work. We loved challenges. This seemed to be the perfect next challenge for our life!

SURROGACY

"Some beautiful paths can't be discovered without getting lost."

—**Erol Ozan**

*I*n an age where people can search for anything online, I found a website called FindSurrogateMother.com. There were so many women posting their photos, information, and desires to become a surrogate. *Maybe we would have some luck?*

Still burned by my non-response Match.com experience, I wrote a heartwarming post on our profile introducing us to the world as intended parents. I carefully picked the best photo I could find of Bryan and me. It was from a Halloween 5K run a year ago. Bryan dressed me like Pee Wee Herman, the main character of his favorite show when he was a kid. The red bowtie, gray suit, and big, shiny white shoes we got from Value Village might make potential surrogates find some humor and like us.

I started to browse all the surrogate mothers' profiles. This was like Match.com. The photos were beautiful, and the descriptions beyond imagination. There was always a love letter to intended parents at the end talking about why they wanted to help another couple have kids through surrogacy. Some of the stories about their experiences helping gay couples not only brought tears to my eyes but also infused me with the

151

confidence that we could do this. I selected a few profiles that I felt good about and sent them a greeting.

That evening, sitting in bed, I was so excited showing Bryan all the profiles I liked. "This one lives in Olympia; we can visit her next weekend." Flipping through the web pages, I couldn't hide my excitement. "Look at this one. She has a big butt. In China, that means she is great at carrying babies." While Bryan was still laughing at my last comment, I continued, "This one is so beautiful! Look at her kids! She has two already! She will take care of our baby in her belly for sure!"

While I was overjoyed with my progress at finding a surrogate mother, I also started doing more research online. The devil was always in the details. It turned out that deciding on surrogacy was the easiest part of the entire process. The price tag was high, and the process was complex. We tried to understand. But the amount of information soon overwhelmed us.

Gestational or traditional surrogacy? Anonymous egg donor or not? Agency or independent journey? And in what states did we want to do this? Washington? California? Texas? I thought we had avoided the multiple-choice way of having a baby.

Whether it was Bryan's charming smile or my Pee Wee Herman outfit, we received several enthusiastic responses from FindSurrogateMother.com. I messaged back to learn more about them and why they wanted to become surrogates. But our conversations mostly ended there. What was the next step?

At the same time, I received a message on FindSurrogateMother.com from Melissa at an agency called Tiny Sprouts. Just like we hadn't thought about using a surrogate before, using a surrogacy agent was not an option for us before either. An additional $15K-$30K agency fee would definitely make surrogacy out of reach.

Always believing in karma, I tried to respond to all the messages I received. I replied to Melissa without thinking about taking the conversation any further. She, on the other hand, insisted on having a quick phone call. Thinking there was nothing to lose, I called her cell.

The conversation with Melissa turned out to be amazing. Although she lived in LA and ran the agency there, Melissa was actually from Washington State. For a person who was always moving and looking for a sense of belonging, the geographic connection helped. She had been a surrogate mother too, so she understood the process. Her voice was sweet and calm. She used "hon" and said, "You will be fine," every few sentences, which made me feel even better.

Melissa had oceans of knowledge about the surrogacy process. She could help to find a surrogate mother based on our criteria, and an egg donor too! To make it even better, her agency cost for surrogacy was only $8K, and the donor cost $1.5K. It was pushing our budget, but it was reachable with more ramen noodles.

I told Melissa that Bryan and I needed to do more research before making a decision. However, hanging up the phone that night, I already knew that we were going to work together. I trusted my gut feeling. The older I got, the truer that became.

* * *

TWO WEEKS LATER, we signed the retainer agreement with Melissa.

Melissa had explained the entire process to us at least three times, but we still could not grasp the complete journey and feel confident. Melissa asked us not to think about having a baby or when we could have a baby; instead, we should focus on the next thing she asked us to do. "A journey of a thousand miles begins with a single step; remember the Chinese saying, Nick?" Melissa giggled on the phone.

In our next call, Melissa asked what kind of surrogate mother we wanted.

"Healthy? A good family?" I tried to remember what I saw on FindSurrogateMother.com and visualize the ideal woman who would carry our child for nine months.

"Maybe live not too far from us so we can visit," Bryan added.

"All good points." Melissa continued, "We will also try to find somebody who has her own kids. This will make the process easier. Do you want an experienced surrogate, or are you okay with new ones?"

"What's the main difference?"

"The price goes up for an experienced surrogate. For a first-time surrogate, the basic compensation could be $25–$32K in California. The experienced ones could be $30–$40K." She paused and gave us time to let the information sink in, and then continued, "I think a first-time is totally fine, as long as she has her own kids." Melissa knew that controlling costs was important to us. I felt great about our decision to work with her.

"Finding a surrogate mother could take a while, but I have somebody that may work for you. Let me look more and get back to you."

"Thank you so much!" Hearing that, we were so excited. No more matchmaking by ourselves online.

"You are totally fine, hon. So, how about the egg donor. Any thoughts?"

"Could it be from the surrogate mother?"

"Everything is possible. But I wouldn't recommend it. If the surrogate carries a baby with her genes, that's traditional surrogacy, which is very complicated and not allowed in lots of states. If we have a different egg donor, the surrogate mother becomes an oven to cook your buns."

"Oven for our baby buns." I looked at Bryan, and we both burst into laughter.

"Yes, hon. I highly recommend a separate egg donor. That's called a gestational surrogate."

"Sounds good to us! Let's do it. Thank you!" We said too many thank-yous, just like Melissa's you-are-fine-hons.

"You are totally fine, hon. So what do you want in an egg donor?"

"Needs to be beautiful! Blue eyes! Blond!" I didn't even hesitate. Very insecure about my looks, I needed some good genes to balance out my small eyes and big nose.

"Definitely needs to be healthy, no genetic diseases." Bryan was taking a more practical route.

With a gentle laugh, Melissa said, "All good points! That's all doable. You guys are easy. We also want them to be young, ideally less than twenty-three years old so they can produce more eggs. We have lots of egg donors; we can send you some profiles right after the call."

"What! That's amazing! You are amazing!" I yelled.

"Thank you, hon."

Melissa sent us the files of four women who could be the genetic mother of our kids! Wow! We printed all sixty pages. Bryan read all the information about who they were, where they were from, their height, weight, personality, family history, etc. I went directly to what I cared about the most, the photographs.

Since all of them wanted to be anonymous and didn't want to have any future connection with the babies or us, we labeled them "Hollywood Superstar with a Horse," "Cute Girl Next Door," "Successful Real Estate Agent," and "PhD."

Bryan and I complemented each other in every possible way. We thought from different angles 99 percent of the time. When we caught a cold, Bryan would suggest taking Dayquil and Nyquil to stop the symptoms, while I would dig through my Chinese medicine boxes and cook a brown sugar ginger soup to help to infuse the body with heat.

There were lots of times our different approaches turned into an argument between us. Bryan hated me dumping cooking grease into the garbage disposal, and I couldn't stop Bryan from throwing away all those perfectly reusable glass drink containers that I could put food in.

However, making this decision was easy. I cared about looks, and Bryan cared about the fundamentals. After reviewing the profiles a few times, we decided on "cute girl next door," who met both criteria. She was a stunning blue-eyed blond. She had a college education, no family genetic disease history, loved music, and enjoyed reading. As Melissa said, we were easy. We didn't need more choices.

We started to dream about what our future baby would look like. Blue eyes, long nose, blond hair, dark skin, skinny body. At the same time, Melissa sent us three surrogate mothers' profiles.

It had only been a week since we started working together! She was so efficient! What I loved about working with Melissa was that she didn't just present us choices and leave the decision-making to us. Instead, she had already made an analysis and told us what she thought.

For surrogate options, she told us Isabella could be a great fit for us. She was thirty-one, healthy, and had a husband and three kids. She was a first-time surrogate, so her compensation was only $26.5K. She was from San Jose, California, and lived in Colorado at the moment, but was planning to move to Fort Lewis in Washington in a couple of months because of her husband's military assignment transfer. When she was pregnant, she would be in Washington State, so it would be easy for us to go to all the doctor's appointments with her. At the same time, she would go back to San Jose for the birth, which would allow us to have a California pre-birth order.

California was one of the few states that allowed a pre-birth judge's order. That meant that we, as intended parents, were granted the right to the baby as soon as it was born. The hospital would allow us to go into the delivery room and start taking care of the baby immediately. To make it more amazing, Bryan and I would both be listed as "parent" on the birth certificate. We didn't need to fight for who would be listed as "father" or "mother."

The only red flag we saw on Isabella's profile was the three C-sections from her three deliveries. Melissa told us that three C-sections could be a problem for some clinics, but Isabella's initial screening doctor said it should be all right.

At this point, Melissa had gained our trust. We decided to schedule a Skype call with Isabella.

Isabella was a doll. She talked from her heart. She had been married to her high school sweetheart for eleven years. She loved being pregnant. After having three kids, she was done. Three kids were enough for her family.

Maybe one day we will have three kids too! I thought. *Since she liked being pregnant, she was ready to help another couple. It could be us!* During the call, she listened carefully to our stories and nodded with a gentle smile. Although the connection through Skype was flaky, we felt an immediate bond.

Isabella it was! We were continuing to trust our gut. There is an old Chinese saying, "trying to pick bones out of an egg." It means that when people want to be difficult, they can always find a reason. For us, when a surrogate fulfilled most of our criteria, there was no need to delay the decision for some potentially better choices.

* * *

THE NEXT BIG step was to pick a clinic. According to Melissa, there were three main factors going into this one – success rate, location, and cost.

Looking at the clinic success data online, we were puzzled. *How could one clinic's success rate be 60 percent, while the other one was 85 percent?*

We later learned from Melissa that it was because some clinics took on couples who had fertility problems, or helped older couples who wanted to get pregnant, while other clinics focused on surrogacy cases with young, healthy donor eggs and healthy sperm. This was definitely a "it's me, not you" case. For a typical healthy egg and sperm surrogacy situation, the success rate was around 75–85 percent. This made us feel good.

Location was also critical. Both the egg donor and surrogate mother needed to travel to the clinic multiple times. If the clinic location was not ideal, the travel costs would add up quickly. Our egg donor, "Cute Girl Next Door," lived in Palm Springs, while Isabella was in Colorado, Fort Lewis, and San Jose,

California. In this case, a clinic that was close to either Southern or Northern California would to be a good choice.

The last but very important factor was cost. Clinics charged widely varying amounts. Some clinics charged per transfer of embryos. What we saw most often was $15K–$20K. Some provided an "all-you-can-eat" package. Paying $40K guaranteed us a baby, no matter how many times we transferred.

Most of the clinics told us that health insurance would not cover the medical expenses for the surrogate and egg donor during the IVF process. Luckily, I realized that our health insurance at Microsoft covered infertility treatment, including surrogate and egg donors, up to $15K per person. How lucky we were! This meant that Bryan and I would have $30K in total for the entire IVF process. I was thrilled to hear about this new savings opportunity!

It was clear that our next step was to find a clinic located in California, with a good success rate for surrogacy cases, that took our insurance. Sounds easy given how popular the surrogacy industry in California was, right? Not really.

Melissa recommended a couple of clinics. I also found a great clinic rating list on MenHavingBabies.org. The rating was based on survey data from intended parents who had been through the journey. I started scheduling calls. This was not as speedy as I wished. We wanted to talk to the doctors, and the doctors were always busy. Our call was always one to two weeks down the road. There were even some clinics that charged $150–$250 for a half-hour call with the doctor.

When we were finally on the calls with the doctors, we were overwhelmed by the terminology and further decisions to make. "How many embryos do we want to transfer? Do we want to do genetic testing? Whose sperm are we going to use more of? Do we want to make the embryo naturally or with sperm injection?"

While we were frantically thinking of answers to the new questions, we heard from several doctors that they had serious concerns about using Isabella as our surrogate. Three C-sections could have thinned the uterine lining. Our little embryos might not be able to stick well enough. There could be other implications throughout the pregnancy.

We were disappointed. We talked to Melissa about it. She asked us not to share our concerns with Isabella yet because we didn't need to create unnecessary drama. We agreed. Until we receive a final decision on the clinic and a firm answer from the doctor, we were not going to say anything to her.

This made our calls with Isabella uncomfortable. We had developed so much emotion for each other. Now we knew that there was a good chance we didn't have a future together but needed to pretend there was nothing wrong. This reminded me of those early coming-out dates and the open relationship quandary.

Growing up as an only child, I always craved a bigger family. Since I was born in the early 1980s in China, all my friends were only children. Being an only child was never a problem for me. I never had play time; I was always studying and studying. But as I started to watch Hollywood movies and realized that in America, most families have more than one kid, my heart opened. *How wonderful would it be to have brothers or sisters? To have somebody to laugh with, play with, and be sad with?*

But for so long, just like my sexuality, I buried the fantasy of having a bigger family deeply. There was no point in thinking about it since I was gay and couldn't have kids.

Now we were on this journey of surrogacy, we learned that we could transfer two embryos, which meant we could have twins! To make it sweeter, while having one baby could be $80–$100K, having two would only incur an incremental cost, making the total bill $100–$120K. Since we were strained financially, transferring two embryos was a better decision.

At that time, I realized that some clinics didn't want to transfer two embryos because of the risk and potential complications during pregnancy. "Our success rate is 85 percent; there is no need to transfer two embryos." This eliminated almost half the clinics. The decision to transfer two embryos and the need to find a clinic that would take our insurance became our constraints, which led us to only one choice – Fertility Associates of California.

* * *

JUST LIKE WHAT *The Alchemist* said – when you want something badly, the universe will send the best person to help you. Dr. Kumar and his team were beyond amazing. My initial call with them was scheduled within forty-eight hours of my first contact. They always returned my calls and emails on the same day. Dr. Kumar even gave me his personal cell number to make sure we had a way to reach him in case of emergency, although we were lucky not to have to use it.

To make it even more magical, the coordinator, Kim, who was assigned to my case, was from Hunan and grew up in Guangzhou, China. That was the journey I followed when I was a kid. It could not be more perfect! This was destiny!

Dr. Kumar was a great doctor. Wearing a pair of big plastic glasses, he always looked like he was deep in thought. His smile was gentle. His voice was always, *always* calm. He listened to our concerns and openly shared his thoughts. He never used jargon or professional expertise to push us toward something we weren't comfortable with. He gave us direct and honest feedback. He told us that he had viewed Isabella's exam report and had a lot of concern about the three C-sections. If we were his brothers, he would recommend we choose another surrogate.

We were sad to let go of Isabella. We had developed a strong bond with her. "I know this is a tough decision. But you need to make the best decision for your kids even before they are born. Those best decisions can be tough ones. Being parents is all about making difficult decisions." Melissa noticed our hesitation and gave us a clear recommendation.

The benefit of an agency was more than guidance; the agent was also the mediator and bad news deliverer. Melissa asked us to focus on reviewing the new surrogate profiles that she sent us and let her take care of Isabella.

Two days later, we received a heartwarming email from Isabella. She gave us an update about herself, her kids, and her husband's job. She told us she understood the situation and wished us all the best. We cried and told her that we would be in touch.

Melissa worked really fast. We liked it. We had already received two more surrogate profiles. My friends said we were too easy – whatever our agent recommended, we just went along with it. One friend even suggested we be more like "picking bones out of an egg." She believed that pushing more would get a better result.

As type A as I could be, it didn't feel right to follow this advice. *Wasn't that why we hired an agent?* She understood our goals, needs, and criteria. She helped us filter and connect. We trusted her proposals and then made our decision.

We scheduled a call with each surrogate mother. The talk with Jerrie went well, but there was something missing. We were not connecting as we had with Isabella. Bryan and I were going back and forth on whether we made the wrong decision by giving up on Isabella, but the call with Chelsie erased that doubt.

At the age of twenty-three, Chelsie was young, sweet, and had kind eyes. She had one daughter who was two years old. She lived with her boyfriend in Fresno, California, and her parents were just a few miles away. Fresno was a four-hour drive from Dr. Kumar's clinic in LA. She was also perfectly healthy. She had her daughter naturally, and she used to be in the army and left it two years ago because of an injury. Her favorite flower? White rose! How beautiful and calm was that!

In our Skype call with her, Chelsie listened to us patiently and talked to us calmly. We asked her whether she needed to let us know anything else. "Just my name. It's not the normal spelling of Chelsea, but with 'sie.'" She gave us a shy smile. After the call, we told Melissa that Chelsie it was! That decision was on November 15, 2014.

* * *

EVERYTHING WENT REALLY fast from then on.

Nov. 17 – Our egg donor's bloodwork to make sure she was perfectly healthy and genetically compatible with our sperm.

Nov. 20 – Chelsie's bloodwork to make sure she was ready to be our surrogate.

Nov. 21 – Bryan and I visited Dr. Kumar in LA to do our bloodwork and deposit our sperm.

At the same time, the lawyer that Melissa recommended was busy working on contract terms for our egg donor and Chelsie.

The time after the bloodwork was the first of many anxious waiting periods that we went through in the surrogacy journey. The FDA required all parties involved in the process to test for sexually transmitted diseases. We also needed to test the egg inventory and any genetic risks from the egg donor side.

On Nov. 24, our coordinator, Kim, from Dr. Kumar's office emailed us saying that "Cute Girl Next Door" had level 5 AMH (anti-Müllerian Hormone). I asked her what that meant. She told me that the egg donor could produce lots of eggs.

The surrogate journey was ironically an experience of learning about women. Thanks to Google, I learned that women were born with a finite number of eggs. When a girl is born, she is born with up to two million eggs. By the time she reaches puberty, she's down to about 400,000. During a woman's reproductive years, those numbers continue to fall, and by the time she's thirty, that number has diminished by a whopping 90 percent! By the time a woman hits menopause, she has less than a thousand eggs left, and not all of them are good. Anti-mullerian hormone was a substance produced by granulosa cells in the ovarian follicles, which are specific cells which surround each egg in a woman's ovary. The more eggs, the more granulosa cells, and the more cells, the more AMH.

There were five levels of AMH. Our "Cute Girl Next Door" had the highest level! We were excited about the news. But my mind was still shadowed by the thought of our own bloodwork.

The scary feeling of having AIDS from my college days lingered. I talked to Bryan. He assured me that he had been tested right after we went into our exclusive relationship. But the feeling would not go away completely.

Two days later, I got a call from Kim. She normally did not call me unless it was something important.

"I need to share some bad news..." Kim said.

I pushed my breath down to my stomach. "Okaaaaay..."

"Your egg donor has an STD."

"What?" I happily let go of my own worry, but I instantly was pulled into this new situation. "What does that mean?"

"This is also news to her. She was surprised. Her boyfriend is breaking up with her."

"I am sorry to hear that... but what does that mean for us?"

"We can treat the STD first and then redo the test, and then egg retrieval."

"How long would that take?"

"Three to six months at least."

"Let us talk to Melissa about it."

I hung up the phone and speed dialed Melissa. She was surprised too. She must have felt bad because she introduced "Cute Girl Next Door" to us.

The more I was letting the results and reality sink in, the more annoyed and angrier I became. *Why was this not identified before? Shouldn't being STD-free be a requirement of becoming an egg donor? There were so many free STD exams in clinics all over the country. But we had spent thousands of dollars on the blood and genetic testing, let alone the egg-donor retaining fee.*

And the delay! We didn't want to wait another three to six months and spend thousands more dollars to test again. What if the STD wasn't cured?

Never a fan of confrontation, I decided to keep my anger from Melissa and talk to Kim instead. Kim told us that they had lots of egg donors in-house. They had all been tested before and wouldn't have a problem like this.

Bryan and I discussed it. We decided to move forward instead of playing the blame game. We messaged Melissa that we would find an egg donor from Dr. Kumar's in-house pool. She agreed that was the best route.

Kim sent us a list of twelve egg donors in one email. We were happy about the efficiency and quickly dived deep into the filtering process. After reviewing every single profile, we realized that we needed to change our criteria, especially mine – blond and blue eyes. Yes, who was I kidding? Did I really care that much about the hair and eye color?

Bryan and I agreed on our new criteria with the following order of priority: (1) healthy, (2) a good family with no genetic disease, and (3) needed to pass our beauty test in the photos.

We soon picked out donor #910. We didn't have the energy or the will to create a lovely nickname for her, let alone imagine what our future babies may look like. We tried not to be too emotionally involved.

It turned out to be a great decision! Donor #910 had had unprotected sex two days before the bloodwork and genetic testing. It was great that she was honest and told us this three days before the blood test so we could decide against moving forward and save thousands of dollars, which could be wasted due to pregnancy or an STD.

However, we were still recovering from the "Cute Girl Next Door" incident. This news definitely shot us to the bottom. My mind was constantly running and distracted. I developed the habit of looking through phone alerts when driving. Any notification or phone call would send a shiver up my spine. Driving home one day right before Christmas 2014, I rear-ended the car in front of me.

* * *

BRYAN AND I decided to take a break. We need some breathing room. We went on a short vacation to Cabo San Lucas. Traveling is not about where you are going, but who you are going with. Now we felt like it was also when we were traveling.

Instead of just staying at the Sheraton and enjoying the beach, we rented a car and drove all the way to Cabo Pulmo National Park. There were two roads leading to the park, south and north. Going in from the south is a 95-kilometer drive, while going in from the north would be a big circle with a 135-kilometer drive.

Reading on TripAdvisor, we understood that part of the southern road had been destroyed by landslide and sinkholes. However, some brave soul on TripAdvisor said that it was still doable.

Thirty minutes into the south road, we started to doubt our decision. No cars coming from the other direction in thirty minutes should have given it away. But we stuck to the plan until we saw half the road was collapsed on one side. I jumped out of the car, got off the road on the desert landscape, and saw the other half of the road was also in the air with no support underneath.

"We can't let our future babies be fatherless," Bryan joked. We decided to turn around.

The road coming from the north was longer and not that much better. Dirt and sinkholes were everywhere. But the occasional passing car gave us confidence that it was the way to go. The cars also created clouds of dust that blinded us and made us stop our car to let the dust settle. Sometimes we just need some time to let chaos settle.

After an additional two-hour roller-coaster ride, we finally reached Cabo Pulmo. We were starving. We found the only "restaurant" open. It was a washed pink clay house sitting in somebody's private yard. The owner lived in the house and served food on the three tables that were casually placed in the living room. You could not get more local than this. Using his Spanish from high school, Bryan ordered us some tasty fish tacos.

Stomachs stuffed, we chose not to do anything but just wander on the beach. The white sand beach was miles and miles long and nobody was on it. The wind was high that day. Waves kept crashing to the shore. I took Bryan's hand.

We looked back at how much we had accomplished in the past three months. In September we were still debating whether to go on the surrogacy journey. Now in December, we already had a surrogate mother ready to go. We realized that we were so beaten down by the egg donor issues we were facing, we forgot the things that we had gained. Sometimes, we just needed to be pulled away from reality and to have a thirty-thousand-foot view to find a holistic perspective.

We also joked about the sex adventures that our egg donors had been through. Young and reckless. That reminded me of when I first came out to myself and started meeting guys.

The next evening, we finished our quarter-kilo shrimp and quarter-kilo lobster combo dinner at Maro's Shrimp House and ran into a local event in downtown Cabo. It was a Christmas celebration in a square that was like a hotel courtyard. The sun was down. The heat had dissipated. People were all dressed in colorful clothes that were made of canvas. They were dancing and singing, immersed in pure joy.

The music was fast and upbeat. Not knowing any words in the lyric, I couldn't help but jump in and start shaking my body and waving my hands high. Never a dancer, Bryan stood outside of the circle and cheered for me in his broken Spanish. "Join me, Bryan!" I ran to him and pulled him in.

After we sweated out all the calories from the dinner and the worries about the future, we wandered around the square. There were lots of local artists making crafts. We saw a pair of ornaments decorated with sea turtles.

"Let's get them!" I said. "Hopefully we will hang them on a tree next Christmas, with our two babies in our arms!"

Looking at my excited face, Bryan leaned forward and gave me a gentle kiss on the cheek.

PHOEBE

"You will always be the miracle that makes my life complete."

—George Strait

Coming back to Seattle from Cabo, we went directly into the busy schedule that Melissa and Kim carefully planned.

Jan. 6, 2015 – We had the contract terms reviewed with our lawyer, Doug.

Jan. 12 – We chose our new egg donor, #871. We were still refusing to use creative names. The distance with the numbers felt just right.

Jan. 30 – This was our surrogate Chelsie's medical start.

Feb. 6 – We retrieved twenty-five eggs from our egg donor! Twenty eggs were good!

We were thrilled! Six weeks ago, we were still whimpering on the roller coaster ride of our egg donor journey, and now there were twenty living and thriving eggs! Maybe two of them would give us reason to hang the sea turtle ornaments in the coming year.

It wasn't time to celebrate yet. The next phase was one of the most critical. It was also where the magic happens.

When Dr. Kumar was retrieving the eggs, he also thawed our sperm. He then split the eggs in half. Half for Bryan's sperm and half for mine. To ensure success, he would further split the eggs in half for each of us. Half the eggs and sperm would be allowed to find each other naturally. With the other half, Dr. Kumar would inject the sperm into the egg.

All of this happened on Day 0. That's all that we could control. The results were left to Mother Nature, to God, to a higher power. We were waiting for the magic to make the individual sperms and eggs, each with its own distinct complement of genes, to become embryos with new, unique, and unified genes.

We then needed to wait five days for the embryos to develop. Quickly searching online, this was what I found (on the Houston Fertility Center website) on what we should expect for our precious little ones:

Day 1 – Fertilization
Fertilization refers to the sperm entering the egg. At this time, the genetic material of the egg and sperm begin to fuse together, creating a zygote.

Day 2 – Cleavage
Cleavage is a term used to describe the process of cellular division, with the zygote going from a single cell and dividing into multiple cells. The first split means a single cell becomes two cells, with four cells developing with the next cellular split, then eight cells, and so forth. If you remember your biology class, this is a process known as mitosis.

Day 3 – Compaction
As cells continue to divide, the shape of the embryo begins to change. Rather than a round embryo, it's more likely for an embryo to have a shape that resembles a berry. This is known as compaction. It's much more difficult to count the number of cells

given the shape change, but generally by the compaction stage, between 20 to 30 cells is common.

Day 4 – Differentiation
Differentiation refers to a type of process in which a cell changes from one type of cell into another type of cell. When it comes to zygotes, this means the change from simple cells to more complex cellular structures to help build human tissue and other cell types.

Day 5 – Blastocysts
By day 5 or day 6 of the growth of the embryo, the cells will have divided further, with approximately 200 cells present as well as cavitation of the cell itself. This cluster of many cells is known as a blastocyst, and it is the furthest stage of embryonic development. Outside of the IVF process, this would be the time that the embryo would implant itself along the lining of the mother's uterus.

Waiting for Kim's call becoming my new addiction. Day 1, we had nine fertilized eggs each. Eighteen out of twenty, not bad! Day 3, Bryan had four and I had six embryos! Day 5, those ten embryos all went into the blastocyst stage!

Dr. Kumar froze all the ten little lives and picked one cell from each of their outer walls to do pre-implantation genetic screening and testing, PGS for short. He told us that the main reason for miscarriage was that the embryo had genetic issues that made it not viable. Doing a PGS would tell us the genetic info upfront and dramatically decrease the chances of miscarriage.

Doing genetic testing on the cells from the embryos also meant that the embryos needed to be frozen. *What! That's just like science fiction! Are we in 2050 yet?*

Dr. Kumar told us that freezing embryos was very common. He had implanted embryos that had been frozen for over ten years, and they grew into healthy babies.

We also learned that freezing embryos was better than freezing eggs. It caused the least damage to the cell and had a higher success rate. That's why all of the scheduling and planning need to be centered on the egg donor's menstrual cycle.

PGS testing was normally done in a set of eight. Each additional embryo tested would cost us $500. We decided to stick to the eight and asked Dr. Kumar to pick four of mine to test.

While we were nervously waiting for the test results, Dr. Kumar's office scheduled a transfer date for us. It was based on the cycle of our surrogate, Chelsie.

Feb. 20, 2015! That was one week away! Be careful what you wish for. I asked for an efficient and fast-moving process; now we were transferring in just eight days.

Feb 16, four days from Day 5 stage, Kim sent us the report. It was less encouraging. Bryan had only one normal grade AA embryo, while I had three normal ones. Mine included one AA grade; the others were BB. The remaining embryos either had noisy signals or abnormalities on monosomy 14, 15, and 21.

"You only need two good ones, right?" Melissa reminded us. Yes, that's right! This was perfect for us. In total, we had one good embryo from Bryan and three from me. We each had one AA grade. We should just transfer the two AA embryos.

To make it more perfect, Bryan's was a little boy, while mine was a girl. "They will be dragon and phoenix twins." Mom was thrilled. In Chinese culture, it is said the best is to have boy-girl twins. It represents the balance of yin and yang and creates harmony and prosperity for the family.

* * *

FEB. 20, 2015, was the official transfer day. We got up at 4:00 a.m., caught a flight to LA, and then drove to the clinic. At 11:20 a.m., with our hearts in our throats, we went into the clinic.

Chelsie's boyfriend, Steven, was playing with their daughter, Delia, in the lobby. We said hi to each other. I tried to talk about the ridiculously long TSA line and the complimentary upgrade of our rental car. When I was nervous, I talked too much to fill the void and cover my emotion.

"We are ready to go!" Kim came out of the door. We gave her a hug and followed her into the back.

Chelsie was already lying on a bed. Dr. Kumar wore a surgical mask. He saw us and said with his normal calm voice, "Are you excited?" I didn't respond. I was too excited and nervous.

"Do you want to see the little ones?" Dr. Kumar handed over the dish with a cover. "The two embryos are right there. Fresh and ready to go."

Tears started running down my face. It was like a little stream that carried all the memories. Images of my past life played in front of my eyes like a movie.

The little boy moving with his parents to a new city for a better life. The rejections from the teacher. Laughter from the new classmates. The boy touched by his deskmate. The sleepless nights. The depression. The first night with a guy. The fear of AIDS. The struggle over who I was. The collision of the environment with the inner me. The first time in America, the land of freedom. The dark Vancouver night when I decided to live true to who I was. Meeting Bryan. The conflicts between us. The fight for our life together.

In any of those moments, I could not imagine today, the day when we were going to create the next generation of Bryan and me.

"We are done!" Dr. Kumar said.

"That's it?" I was deep in thought, but it must have been only two or three minutes.

"They are planted now. We just need to make sure they will stick," Dr. Kumar said.

"Anything we should do?" Chelsie asked.

"Yes, you have three items of homework: (1) Do not go on a diet. Eat normally. Drink lots of water. (2) Don't go on excursions. (3) Be positive and have positive and sticky thoughts."

Like when I was a student back in China who was eager to write down every piece of information that could help me get into a great college to change my life, I quickly grabbed my phone to write down the homework for Chelsie.

We booked a hotel right by the clinic for Chelsie to stay in for two days. Kim told us that it was beneficial not to travel and to lie in bed for the first forty-eight hours post-transfer. We definitely did not want Chelsie and Steven driving four hours home to Fresno.

Bryan and I had dinner with Chelsie at the hotel that night before we departed early the next morning.

Though she used to be really skinny before leaving the army due to a leg injury, Chelsie was a bigger woman now. Her light brown hair was as curly as Keri Russell's from *Felicity*. She had smaller eyes, like me, but her eye color was a mysterious blue, green, and brown, just like her racial identity. She told us that she might have some Native American in her.

She moved her body slowly as she sat at the table. "Burger and fries." Her order was easy, and she was definitely following Dr. Kumar's recommendation of eating normally. I took out my phone and reviewed Dr. Kumar's homework assignment several times. We tried to joke around and be cheerful. But we all knew that the next few days were critical. This was a pivotal point in our life. "Sticky thoughts!" Chelsie said to me when she gave me a goodbye hug after dinner.

Maybe it was because we woke up too early that day, maybe it was because of the letdown after a big moment, but when we got back to the hotel room, negative thoughts flooded my mind.

I remembered the dead black animal we saw on the way to the airport in the morning. It was very unlucky according to Chinese culture. When we were driving to the clinic, the highway exit we took was 44. I told Bryan that 44 meant double death in Chinese. During dinner, Chelsie told me that she had had a dream last night that she became pregnant on Day 2. Dreams were always, *always*, the opposite of real life.

Bryan asked me not to think. "Just go to sleep," he growled. I shut my mouth and put a pillow over my head.

The next few days were difficult even for Bryan. I knew he was very nervous too. The result of this action could change our lives forever. However, at such a pivotal moment, there was nothing we could do but wait. The uncertainty, the fear, and the nerves made us pick on each other a lot. We realized that and tried to talk everything over openly.

Every day, I kept praying, "Little Nicky and little Bryan, please stick to Chelsie, please! We cannot wait to meet you!"

For somebody who never prays, this turned out to be my only solution.

We told ourselves that we had already done everything we could. We just needed to let life and fate unfold. If we weren't successful this time, we still had some embryos frozen. We could try again. If we still didn't succeed, we would just quit our jobs and travel around the world. If the higher power didn't give us a chance to have the next generation, we would make sure that we lived our lives to the fullest.

We filled our time watching the TV show *Parenthood*. We had been watching it the last few months. We laughed and cried, were happy and got angry with the show every night. Seeing the grandfather's name was Zeek, I asked Bryan, "Is that why you like Zeeks Pizza?" Bryan was as speechless as when I asked him who Aretha Franklin was.

To him, I was sometimes like a real alien who had had no connection with the world that he grew up in. For my part, I was thrilled to learn another culture – the food, the language, the social norms, the movie stars and singers.

What the show gave us was an education about being good parents. Adam told his niece Amber, "Life will knock you down more times than you can possibly imagine. Don't knock yourself down." We stored that in our minds because we would definitely use it one day. We imagined what it would like for us to be parents. *What could we share, what would we have to teach our little Bryan and little Nicky?*

We were also a bit sad because we were already on the last two episodes of the show before heading down to the transfer. Not having the show to watch every night, *what would we do? How did we learn about parenthood? Maybe we would welcome the end of* Parenthood *with our own parenthood?* We sure hoped so.

* * *

AT THE DINNER table after the transfer, Chelsie told us that she planned to do home tests before the official blood test. "Do you guys want to know when I test?"

We quickly told her no. Melissa had told us that those home pregnancy tests could be unreliable. It was better not to have our hopes up if the test gave a false signal. Also, the official blood test was just seven days away. We could wait.

In the next few days, I tried not to text Chelsie. If she had done her home test, she might subconsciously give an indication.

Not communicating with Chelsie, even for a few days, created a void in our life. Bryan and I normally talked during dinner. Now, we just sat there silently, our minds wandering.

On Wednesday, four days post transfer (4DPT), Chelsie texted me, "Do you guys really not want to know?" My eyes lit up seeing this message. If it was negative, I didn't think Chelsie would send such a text. This must be good news. Bryan and I decided we had to know.

"Yes, we want to know," we texted back fifteen minutes later. Literally in two seconds, we got a FaceTime request from Chelsie.

"It's positive!" she yelled.

"It's positive! Oh my God!" We all started crying. Subconsciously, I switched all the yelling to, "We are pregnant! We are pregnant! We are pregnant!" The word positive still had too much negative meaning to me.

"I started testing on Monday, which was three days post-transfer..."

"Shouldn't it be four?" I didn't always know the best way to interrupt and ask the right questions.

"Friday was transfer day; that day doesn't count. So Saturday is Day 1, Sunday is Day 2, Monday, when I tested at 10:30 in the morning, it was three days post transfer..." Chelsie also told us that the reason she felt comfortable telling us was that she switched to a digital pregnancy test kit on Wednesday. Digital testing was more accurate. Since the result was yes, she was more confident and comfortable telling us. What a thoughtful person!

In the following days, Chelsie kept texting us photos of the test result. To show progress, she sent one photo of the traditional test result to us every twelve hours. As the line grew darker and darker on the tube, our confidence grew, and our spirits were high.

We were going to be dads!

On the radio, the meteorologist said that Seattle was having the warmest winter in history. That was just like the feeling in my heart. Filled with joy, happiness, and hope.

Our first beta test result confirmed that. We got our first beta result on March 4, which was twelve days post transfer.

"You guys are definitely pregnant!" Kim said on the phone. We smiled although she could not see. "HCG was 345, which is pretty high." She continued, "It could be twins."

For the first time ever, I didn't bother asking what the new term, HCG, was. "Really? How will we know for sure?"

"We can only confirm with the ultrasound, which will be on March 30. But the number is high and in the twins area. We want to see the HCG number double every day from now on."

We got our second HCG the next day: "It was 1,014!" more than double the first number. Kim told us that it was very likely to be twins.

We were thrilled. Chelsie was excited. She knew how much this meant to us and really wanted to know whether we were having twins. She was not communicating any worry about the risk of having a twin pregnancy. Instead, all she showed us was support and love for the creation of our family with little Bryan and little Nicky.

She scheduled an OB visit for March 9. At first, her OB didn't want to do an ultrasound yet because she was still with Dr. Kumar until week twelve. It could have been Chelsie's charming smile and personality, it could have been the doctor's understanding of the special surrogacy situation, but two days later, Chelsie had an ultrasound.

"There were two black holes! Two! There were two!" Chelsie was literally yelling in my ears. I loved the energy, loved every word, and every enunciation of every bit of it!

Chelsie texted us the photos from the ultrasound. They were labeled Baby A and Baby B. Baby A was skinnier and longer. Baby B was round and bigger. A must be little Nicky, and B must be little Bryan, we told each other.

For the first time in months, we slept really well. No dreams. No sudden waking. We didn't even receive our normal morning bark from JD to take him outside. Looking at JD and Jack, who were sleeping next to us, I smiled. "You guys will have a younger brother and sister in seven...hmmm... eight... months..." I still didn't know how the due date post-transfer should be calculated. Melissa told us that on the transfer day, we were already five weeks pregnant. Really? We couldn't believe that.

One thing we knew for sure was that our due date was November 7, 2015. Dr. Kumar warned us that twins may come early. It was possible that they could be born at thirty-seven weeks, which make it around October 7. I carefully marked the two days on every single calendar I had – work computer, Gmail calendar, calendar at home and at work. I also asked Mom to do the same. Mom and Dad planned to visit us around thirty-seven weeks so if the babies came early, they could help us.

* * *

CHELSIE WAS BACK to school a week after the transfer. Everything was fine. She resumed her life. We texted every day. "Do you feel tired?" "Do you want to eat spicy food?" "Do you want to throw up?" Chelsie was bombarded with all the questions I heard when people talked about the first trimester of pregnancy.

"I wanted something spicy."

"That must be little Nicky!"

"I also want something Mexican."

"That's definitely little Bryan." Since Bryan was half German and half Mexican, whenever there was mention of either of these two countries, I would pin that on him.

When we were happy, time passed so fast. It was the big day, March 30, the ultrasound day. Same hotel. Same rental car agency. Same clinic location. I was superstitious sometimes – ah, okay, all the time. Could you blame me? I just wanted to continue the good luck train and let little Nicky and little Bryan grow healthily.

"Are you excited to see your babies?" Chelsie asked, lying on the ultrasound bed.

"Yes! We cannot wait to see them." I looked at Bryan and smiled.

"It is going to be a little cold..." Dr. Kumar put some gel on Chelsie's belly, and the scanning device followed.

A white mass showed up on the screen; that must be Chelsie's uterus. "That's one," I cried out when I saw one black hole. "Oh, the other one!" as Dr. Kumar was moving the wand around.

Dr. Kumar kept moving the scanner, and the screen kept changing. He didn't talk. Seconds went by. There was no talking. It turned to a minute, and then two minutes, and then more. There was still no talking. The air became heavy. The happiness in the room evaporated and was replaced by questions and uncertainty.

"How... are... little... Nicky... and Bryan...?" I squeezed out those words one by one. It was like the first time I answered a teacher's question when I moved to the new school in the fourth grade.

"I could not find a heartbeat in one of them... Let me try to move around more..."

I felt like I was falling, free falling, from the tallest building in the world, from the highest mountain, from the moon when there is no friction to stop me falling. What Dr. Kumar said after that became background noise.

No heartbeat. What did that mean? How could you die before you were born? The HCG level was growing so well! It more than doubled every day from the first test!

"But the other one is growing well," Dr. Kumar switched the focus. There was a little person in there. I could see. The heart was jumping up and down. "Do you want to hear the heartbeat?"

"Em..."

"Pudong... pudong... pudong..." A strong wave of sound filled the silent room with life.

I should have been excited. I should have been happy, moved, thrilled. So many times I had imagined seeing little Nicky and little Bryan and hearing their heartbeats for the first time.

I couldn't focus, couldn't find my way out of the grief. I didn't cry though. I kept my tears inside. I told myself that Chelsie could not see me crying. Only happy tears in front of her. She needed support. She needed to know I was okay. She still had a long pregnancy journey to go through.

"You have a very healthy baby," Dr. Kumar said. "Because the other one was still very early, it will be absorbed and just come out as blood in the future." I knew Dr. Kumar was trying to calm our worries about the health impact of the black hole (later I learned it is called a *sac*), but I was just not there. I couldn't stop falling and grieving. I wasn't ready to move on.

We had planned to go to In and Out Burger to celebrate little Nicky and little Bryan. We were not in the mood. Trying to stay strong, I squeezed a smile to Chelsie. "Do you want to go to Deli for a quick bite? I heard they are good." That was the closest restaurant I could find on Yelp. I just wanted the lunch to end quickly because I didn't know how long I could hold on in front of Chelsie.

I don't remember what we talked about over lunch. It must have been whatever comforting and encouraging words I could spit out to let Chelsie know that we would be fine and that she and the baby would be fine too.

Bryan and I had a few hours to kill before going to the airport. We knew the empty hotel room would drive us crazy.

We decided to go to Malibu. When we were falling apart inside, we just needed to grab whatever shiny object was around to be our lifebuoy. We took a selfie in front of the famous "Welcome to Malibu" sign. The blue sky, the ocean, the beautiful people around, the breeze... and two broken hearts.

On the flight back to Seattle that evening, I took a nap. When I woke up, I could not control myself any longer. My tears started pouring out. I wished it was a nightmare, the worst kind, the kind where you wake up and are so happy that everything is normal.

I pulled out my computer, going to my private blog, Looking for My Way Out, the blog that helped me come out to myself in the cold Vancouver night. I started typing frantically.

Tears dropped to the keyboard and became little puddles. I just needed to let everything out. "Wish you all the best in heaven, our little baby." I heard people say that in the movies. I never imagined I would be the one saying it.

In the next few days, weeks, we were all living on ice. Chelsie and I texted every day. We talked about the baby's growth. She must be the size of an egg now. Chelsie still wanted both spicy and Mexican food. Chelsie told us that she tried to eat as healthily as possible. She stopped drinking soda to make sure no caffeine was going to the baby. We were so blessed to have such a wonderful surrogate mother, Bryan and I always told each other.

* * *

WE HAD A tradition to travel every April to celebrate Bryan's birthday. Before we knew we were pregnant and everything that had happened, to challenge ourselves and to celebrate the parenthood we hoped for, we had planned a four-day hike at Machu Picchu.

Mom heard about the trip and was not happy. "If you have time, go visit your surrogate mother and check on the baby," she said on the phone, her tone upset. I didn't want to protest and argue.

Totally understanding where she was coming from, Bryan and I were craving this trip more than before. We needed a way to deal with the loss of a baby we had not had a chance to say hello to. Maybe a different country, unique culture, new food, and greater than normal physical challenge could make the grieving and healing process easier and faster.

The hiking trip started from Cusco, which was a tourist city at an elevation of 11,152 feet. I had heard about altitude sickness. I just never thought I would experience it until I stepped out of the plane. My head was light and filled with pain. My breathing was shallow and fast. We rushed to a local pharmacy to buy some medicine that I should have procured before the trip. It helped a little bit. I went to bed early, hoping the night would restore me.

The next morning, I was no better. As I chewed the coca leaves provided by the hotel, our concierge told us that it might be good to walk around the city more before the hike that would happen in two days. He also handed me another bunch of the leaves. "Continue chewing on them. It will help."

We started walking around the beautiful city. The air was crisp. The sky was azure. There was not a single cloud. The local people were dark skinned and talked happily. There were so many things happening, just like in Malibu. We needed the noise to keep our minds full. But there was also a sense of peace and divinity that was calming to our souls.

That evening, we booked a nice restaurant to have the highly recommended cui (guinea pig). The lighting was romantic. The seating was comfortable. The menu was detailed and well-crafted. The waiters were handsome and polite. We had been frugal during the trip, but we decided to treat ourselves to a great dinner before the big hike.

"Good day, gentlemen. Do you want to start with some drinks?"

"We are fine. Just give us two *cuis*." We knew what we wanted.

A little bit surprised by our fast ordering, the waiter smiled back. "Okay, that's a great choice."

Ten minutes later, he came back with two plates. Each held a roasted brown guinea pig. The ears, the eyes, everything was still on them. I threw up a little bit in my throat. Growing up in China, I was used to all kinds of weird foods: snake, frog legs, drunken shrimp... But I never needed to see the entire animal before eating it. It was always the taste that mattered. Now, seeing these cute guinea pigs served to us on delicate china plates, I suddenly lost my appetite.

I picked up the quarter piece with one leg (yes, the *cui* was cut into four pieces but put back together on the plate) and took one little bite. Oh, the taste, the sour, bitter, weird taste... I spit it out and rinsed my mouth with water.

I looked at Bryan. He was shocked by the cui too. He was always so calm no matter what challenge was offered to him. He picked up his fork and knife and tried to start his dinner. There was just no way to cut.

"Look at her." I pointed at a blond girl at the next table. She was holding the upper quarter body of her cui and used her teeth to work on the meat between the ribs. On her plate, the other three pieces had nothing but bone left. "That's the right way to eat it."

We tried for another fifteen minutes. I managed to swallow two or three bites. Bryan almost finished one-quarter of a cui. We decided to give up. There are things in life that you shouldn't push yourself on.

Trying to be polite, we asked to take home the cui. Once outside the restaurant, we rushed to a grocery store and devoured some bread. On the way back to our hotel, we saw four or five dogs. Yes, there were many street dogs in Cusco. We decided to give our cui to the dogs.

Each of them sniffed the cui that we left one yard in front of them, and then walked away. "Ha ha! Even the dogs don't want the cui!" I laughed out loud. The feeling of laughter was so good. I missed it so much.

I woke up several times that night. My stomach was not feeling well. In the morning, it became worse. I needed to go to the bathroom every half an hour, and my temperature was rising. We found an international hospital not far away. Fifteen minutes later, a taxi dropped us off at the hospital.

Everything in the hospital was screaming at me all my memories of hospitals in China. I didn't have time to enjoy the familiarity. I was losing fluids fast, and my climbing temperature made my head dizzy and world spin. The ER doctor spoke good English. She asked me what I ate yesterday. The corn on the cob? The cui? I didn't know.

After several rounds of testing, I was given a bag of drugs and instructions to stay in bed and not eat much for the next five days. "But I was going to start my four-day Machu Picchu hike tomorrow!" I tried to stay strong.

"No, you should not go. You cannot go." The doctor was sweet, but she was very firm.

I slept most of the day. Bryan was just sitting in our room, switching TV channels. Bryan and I tried not to talk about whether we were going to hike tomorrow. We knew we should probably cancel the trip and just take it easy. If I called Mom, that's what she would say for sure. She would tell me to take care of myself and be ready to be a dad. Why risk my health when our little baby was growing in Chelsie's tummy? She would tell me to go back and save my time to visit Chelsie instead.

That evening, there was an information session for the hike. I struggled out of bed. "Let's go to the meeting."

"Look at yourself; let's just stay. There is still lots we can see in Cusco." Bryan tried to comfort me.

"I'm feeling better. Let's go see and then decide." My pale face and horrible dry mouth smell were giveaways.

The meeting was held in a small room on the second floor of an old building. We were the last ones to arrive. Having had nothing but Gatorade for the whole day, I was trying to get through it as quickly as possible. There were twelve to thirteen people in the room, most of whom were younger than us.

A middle-aged guy came into the room. He was dark-skinned, just like other locals, but with a lot of wrinkles. Curly hair. He told us that he was Ruben, like a Reuben sandwich, and was our guide.

He talked very loudly. His laughter was loud too. "Welcome to Alpaca Expedition. You are now all part of our green machine family." He handed a green T-shirt to each of us. I unfolded it. The front was a photo of Machu Picchu, with Peruvian sacred animals randomly put into the corners. *So cheesy*, I thought. On the back, just six words: "The journey itself is the destination."

I repeated to myself, "The journey itself is the destination."

I learned that our journey would start at 3:30 a.m. tomorrow. The daily hiking time would range from eight to twelve hours. Most days, we needed to get up around 4:00 to 5:00 a.m. We would live in a tent. We would eat freshly cooked food. The thought of food made me want to throw up again. There would not be a toilet on the entire hike until we reach Machu Picchu on day four. *NO TOILET!* I needed to use the toilet ten to fifteen times a day...

On the way back to our hotel, we detoured to the small pharmacy where we bought the altitude sickness medicine the first day, and bought more medicine. "Let's load up on more Gatorade. Let's go on the hike tomorrow," I said.

"Are you sure?" Bryan looked at me. His eyes showed his concern.

"Yes, I am. The journey itself is the destination." Deep inside I knew that I needed the hike. I needed a distraction to keep from thinking about the baby we lost. I needed to conquer something that was so difficult so that I'd know I could still control something in life, especially during the uncontrollable pregnancy journey.

Our guide, Ruben, was on time the next morning. At 3:30 a.m., the bus was outside of our hotel. With my medicine and Gatorade packed, we joined the group and dived into the darkness of Cusco.

The next four days of hiking was a journey of pushing myself over my limit. Day one, we climbed from a desert-like setting to a mountaintop that was freezing cold. I had a nose bleed in the morning when we were in the desert, lost my voice at noon, fell asleep when I was having a fifteen-minute sitting break, and went to use the "toilet" fifteen times. Before I went to sleep on the hard rock surface in our tent, I reminded myself, "The journey itself is the destination."

Day two was the most hiking of the entire trip. We went up and down from an altitude of 5,905 feet to 13,828 feet, back to 7,000 feet, then ended at 11,000 feet. We passed Dead Woman's Pass, where I almost gave up.

Day three was a normal hike. Surprisingly, by that time, I was feeling much better. Before, when I had an intense stomach flu with fever like this, it took me at least a week to recover. I wasn't sure why, but this time, I felt much better already.

That's also when I had the energy to learn about my companions. Where were they from? What made them come here? What was their life dream? We openly shared our stories about surrogacy. Talked about the baby we lost. Talked about the baby we still had.

Maybe this was because the road we were traveling was the original pilgrimage path for the Inca to Machu Picchu. Or maybe it was because I was focusing on the journey, a journey of survival, of courage, and of love. Whatever the reason, I could openly talk about everything.

Day four, we got up at 4:00 a.m. to line up for the last push to see the sunset at Machu Picchu. We almost ran the entire way to the top of the mountain that was south of Machu Picchu in order to see that first sun ray lying on the cloud-covered stone buildings. When we reached the city of Machu Picchu, my right knee completely gave out. Every step up a stair gave me a piercing pain.

Just when I thought we were done and was ready to take the glass ceiling train back to Cusco, a city that I had not explored enough, Ruben yelled, "Here is your final challenge, Huayna Picchu." He pointed to the tall mountain behind all the buildings. "There is at least one death every year climbing Huayna Picchu." He was not encouraging at all. "But you can do it because you are Green Machine now!"

"We need to do this." Bryan looked at me.

"I've had enough; my stomach, now my knee..."

"No, we need to do this for our baby who is growing every day." Bryan was determined. Bryan was normally very easygoing; I had not seen him so committed to anything before. He must have been going through some internal healing, I thought.

"Let's do it," I said without asking my body again.

This was not hiking. This was rock climbing the whole 1,180 feet. The mountain was skinny. The "trail" was winding. There were so many places that were barely a path. We needed to use hands and feet to climb. There were some parts where the only thing between me and the hundreds-of-feet-high cliff was a rope tied to a rock. "Please don't break. Don't break." It was so dangerous that everybody taking the hike needed to write down their name. When they left, they needed to mark that they were safe and "checked out."

"Let's do it for our growing baby." Bryan's words were circling in my mind. In the past few months, I had been devastated by losing one of the twins. Not seeing and feeling the other baby's development because Chelsie lived in California, we wallowed in grief and sadness. We weren't focusing on what was coming toward us. In five months, we would welcome our baby to the world. The thought of the baby excited me and pushed me to go harder. "Let's do it for our growing baby," I yelled to Bryan who was just ahead of me.

On top of Huayna Picchu, there was a big rock. Always scared of heights, I climbed up shakily with Bryan. Machu Picchu was just on the other side. The view of the ancient city, the seventh wonder of the world, from a different angle was refreshing.

"Wish you all the best in heaven, our little baby! We will take care of your brother or sister!" Cupping my hands as an amplifier, using all my remaining energy, I cried aloud to the mountains, the city, the spirits that surround Machu Picchu.

* * *

THE NEXT FEW months were uneventful. Chelsie told us that this was such an easy pregnancy. "You guys should have given me more of a challenge," she joked. *Hell no!*

We knew that the baby was a girl, which meant that it would be biologically related to me. It didn't matter whose genes were in the baby, Bryan and I would love her with all of our hearts. But knowing the sex gave us more inspiration to imagine what she would look like. She would be half-Chinese, one-quarter Irish, and one-quarter Mexican.

We put photos of the egg donor and me side by side. "Little Nicky should have her eyes, large and round; arched eyebrows; long nose, small ears, and an oval-shaped face," I said. "I also like her hair. It is curly, not like mine, thick and straight... Hope nothing from me..." I gave Bryan a bitter smile.

"At least she can have your intelligence," Bryan laughed.

We were procrastinating on preparing all the baby items. Chelsie constantly reminded us to buy a car seat and shared good brands of strollers or cheap and good-quality bottles. We were just not there. No matter how well it was going, no matter how much we believed that it would be fine, we still protected ourselves by not buying anything until the baby was here.

The only thing we did talk about was the name. Bryan wanted to give me the honor of choosing an English name for our girl. "Well, English is definitely my strength," I said and laughed.

My Chinese name is Yu, which means pure jade stone. My parents wanted me to be a kind person. In college, I picked my name Nick. I watched the movie *Little Nicky* with Adam Sandler. The story is about Satan's third son who decides to become a good devil and prevent his brothers from destroying the world. He travels from hell to earth to heaven to hell and finally settles on earth with a partner and a baby. He fights all the odds and is a rebel. I named myself "Nick" then. Maybe I wanted to be a rebel in my sexuality.

I loved *Friends*. Before coming to America, I had watched *Friends* eleven times. That's how I learned English, American culture, and the way everybody lives here. How wrong could I be! Lol. That's another story for another time.

Phoebe always stood out to me. She was such a character, with the biggest heart and the ounce of cute weirdness that made her unique. "Phoebe," I told Bryan when I was brushing my teeth one day.

"From *Friends*?" Bryan poked his head out of the shower curtain and gave me a look of disbelief.

"Yes!" I gave him a big smile and gave him a gentle toothpaste kiss. I was excited.

"Sounds great!" Bryan smiled back. He was the best husband I could ask for. He supported me unconditionally.

* * *

THINGS WERE GETTING real. November 7, 2015, was coming. We decided to take a road trip to Fresno. Everybody enjoyed our last trip to Yellowstone very much. We packed our newly leased Honda Pilot, including JD and Jack, and headed down I-5 south to welcome Phoebe. Designed to seat eight people, the car was just half full, even with JD and Jack.

Chelsie finally persuaded me to go shopping with her before the baby was here. We went to Buy Buy Baby the day after we arrived in Fresno. "I have this coupon for 20 percent off one item; let's pick a big one." She showed me the coupon and smirked.

Her belly was really big. It looked like it was going to explode. It didn't bother her though. She told me we needed a good stroller. She was lifting strollers off the shelf and pushing them around. She was an amazing woman.

We stayed in an Airbnb townhouse in Clovis, which was close to Chelsie's home. The neighborhood was very nice. Every yard was perfectly taken care of. There was not even one weed. This was so different from the "let nature grow" way of yard maintenance in the Pacific Northwest.

Bryan and I walked the neighborhood every night. It was Halloween. Every house was decorated with fun lights and blow-up figures. "Phoebe will love trick or treating," we told ourselves.

Our protocol with Chelsie was that once she was admitted into the hospital, she would text or call us immediately. We got the call at 3:00 p.m. on November 2. It was her boyfriend, Steven. "Chelsie is in labor now."

We rushed to Saint Agnes Hospital and went straight up to the delivery room. Because my parents didn't have the wristband that identified them as parents, they stayed outside in the waiting area.

"How are you, Chelsie?" I asked.

"Good! Are you guys, ohhhh, excited?" She smiled at us in the middle of a contraction. She was definitely strong.

Bryan and I looked at each other. "Yes, we are. Beyond excitement!"

"Now, we need to push. You hold Chelsie's left leg. You hold Chelsie's right leg." The doctor pointed at Steven's and Chelsie's moms. "Now, let's push with the contraction rhythm."

Six pushes later, our world forever changed.

Phoebe was born at 4:39 p.m. She was seven pounds, eight ounces, and twenty inches. Her crying was loud and clear. Her eyes were barely open but were big. "She's got your eyes," I joked with Bryan. I was always a cry baby. But at that moment, there was only joy, pure joy and happiness.

Phoebe needed to stay overnight at the hospital. The nurses told us we should soak up as much sleep as possible before we took her home tomorrow.

We left the hospital at 10:15 p.m. Driving to our temporary home, Bryan and I didn't speak at all. We just held each other's hands for the entire ride. We knew that a new journey had begun.

Becoming Dads

"Someone told me that having a baby is like having your heart walking around outside of your body, and I didn't understand it until I had a baby. Now, like, everything he does literally crushes my heart. In a great way. And then if he's in pain, it's like my whole endeavor is to make sure he's not in pain."

—Elizabeth Banks

W e didn't sleep well. I blamed it on the Chick-fil-A sandwich we had at the drive-through on the way home from the hospital the night before, but deep inside, I knew it was because of the excitement of Phoebe's arrival.

At 6:00 a.m. the next morning, both Bryan and I were up. He took JD and Jack for a walk. In five minutes, they were back. "Did they pee and poop?" My jaw dropped.

"Yes, they cannot wait to see their sister." Bryan was breathing heavily. His walk must have been more like a run.

Mom and Dad were up too. It was the day to welcome Phoebe back home! Phoebe had checked out well the night before, and the doctor and nurses told us we would bring her home today. None of us could wait. The last eight hours' separation was already too much. Picking up the brand new Graco car seat that Chelsie helped us choose three days ago, we dashed to Saint Agnes Hospital.

Phoebe was sleeping quietly when we arrived at the caring room. The nurse who took care of Phoebe for the night had finished her shift. We met a new nurse, Angie, who told us Phoebe did great last night.

"She drank milk four times and peed twice. We are just waiting for her first poop, which will be completely dark green because she's passing the amniotic fluid, bile, and other things from her mom's body," she said.

"We cannot wait too!" For the first time, I was eager to see human feces.

"Do you guys want to hold her?" Angie said.

"Yes!" I yelled a little bit louder than I should have. Angie picked up Phoebe. I looked at Bryan. He gave me a warm smile. I knew he really wanted to hold Phoebe too, but like always, he let me have the best.

I extended my arms. I wrapped Phoebe's body with my left arm and tried to hold her shoulder on my right. Holding a baby should be so easy, but I just could not get it right. I kept adjusting my arms and tried to cover all her body. It was like if I did not cover her enough, Phoebe might fall out or get hurt.

"You are doing great, Nick." Bryan tried to ease my nerves.

"Just make sure to support her head. Her neck is still very weak," Angie added. "She is so lucky to have two daddies. She will get all the love in the world," Angie continued while getting out the breast milk from the fridge that Chelsie pumped last night. "So, what will Phoebe call you?"

"Baba for me and Daddy for Bryan."

"What time can we take Phoebe home today?" Bryan asked. "We have our car seat!"

"She is almost ready. She failed her first car seat challenge last night, but breezed through the second one easily. We just need the doctor to approve it, and you can take her home this afternoon."

"Perfect!" I yelled again. I couldn't hide my excitement.

I took a close look at Phoebe. All the wrinkles from yesterday had almost disappeared. Although her eyes were closed, I could tell that she had big eyes. And those long eyelashes! Was it normal for a newborn to have such long eyelashes? *This must be Mother Nature compensating me for my extremely short ones*, I thought.

I tried to look for similarities between Phoebe and me but had no luck. Her skin was darker. Her hair was thinner. Her ears were smaller. She was also round with baby fat not like my chopstick body. "Thank God Phoebe didn't get my worst feature." I looked at Bryan and chuckled.

"It must be the half Mexican gene from the egg donor. I heard that Mexican genes are very strong," Bryan said.

"Are you ready to hold her?"

Bryan nodded. I carefully extended Phoebe to him. He was the handy person in our family. Bryan personally worked on our house flips and was in charge of organizing our home. But now he was so careful and moved his arms so slowly until Phoebe was completely wrapped by his upper body.

Bryan was always a passionate lover, but now his love was so gentle. He stared into Phoebe's eyes, which had just opened because of our talk and movements. Phoebe gave a few protesting cries. "Shu... shu... shu..." Bryan hummed to Phoebe and moved his arm a little bit. I took out my phone and snapped a photo of them.

"Since Phoebe is awake now, are you guys ready for some more care practice?" Angie said.

"Definitely!" The hundreds of times we watched YouTube videos of changing diapers and feeding babies were not enough to make sure we gave Phoebe the best care possible. Bryan wanted to do the care first. He put Phoebe down and opened the tightly wrapped blanket. The blanket was blue with red stripes, just like the American flag. He opened the tiny diaper.

"She pooped! Green poop!" Bryan yelled. Bryan did not get excited easily. He was definitely thrilled by changing Phoebe's first poopy diaper.

"Here is a wipe." Angie handed over the wipe package and continued. "Make sure to wipe down. We don't want anything dirty to go into her wee-wee." Bryan was slowly wiping down Phoebe several times. It reminded me of him working on his 1970 Cadillac. He sanded every single corner of the car and restored it completely.

As Bryan was finishing up and putting a new diaper on Phoebe, Angie said, "Now let's wrap up Phoebe to give her some more milk. It is very important to make sure she is wrapped up tight with her legs curled up to her body. This is the position babies had when they were in Mommy's tummy. They feel safe that way."

Bryan and I were taking mental notes of every single word Angie said. "Let me show you how." Angie grabbed the blanket Bryan had just taken off Phoebe. "You make a big triangle first. Lay Phoebe on top. Align the neck to the flat side of the triangle. Left side goes in first. Down side goes up. Tuck together tight. And then follow by the right side. Make sure it is all tucked tight." She magically put Phoebe back in the blanket in thirty seconds. "This is called burrito wrapped." She smiled. We burst out laughing.

Because the hospital had a policy that only parents could come into the baby care room, Mom and Dad were outside waiting. After the feeding, we took Phoebe to the giant glass wall by the waiting area, so that Mom and Dad could see Phoebe for the first time.

Tears started running down Mom's face. I knew that this time her tears were of pure happiness, not disappointment at me being gay or fear for our future.

We put Phoebe back into her clear plastic bassinet. Angie asked us to put the side with Phoebe's head higher because that was good for her digestion right after feeding. Maybe it was the warm milk or the exhaustion from meeting her family, but she went back to sleep very quickly.

Bryan and I were still experiencing the feeling of holding Phoebe. We sat by Phoebe's bassinet. I reached out my hand to Bryan's, and he squeezed tightly. I turned my head toward Bryan and gave him a gentle kiss.

* * *

AS WE WERE enjoying looking at Phoebe's chest going up and down and up and down, a doctor charged into the room. Bryan let go of my hand. Even today he was self-conscious about public displays of love. He always felt that other people didn't need to see anyone's intimacy, no matter gay or straight. I had learned to respect and accept Bryan's point of view, although sometimes I protested by holding his hand tightly or giving him a surprise kiss in public. I let go of his hand today.

"Hi!" I gave a cheerful greeting while trying not to wake Phoebe up. *This must be our discharge order*, I thought.

"En." The doctor didn't say anything but squeezed a sound out of his throat.

"What time can we take Phoebe home?" I asked impatiently. No response. He glided to the top of Phoebe's bassinet and turned around. "Bang!" The bassinet was dropped from the higher side. The at least fifteen-inch drop shocked the sleeping Phoebe but luckily didn't wake her.

My mouth opened. "Is she all right?" I yelled. No response. He seemed not to be bothered by what had just happened. He took Phoebe's temperature and wrote down some numbers. Then he turned around and stormed out of the room. The whole process took less than five minutes. Bryan gave me a look of surprise and loss. I felt the same way and even a little bit of anger. Not even a word? The only thing I got was his name tag: "Dr. Lucas James."

I stood up and tried to understand what just happened. *Was Phoebe all right?* I tried to reach Angie to check on her. Just as I was walking to the door, I heard Dr. James talking to Angie. "Two dads?"

"Yes, we are supposed to discharge today," Angie answered.

"No mom? Do they have experience taking care of kids?" I tried not to listen too much, but what I heard created a storm in my mind and an ugly feeling in my heart. I quickly walked back to Bryan and told him what I just heard.

"What?" He paused and continued, "Don't think too much. It should be fine." Bryan was always the calm one and didn't worry about problems before they arrived.

Five minutes later Angie came in. She walked to our bed. "Bad news. You guys can't take Phoebe home today." Her words were soft and hesitant, but also decisive.

"Did something happen to Phoebe? Is she all right?"

201

"No, no. Phoebe is completely fine." Angie waved her head quickly. "It was the doctor's order. You guys have not had kids before and also have no maternal instincts to take care of the baby..."

"What?" I could not believe what I just heard. For my entire life, I had been fighting for acceptance. For the first day of my daughter's life, I didn't qualify to be a dad because I had not been a dad before and had no maternal instinct. I thought by crossing the bridge from China to America, I had crossed the bridge from judgment for being gay to acceptance. This was California. One of the most liberal states in the country. I was treated differently because I was a new gay dad.

I looked at Bryan. I was just speechless. I couldn't say anything; I didn't want to say anything. The feeling of rejection and shame overwhelmed me.

"Angie..." Bryan turned to Angie. "Never mind..." Bryan reached out his hand to mine and held it tightly.

Bryan and I went outside to tell Mom and Dad the bad news. Growing up, Mom always stereotyped male and female. In a very traditional Chinese way, she had opinions that I had no choice but to listen to when I was little, but hated when I was battling my sexuality. "Women do dishes better than men," "A man should care about his career more," and so on.

To me, gender, just like sexuality, was fluid. There were feminine men who liked decorating their houses and making their kitchens spotless, and women who liked nothing but physical challenge and to prove their strength like on *Ninja Warrior*.

But even now, Mom couldn't believe what the doctor said. "Both women and men have the ability to take care of their babies." She was angry. "If the doctor really needs a mother figure, I was and still am a mother." Mom used that as her last resort.

I also called Chelsie to tell her the doctor's decision. She was angry for us. Chelsie was already discharged and at home early that day. Her bed was returned. We also didn't have a bed in the hospital. If Phoebe stayed one more night, she was going to spend it in the care unit.

"Spending time in your arms is much better than in the care unit following a care schedule, no matter how lovely the nurses are," Chelsie said, speaking from experience.

At this point, the shame and rejection started to fill me with anger. *How can the doctor judge me without knowing who I am? How can he know that we cannot take care of the baby because we are two dads?*

I thought about what our agent Melissa said when we faced the difficult decisions throughout our surrogate journey. "You guys are going to be great dads. That means you need to make tough decisions that are the best for your kids. That starts today, even before the kids are born." Now, Phoebe was here. We could not just accept what the doctor said. We were determined to bring Phoebe home.

I talked more to Angie and other nurses throughout the afternoon about the doctor's decision and what we could do. Some told me that I could sign a waiver discharging the doctor and hospital from responsibility. In that case, we could bring Phoebe home because she was healthy, and it had been more than twenty-four hours. Bryan and I were excited. We had a plan.

While we were eating dinner in the cafe on the first floor, we saw Dr. James walking by. "Dr. James," I cried out in a high-pitched voice, "do you have a moment?"

He approached our table. "Yes?" He seemed to be in a good mood.

"We know that the current plan is to have Phoebe stay one more night. But we were told before that if Phoebe was healthy, we could take her home after twenty-four hours. Our surrogate, Chelsie, has been discharged already, and we don't have a bed in the care room. We really want to spend every minute possible with our daughter." I dumped all my thoughts out nervously. "We understand that we can sign a waiver so that if anything happens to Phoebe, it will not be the hospital's responsibility. Can we sign that?"

Dr. James gave us a smile. "I understand. Yes, you can do that. I am going back to the fourth floor now. I will prepare the paperwork."

"That was easy!" I laughed and turned to Bryan.

"That seemed strange..." Bryan was not buying it.

"Let's not overthink it. Let's go bring Phoebe home! I can't wait to have JD and Jack meet their younger sister!" I yelled.

We quickly cleaned our table. Bryan threw the garbage in the can, while I put the empty dishes on the cleaning tray. I skipped in front of Bryan all the way to the elevator. Pressing the up button on the wall, I turned to Bryan. "I am going to spend the first night with Phoebe!"

Twenty minutes later, Dr. James walked into our room with a few papers in his hand. I was thrilled. "We are ready to sign and take Phoebe home!" I gave the most cheerful statement ever.

"I cannot let Phoebe go." He did not waste time. "She has a heart murmur. We cannot let you leave and sign the waiver. If you do, I will call Child Protective Services."

"What!" I was shocked again. *Heart murmur, what was that? Was that serious? It was heart-related. Would Phoebe be alright? Child Protective Services? If we take Phoebe home?* Shock and worry were battling for the control of my emotions.

"You can take Phoebe home tomorrow. You need to schedule an ultrasound within twenty-four hours of the discharge to check on the heart murmur. I've recommended a doctor in Children's Hospital whom you can go to. The nurse will give you the name in the discharge papers." He walked out of the room after he finished speaking. No further explanation. No Q&A. Not to mention, no comfort.

Right after Dr. James left, Bryan and I pulled out our phones and started frantically searching for information related to heart murmurs. We had so many questions. Right after talking to a doctor, the internet became our only source for information. We quickly found that it was normal for a newborn to have a heart murmur. It's called an "innocent heart murmur," affects 75 percent of babies, and would go away in a few weeks.

Reading this information and what other parents shared about their children's heart murmurs going away by the next checkup gave us some respite from worry. "Phoebe should be alright," we told each other.

As I was on the phone, I also started searching Dr. James on Google. One-star reviews were all over. "Suck." "Hella rude." "Not going back, unprofessional and doesn't take a personal interest at all." Mostly negative reviews. I showed Bryan all the reviews and people's feedback.

Somehow, the negative reviews comforted us. Phoebe might be all right. It was also not us who didn't qualify to be new dads or have the right instincts to take care of our daughter. We understood the reality. We could not take Phoebe home tonight. He even mentioned Child Protective Services. Was that necessary? Bryan and I agreed that the doctor just wanted Phoebe to stay one more night so the hospital could make more money. True or not, that made us feel that it was not us to blame for another night of not rocking Phoebe to sleep.

The ultrasound the next day confirmed our suspicions. The doctor at Children's Hospital was also a little bit surprised at the ultrasound appointment since he said it usually wasn't done unless the murmur didn't go away in a few weeks. We weren't surprised when we saw the bill later though – over $3,000 for the entire bill. We had to pay $950 out of pocket.

I loved leaving five-star reviews online. I always believed that sharing love was more important than spreading hate. However, maybe I wanted to be a rebel and maybe wanted to protect other new parents or gay parents. I wrote a one-star review for Dr. James.

* * *

THE ROAD TRIP from Fresno home to Seattle was uneventful. We stopped every three hours to feed Phoebe and change her diaper. Everybody was enjoying their new promotion in life. Bryan and I were dads now. My parents were grandparents. Even JD and Jack were now older brothers. Bryan and I were still overjoyed with Phoebe, and we made sure that we did all the caring while my parents walked JD and Jack.

The new roles and responsibilities were the same when we got back home. Our house was a typical northwest contemporary style that was built in 1979. At the end of a fifty-foot-long, dead-end driveway, our dark green house was tucked away in the forest.

From the front, it looked like a little cabin with brown cedar roofing: Snow White's house. From the back, where the ground sloped, it was a gigantic three-story building with windows from top to bottom.

The northwest contemporary style respects nature and prioritizes the concept of the master bedroom. In our house, the master was a loft that oversaw the entire living space on the main floor. There were twenty-foot floor-to-ceiling windows around the entire back of the house. That was the only thing between us and the woods. In the summertime, we enjoyed having dinner on the deck, the song of big fir and cedar leaves brushing against each other putting us in vacation mode every day.

The master bedroom was also the room where we would take care of Phoebe. After talking to our pediatrician, Dr. Manfred, we decided to put a crib right next to our bed so we could reach Phoebe easily at night.

Before we got on the road back to Seattle, with Chelsie's help, we made a shadow box with Phoebe's first blanket, blue-and-red striped hat, first onesie, and also her name tag with two cute footprints. We hung the box on the master bedroom wall, right next to all the beige wood-framed travel photos we printed out every Christmas as gifts to each other. The photos added lots of color to the white-and-wood tone of the room.

We bought this house by accident. Bryan's sister Julie was looking for a house in the summer of 2014. This was the last house on the tour. Julie loved the big windows and the trees on the listing photos. But when we turned up to the house, she said the long, steep driveway would not work for their RV.

For Bryan and me, though, it was love at first sight. We were amazed by how isolated and protected this 2,400-square-foot house was, while also being only five minutes from the Lake Forest Park shopping center. The big trees were like guardians protecting the house. There were only trees, sky, and us.

I called Mom immediately after seeing this house. They joined us for the tour, and we sat in the house for over two hours. It reminded us of the nature in Yellowstone and Grand Teton National Parks. The harmony between natural forces. This would be a great place to call home.

One month later, we moved into the house. Still using my old $500 couch I got from Craigslist, we decided to have some upgrades to treat ourselves a little bit nicer. We printed out the listing photos with all the staging furniture, drove to Macy's Furniture Gallery in Lynnwood, and spent hours finding a perfect mid-century modern orange-and-bright-green leather couch set. We made peace with the price tag with the excuse that it was important to have a comfortable couch to get us closer to nature.

We called the house a "Gem of the Pacific Northwest." The northwest contemporary style brought us closer to nature but also increased our energy bill dramatically. The house had a thirty-year-old electric furnace. The windows were double-paned but too large to keep out the cold air from Alaska in the winter. The roof and Northwest signature exposed-wood-beam design did not include insulation.

Before Phoebe, we had been careful not to turn up the heat too much. "Sixty-five degrees is enough. We can just bundle up," I told Bryan. Bryan was not bothered by this at all. He was in shorts and T-shirts even outside occasionally. But I dug out an old puffy jacket that I bought back in China. It was oversized and covered me from my head to my toes. The hood was so big that when I put it on, it hid my entire face. Bryan called it the "penguin jacket" because when I was wearing it, the weight and lack of eyesight made me walk slowly and in a waddling fashion. This was perfect for living in the new house.

Like any good parents, we were not bothered by spending money on our kids. We turned up the heat to seventy-two degrees – the temperature it was in the caring unit in Saint Agnes. This made me miss my penguin jacket for a while and gave Bryan an excuse to consume more Tillamook Rocky Road ice cream. When we received our first monthly energy bill ($795), we realized this would not work.

We decided to switch rooms. There were two bedrooms in the daylight basement that also had perfect views of the forest in the backyard. One would be Phoebe's when she was older, and the other one was my parents' when they were visiting us from China. There were small wall-mounted electric heaters and separate thermostats for those two bedrooms.

The two-zone heating system helped. We could set the whole house to sixty-five degrees while setting the small bedroom at seventy-two degrees. Mom and Dad gladly agreed to move into the master bedroom. They were willing to do whatever they could to help their son and his family.

The arrival of Phoebe induced my parents to stay longer with us. Previously, they visited us one or two months each year. That was enough, for them and for us. The first few days of their arrival were always exciting and happy, but soon we started arguing about even smallest things, such as I did not take off my shoes coming into the house or Dad hoarded all the empty drink bottles and Amazon boxes in the yard. He thought they could be useful in the future.

This time, with Phoebe, it was different. They planned to stay six months. My previous worry was soon washed away by how helpful and efficient they were.

Mom took on the duty of cooking dinner. To keep Bryan's sanity intact, though he loved Chinese food, we decided to create Pizza Tuesday and Burger Thursday. That also became a way for my parents to explore American food, although I always saw Dad secretly eating noodles and King's Hawaiian bread before dinner on those nights.

Dad took on the responsibility of walking JD and Jack. He tried to take both of them together at first but soon realized it was an impossible feat. The free thinker and crazy thinker pulled so hard, they made him fall on the hilly road once.

I also enjoyed my parents' presence. After I lived so many years alone, in Shanghai, in Durham, and in Seattle, Mom, Dad, and I were like a family again. The people that brought me up now joined Bryan and me to bring up Phoebe. Mom and Dad started to use the Google Translator app to have some long conversations with Bryan. Bryan also surprised me with some random words, such as *jiangyou* (soy sauce), picked up from my parents here and there.

My favorite part was dinner time. Four adults, two sniffing-around-for-dropped-food doggies, one hungry but picky kid: three generations and two cultures, all sitting together around the black dining table I bought from IKEA after graduation. It was magical to see two sides of my life finally coming together.

* * *

LESS THAN ONE month old, Phoebe was on time to wake up at 12:00 a.m., 3:00 a.m., and 6:00 a.m. every day. Bryan and I took turns doing the care at night. This was supposed to help the other person sleep better, but it didn't help me. I used to sleep like the dead. Even loud thunder during summer storms in southern China couldn't wake me up. But now, every tiny noise from Phoebe kicked me out of sleep instantly.

At our one-month checkup, we heard some relieving news from our pediatrician, Dr. Manfred. He was over sixty years old. Originally from Germany, he had lived in Seattle for decades. He was trained at Seattle Children's Hospital, which was one of the top ten hospitals in the country.

He had a philosophy that we were too protective of our children. "Eating dirt can only help their immune system," he always said. I thought he said that to make us feel better as parents and to forgive our mistakes. But somehow there were many truths in that statement.

He was a big guy with a huge body. The small exam room made him look even bigger. He had an energy that I loved. He always smiled with his mouth wide open. In our appointments, he always talked about life, talked about how he taught his daughter to raise his granddaughters and about how to become a parent. Every time I left his office I knew more about raising Phoebe and felt better about myself.

He told us that Phoebe should be able to sleep through the night now since she was one month old. He grabbed his pen and started writing on the checkup result sheet that was marked "A+."

"An average full-term newborn needs to consume 120 calories per kilogram of weight each day to grow into a healthy child. Phoebe is 8.7 pounds now. So she is 3.95 kilograms. In this case, she needs 474 calories a day. Phoebe's stomach can take four ounces for each feeding now. Each four-ounce formula equals 80 calories, and 474 divided by 80 is 6. In this case, you just need to feed her at 6:00 a.m., 9:00 a.m., 12:00 p.m.,

3:00 p.m., 6:00 p.m., and 9:00 p.m. It's that easy." My eyes were wide open at Dr. Manfred's fast math.

Coming back from the one-month checkup, I told my parents the new feeding schedule in order to have all-night sleep for Phoebe and us.

"No way that will work. You drank milk all night long when you were a baby. That's how you grew up," Mom protested.

Bryan and I decided to give it a try. It was difficult for the first week, but on day eight, all of a sudden, Phoebe could sleep from 9:00 p.m. to 3:00 a.m. without crying for food. We were encouraged. On day twelve, she could sleep from 9:00 p.m. to 5:30 a.m. We couldn't believe the result. It was that easy.

As we were celebrating our newfound freedom of sleeping at night, I spent more time learning about raising kids. I had resisted reading any books before Phoebe was born, but I finally could start working on the stack friends and family had brought us.

I purposefully stacked them on my desk – the left stack was to be finished, the right stack was done. The familiar feeling of accomplishment of my school years in China returned. At that time, I hated the books that teachers asked me to read. But now, I loved all the books. They were my bridge to becoming an amazing dad, or at least I hoped so.

Growing up with a mindset that everything in the West and in America was better, I treated the books as bibles, especially *What to Expect the First Year* and *Healthy Sleep Habits, Happy Child*. All my American friends told me that they got so much from the two books. They learned how to read their baby's cues to know when to feed and when to change the diaper, and the books saved their lives during nonstop crying nights.

Although Phoebe was sleep trained now, she still occasionally cried in the middle of the night. The books provided a step-by-step guide on what to do. They said there were three things that needed to be checked. "Is she hungry?" "Does the diaper need to be changed?" "Is she sick?" If none of the answers was yes, just let the baby cry for a few minutes. Don't try to hold the baby unless the crying goes on for more than fifteen to thirty minutes. We shouldn't reinforce that they will be held if they cry. It seemed logical to us.

However, this created a huge conflict between my parents and us. Mom and Dad believed in holding Phoebe while she cried. "We need to let her know that she is loved all the time," Mom claimed. Bryan and I, especially I, believed in following the book. I told them that their method was uneducated and old-fashioned. They should be open-minded enough to try new things, especially now that we were living in the land of freedom. They agreed, hesitantly. It was not like they had a choice. Phoebe's room was right by ours, while they were two floors up. Phoebe's crying at night could not reach them easily.

One week later, I realized that we had a baby monitor installed in Phoebe's room. Bryan was the least tech-savvy one in the family, so it had be Dad who put it there. I confronted him, and he said that this gave them peace of mind. They loved watching Phoebe breathing while she slept. Looking at her chest going up and down was comforting. I resonated with the feeling a lot. Sometimes when I looked at Phoebe sleeping, her moving chest was the only thing that assured me that she was alive and all right. Bryan and I both installed the Yiqi baby monitor app that Dad shared with us on our phones.

The next night, Phoebe started crying at around 2:00 or 3:00 a.m. I heard it clearly through the wall. She had done so the last few nights. She normally went back to sleep after fifteen to twenty minutes.

Telling myself not to hold Phoebe when she cried was easy. Doing it was really hard. Every cry was a deeper cut into my heart. Phoebe was so precious. She was so little. I thought about the old Chinese tale about a girl who cried until she lost her eyesight. I didn't want that to happen to Phoebe.

I turned to Bryan. He was awake too. "Did you want to pick her up?" he whispered.

"No."

"But it seems to be longer than fifteen minutes."

"It should be all right." I went through the checklist quickly in a mind that was struggling to be awake. Food – well-fed before bed. Diaper – changed. Sickness – not that I was aware of. As we watched Phoebe crying on the tiny phone screen, I heard her door gently open and close. Three seconds later, Dad was holding Phoebe in his arms.

I was furious. We were trying our best to fight our urge to hold Phoebe and follow the right approach, and here came Dad completely not following the book. I jumped out of bed and charged into Phoebe's room. I asked Dad to leave and held Phoebe in my arms. As I was rocking her, Phoebe went back to sleep very quickly. I put her down in her crib and crawled back to bed. All my guilt and anxiety about not holding Phoebe turned into anger toward Dad. "What should I do?" I asked Bryan. No response. "Bryaaaaaaannnnnn." I pushed his shoulder.

"What could you do? You cannot change your dad." Bryan was half sleep. "The only thing you can do is change yourself, or maybe the lock."

The lock! Yes, I could install a lock on Phoebe's door so Dad wouldn't be able to go in at night.

The next morning, I told Dad about the new lock that I planned to install. I gave him a few days to keep his "privilege" of entering Phoebe's room freely. "If you still go into her room at night, I will change the lock," I threatened.

Dad was obviously surprised. His lips moved a little bit, seeming to try to squeeze some words out, but he kept silent and walked away.

Since I can remember, I have never had much conversation with Dad. Each of our conversations were limited to less than two sentences. Even when I knew Dad had an opinion, he would communicate that through Mom to me.

From my side, I didn't know how to talk to him either. He lived in his own universe, never listened, and always did what he wanted. That made me angry at him all the time.

The next few days, Phoebe didn't cry at night. However, the next time Phoebe cried, Dad was there again. I was still angry. I complained to Bryan and yelled at Dad the next morning. I told him that I really wanted to hold Phoebe too, but we shouldn't. We needed to train her to be independent. We needed to have positive reinforcement. I threatened to change the lock, again.

Dad continued to sneak into Phoebe's room when she cried at night. I continued to see everything on the phone while hearing the door opening and closing. However, the lock was never changed.

On some level, having Dad going to the room to hold Phoebe was an easier way to deal with the situation. It erased the conflict between following the book strictly and the heartache of listening to Phoebe's cries.

Secretly, I was happy Phoebe wouldn't be tortured by continuous crying while I didn't break the rule. And if Phoebe turned out not to be independent, I could blame Dad.

Two months later, Mom and Dad left Seattle and went back to China. They had stayed with us on tourist visas, which only allowed them to be in the U.S. less than six months in a calendar year. Any longer than that would make it an illegal stay. They could be banned from entering the U.S. for more than ten years.

Ever since Phoebe was born, they had been carefully calculating how many days they could stay. To assure the immigration officer would approve their entry to the U.S. next time, Mom and Dad needed to go back to China for at least six months.

"My home in Guangzhou doesn't feel like home anymore," Mom told me. "You are here, and now Phoebe is here. I feel more at home in Seattle than back in China."

Sending Mom and Dad to the airport with Bryan and Phoebe and seeing them fly eight thousand miles away to the other side of Pacific didn't mean they weren't involved in Phoebe's day-to-day life. On the baby monitor app, I could always see who else was watching. Dad was always on there.

At night, whenever Phoebe cried more than fifteen minutes, I would receive a courtesy call from Dad asking me to check on Phoebe and rock her to sleep.

* * *

BRYAN AND I were adjusting to this new era of fatherhood while juggling working hard to build a career in real estate. I was still on parental leave from Microsoft. So I was taking care of Phoebe more while Bryan focused on selling houses. The real estate market in Seattle was booming like no other place in the

U.S. Amazon continued their expansion and hiring frenzy. Seattle had the most construction cranes in the country year over year. People started to crown Seattle the valley of "cloud" services. Seattle was the next Silicon Valley.

Thanks to the booming economy, our real estate sales volume increased dramatically quarter over quarter. I created a Chinese blog that documented my journey of investing in real estate in Seattle. That attracted a large number of investors from China, California, and Canada.

Sometimes, on a busy day, each of us needed to show three customers houses. Each customer toured six to eight houses. That was roughly forty house showings a day combined.

Bryan would show customers houses with Phoebe in tow. He could change her diaper in the front seat in less than forty-five seconds. He could hold a phone in one hand, using the eKey app to open the door for the house tour. He could hold a bottle in Phoebe's mouth while explaining to a customer the room layout and the problem of old wiring and plumbing. He made taking care of Phoebe while working seem graceful and easy.

This was when I met a different Bryan. While I had never brushed my hair in my entire life, Bryan started taking care of Phoebe's hair. He went to Claire's in Alderwood mall and bought all kinds of hair ornaments. After Phoebe was bathed, Bryan would spend at least a half an hour blow-drying her hair and putting in beautiful hair ornaments while dressing her up in her favorite pink polka dot Minnie dress.

"Go show Yuyu Baba your beautiful hair and dress." He always said that to Phoebe when they walked out of the bathroom. Phoebe was always happy after the private and special beauty treatment, and Bryan was very proud. He later told me that they did a professional assessment when he was in elementary school. His number one career was hairdresser. Completely closeted, he hid it well and buried all the urge to play with Barbie's hair.

Our beauty collection was pushed to a completely different level once I saw eleven bottles of nail polish on Phoebe's bathroom counter. Hot pink, neon yellow, purple, red, orange, sparkling dark red, turquoise, and so on. This extended the beauty session to almost one hour. I was totally fine with it. I could use the sixty minutes for me time.

Phoebe was such a girly girl. She loved having her nails painted. She always showed them to me proudly and tried to avoid touching anything with her freshly painted nails.

Bryan and I started singing and reading to Phoebe before bedtime. Bryan would sing the American songs, such as "Wheels on the Bus," "Head, Shoulders, Knees, and Toes," etc. I enjoyed listening to the songs, not only because Bryan had a beautiful voice, but also because the songs were new to me. I enjoyed learning. I would sing the traditional Chinese lullabies "Little Swallow" and "Two Tigers," and the wordless one that Mom always hummed to me when I was a baby.

However, it seemed that we were each other's only audience. Phoebe always got fussy and cried when we sang. When we stopped singing, she would become calm again.

It was the same with reading books. I bought so many books for Phoebe, but whenever I started reading, she would try to grab the book and throw it away. If I insisted on reading, she would protest by crying so loudly that I could barely hear myself. To this day, I still have not had a Hollywood movie bedtime story scene with Phoebe.

While it was not movie-script perfect, we were soaking up every single second with Phoebe and finding happiness and enjoyment from even the worst moments. We laughed until we fell down at Phoebe's accidental poop in the bathtub. I even enjoyed the sleepless night when Phoebe was having her first fever. Holding her tiny, hot body against mine, hearing her breathing loudly through her wide-open mouth, patting her back when she made a noise of discomfort, I felt complete and calm. The night was a heartening contrast to the sleepless nights back in college. At that time, there was only fear and worry. Now, there was still worry about when Phoebe would be well, but the worry was no match for my profound sense of love and responsibility.

Quiet time with Phoebe was precious. Staring at her sleeping become my new addiction. She loved sleeping on her tummy, head turning to either side. Her long hair naturally dropped in front of her eyes, mixing with her tiny eyebrows. Her cheek turned a little bit red when sleeping. She loved breathing through her rosebud mouth. I sometimes just put my face near her head to feel the air on my skin. It was like a summer breeze, bringing comfort and happiness.

* * *

SPENDING ALONE TIME with Phoebe gave me room to think about what kind of dad I wanted to be. I didn't have a good relationship with Dad. We barely talked while we were living under the same roof.

Everybody said that I look exactly like Dad – the chopstick-thin body, the small eyes, the short and thick black hair, and even the lifted-eyebrow expression when talking excitedly about something. However, I couldn't find any mental similarities. I had never thought about this before. I had enough issues – studying, job, sexuality, love, and surrogacy.

I also never thought that I would have problems with my parents. I was completely ignoring the elephant in the room. "Those people who never talk to their parents" only existed in other families, not mine.

Now, in front of the sleeping Phoebe, who looked nothing like me with her big eyes, long lashes, and fine brown hair, I could not resist asking myself, "What kind of father do I want to be?"

The question pushed me to think about Dad, the only dad I knew well other than my grandpa. I realized how little I knew about him. Mom and Dad always talked about when I was five, Dad took me to his work to play with the Apple computer. It was the car-driving game, as they recalled, which was several cars that looked like blocks moving along the screen. My little hand was supposed to help the cars avoid all the roadblocks.

They also talked about Dad faking spanking me to make me recite a Chinese poem that was written a thousand years ago, that every kid in China needs to be able to recite in their sleep, that parents would ask their kids to recite in front of other parents to show off.

Dad always said that he never spanked me and always talked to me and tried to care for and love me with reason and patience. I never doubted the truth of all the stories, but that didn't make my relationship with Dad better.

Most of the memories I had of Dad were of him not being there. I remembered Mom took me to the street market to buy grapes for my exams. Mom knew how much I loved the big green grapes and saved two days of grocery money to buy me 500 grams of grapes that were imported from California.

I remembered going on school trips with my parents during summer break. The college that my parents worked at organized summer trips from time to time to nearby tourist spots. This was a good way to provide relaxation for the employees and bonding for the families. I remembered the trip to Qing Ao Bay, playing on the beach. I searched for a memory of Dad. The only thing I could find was the night he argued with Mom for whatever reason and then stormed out of the hotel room. I saw Mom sweep her tears away. Then she took me for a walk outside and bought me some delicious local dessert – double skim milk pudding.

I was shocked by the discrepancy between what I wanted to remember and what I could remember. *Why were all the good memories of childhood those Dad was not in?*

I picked up the phone and called Mom. As usual, Mom picked up the phone within three rings. No matter what she was doing, she always picked up my calls immediately. Sometimes I trusted that reliability more than I trusted myself.

"How is Phoebe? Did she eat enough today? How was her sleep last night? I saw that she cried a little bit at 3:00 a.m...." Mom didn't give me a chance to speak.

"Phoebe is doing well." I tried to direct the conversation to my questions. "Can I ask you something about Dad?"

"Oh?" She was definitely surprised and not expecting this question from me.

"What was Dad doing when I was little? I can't find many good memories of him..."

"I see." Mom seemed to know where I was going. "He was always busy. We moved to Guangzhou because we thought the big city would provide a brighter future for you."

"You guys moved for me?" I couldn't believe what I heard. The fourth-grade memory rushed into my head. I always felt that the move was the beginning of a miserable chapter of my life. The principal's cold voice. The avoidance from the students. The dialect that I couldn't and didn't speak. Ever since then, I was always begging and searching for acceptance.

"Yes, we did. Actually, your dad initiated it. He thought education in Guangzhou was way better for you than in Hunan. Your dad had a great career with the steel factory in Hunan. Because your grandpa was a founding father of the factory, your dad was guaranteed a leadership position. But we moved to Guangzhou and became teachers in a local small college."

Mom paused a little bit and seemed to recall more memories. "We needed to start everything from scratch. I worried about what to feed you every day while your dad was struggling with his new career as a teacher. That's why he started a side business. He had big dreams and always wanted to do something more..."

As I hung up the phone after Mom helped me relive some old memories of the early days in Guangzhou, my mind was going two hundred miles per hour.

The story seemed so familiar. A young dad left for a better place and started everything from scratch. A young dad who believed that he was unique, maybe with some pieces of sun in him, who tried to make the most out of his life while struggling to be a good dad and to spend time with his kid. And now, the grownup kid didn't have many good memories of the dad and didn't even talk much with him other than fighting with him for sneaking into his crying granddaughter's room at night.

Dad was that young dad. I was that kid. Now, I was the young dad. I didn't want Phoebe to be like me when she grew up. I wanted Phoebe to have memories of going grocery shopping, traveling, and tasting interesting new food together, or just lying on the couch, watching TV together. I wanted to listen to Phoebe and let her feel my presence growing up. There would be time to have a better job title and make more money. But Phoebe only had one childhood. Between a career and Phoebe, I chose Phoebe in a heartbeat.

Two weeks later, I wrote a lengthy email to my manager at Microsoft. I planned to resign from my job at Microsoft that I worked so hard for eight years ago. My dream job. The job that provided a living when I was a fresh graduate with $150K in student loan debt.

The job that brought me to the Pacific Northwest, a place that gave me the peace and courage to come out to myself, to meet Bryan and start the journey with Phoebe.

The job that was also the only reliable income that we had at the moment. Although Bryan took the number one spot for sales volume for Berkshire Hathaway Homes Services in Washington State, I knew real estate was seasonal, and everything could change in three months.

My mind was full of fear and uncertainty about the future, but my heart was dedicated to spending time with Phoebe. I pressed the "Send" button.

HANALEI AND CHELSIE

"We can complain because rose bushes have thorns, or rejoice because thorns have roses."

—Alphonse Karr

"And when you crush an apple with your teeth, say to it in your heart:
Your seeds shall live in my body,
And the buds of your tomorrow shall blossom in my heart,
And your fragrance shall be my breath,
And together we shall rejoice through all the seasons."

—Khalil Gibran

Whilе we were still enjoying the fresh new responsibility of being dads, the urge to have a big family came back to me. That urge became stronger after I watched a YouTube video *Isaac and Amy – Yes to Love*. Two families that started with two married couples in the 1940s during the war became one family, ending up with fourteen children, forty grandchildren, and thirty-five great-grandchildren.

I was moved to tears every time during the last scene. The whole family stood together, surrounding the two great-grandmothers who held photos of their husbands, who had both passed away in 2007. Love was floating in the air and through their happy tears. Love was intense. It was abundant.

Watching the last scene, I thought about my grandparents. Every time I called my grandma, who was almost ninety years old, she reminded me that nothing was more important than my family's health and happiness. After spending her whole life chasing a shiny career as the principal at five schools, she realized that simply being healthy and happy was the most important thing. Does aging make you want less or become wiser? I believe the latter.

Grandma had a stroke a couple of years back. After then, her health started failing. Eating less and losing weight, she said that she would not live long. That was changed after she saw Phoebe's photo the first time. It was like the magic spring water I heard from Chinese fairytales that gave people life. Every photo we sent to the iPad we got her gave her more energy and more will to live. She started to eat more and gain weight. We were all so happy about the change.

Seeing the positive change in Grandma made me want a bigger family even more. I showed the *Yes to Love* video to Bryan.

"How wonderful is it to have a family like that!" I said.

"The love part? Yes. The size of the family? Not for us." He smiled. Well, I agreed.

When telling my friends and Phoebe's pediatrician, Dr. Manfred, about having a bigger family, I learned that there were two good choices. Either to have siblings within two years so they could go through everything together, or space them more than four years apart, so they wouldn't fight too much. "Let's make sure our kids will experience kindergarten, elementary, and high school together," I said to Bryan.

"Sounds great." He was still him, a supportive husband. Just like all the big decisions in our life, we made this decision quickly – we would start a sibling journey before Phoebe turned one.

* * *

JANUARY 2016

"We are thinking of starting the next journey." I slipped a text to Chelsie right after the new year.

"Yeah? I am interested! I just need to make sure that physically I can do it and the timeline fits Steven's training for state patrol."

"Sounds good. Let's talk more."

I also reached out to our agent Melissa about the sibling journey. We talked about what we planned to do. I told her I was thinking of working with Chelsie directly to save money. Since Chelsie had not decided yet, I also asked Melissa about other surrogates.

If we were going to work with Chelsie directly, I was going to be the new "Melissa" and manage the process myself. I pulled out my spreadsheet and started to do some planning.

Let's start with the easy ones. Lawyer? Loved the price and service from Doug. Clinic? Definitely Dr. Kumar again. Surrogate? Waiting for Chelsie and Melissa. How about egg donors? Wait, do we need egg donors again?

I really wanted a baby with Bryan's genes. Ever since we were pregnant with little Bryan last time, I kept imagining what he would look like. *Would he have Bryan's long nose? Soft hair? Beautiful eyes? The cute look when he became serious about things? The big toe that was so out of place and poked so many holes in the*

226

socks that we shared? I cherished and adored Bryan so much, and I wanted to see a new generation of him in the world so I could love him or her even more.

After the last transfer, however, Bryan didn't have any embryos left, while I had three with a 3BB rating with normal DNA. If we wanted more embryos, we'd need a new egg donor. The cost would easily be another $25K–$35K.

Our real estate business was doing pretty well, but doing the sibling journey so close to the original one definitely added pressure to our finances.

Maybe we could just transfer two of my embryos? What if we had horrible luck with egg donors like last time? What if there were even fewer embryos produced? What if it was Bryan's sperm's problem? Maybe his alcoholism had damaged the cells?

My darkest and most evil thoughts were pushing me into areas where I didn't want to go. I was too scared to share these thoughts with Bryan. I loved him unconditionally, but saying things I didn't have the right to say would not only hurt him but would also kill me inside. I already felt so small having these thoughts.

I tried to push the thoughts down and called Mom. "No question that you should do another round of embryos." Mom was a little bit angry at what I was thinking. "How selfish are you! It is you and Bryan on this journey to create a family together. Be fair to each other. Your dad and I have been married for thirty-five years..."

"Okay, I got it." I needed to interrupt before the big speech of what it meant to be in a marriage, that I had heard over and over again.

Bryan and I had a talk about the embryos. I was open about my concerns but suggested we try to find a new egg donor to create another round of embryos. Bryan was excited! Who doesn't want a chance to have their genes passed on? Bryan's smile made me happy.

* * *

FEBRUARY AND MARCH 2016

Chelsie and Melissa got back to us almost at the same time. Melissa didn't have a surrogate who wanted to transfer two embryos at the moment. "The surrogate industry has suddenly become so popular and hot, especially with intended parents from China. It may take a couple of months to search," she said. We were not surprised. This was just like the Seattle real estate market with the Chinese investors flooding in.

On the other hand, Chelsie was ready to go! She was cleared with the doctor, and Steven's schedule worked out fine. We were thrilled. Life sometimes magically just puts everything in the right place.

Dr. Kumar was also starting a new practice. His new clinic's name was Western Fertility. They didn't take on infertility treatment anymore but focused on IVF for surrogacy. Given the large number of international, especially Chinese, intended parents that I had just heard about, I understood why. As I was told in China, Western medicine was safer, better, and more advanced. His new office was closer to LA. This made our trip more convenient. We could even find a Poke shop right outside of the clinic. Loving it!

Kim sent us fifteen profiles of egg donors. We quickly picked #932. Twenty-three years old. European and Mexican descent. Blond hair. Hazel eye color. College GPA, 3.8. Favorite subject was marine biology, least favorite subject was history, just like me! She had a smile that reminded us of "Cute Girl Next Door."

She had done three cycles already within twelve months, meaning that she had donated to three families. She produced twenty-two, fifty-nine, and twenty-nine eggs in successive cycles. She was booked for the fourth cycle and would be ready in May or June. Perfect timing for us.

Dr. Kumar also told us that since we wanted to have a baby with Bryan's genes, we should give three-quarters of the eggs Bryan's sperm, one-quarter mine. We thought that was a great plan.

* * *

APRIL 2016

Ever since the start of the journey, I had read information online that some surrogate mothers developed an uncontrollable attachment to their oven babies. That made it hard, or even impossible, to keep a relationship between surrogates and intended parents. I admitted that the thought was elevated in my mind when Phoebe was born, especially when I saw Chelsie holding Phoebe for a long time right before we left Fresno.

The way Chelsie looked at Phoebe was telling the story of the eight-month pregnancy journey that they enjoyed and suffered every day together, that I would never be able to experience myself as a male. I was jealous. *Would Chelsie want to be part of Phoebe's life? Would Phoebe think Chelsie was her mom when she grew up even if they were not genetically related?*

The worries faded soon after we settled into our new life with Phoebe. There was no time to overthink and worry. Instead, I started missing the daily frequent messaging with

Chelsie. And now, as we were about to start our next surrogacy journey, I couldn't wait to get back to our daily texting. We were just like two high school girls.

Chelsie had always mentioned that she wanted to see Seattle. It was not just because of all the great things I said about Seattle; her dad was also a big fan of the Seahawks. We decided to invite her and her family to visit us.

The previous worries completely evaporated when Chelsie arrived. The way she held and looked at Phoebe was still full of love, the same as before. She tickled Phoebe, touched her, kissed her cheek just like how she interacted with her own daughter, Delia.

I realized that it was my lack of confidence and self-doubt that made me have those worries. I thought about how small I was in worrying about Chelsie's love for Phoebe. There could never be enough love for Phoebe. Chelsie was more than just an oven for Phoebe. She was family now, in our modern cross-culture family.

Because Chelsie's family was only staying with us for three days, we wanted to make sure they had a good time in Seattle. We became their tour guides. Space Needle? Check! Aquarium? Check! Breakfast at Pike Place Market? Check! We even jumped on the ferry to visit Bainbridge Island and just relax and let Phoebe and Delia play.

I learned more about Chelsie's dream of a career in the medical field. While taking care of Delia, working at a hotel on the night shift, and being a wonderful girlfriend and great daughter, she was taking courses to pursue her dream. And now, she was ready to add more to her already busy enough plate by carrying our babies again. We were forever grateful for what she had done for our family.

* * *

MAY TO SEPTEMBER 2016

We had some hiccups in the second journey. Chelsie's VA health insurance didn't cover the surrogacy. Because it was not open enrollment time yet, we couldn't get health insurance for Chelsie. If we started the insurance in July or August, we would need to pay an additional $12K for the bridge insurance. That was definitely out of the question.

I talked with Dr. Kumar's office. The earliest we could do the transfer was late October or November. Then Chelsie would be released to her local hospital at twelve weeks pregnant with Affordable Care Act health insurance activated in 2017.

It was a little bit scary since she would be without insurance from the transfer date until the end of 2016. If anything happened and she needed to go see a doctor for the pregnancy, we would need to pay out of the pocket. However, considering the time we would save and Dr. Kumar's expertise, we decided to go ahead with the recommendation of transferring in October or November.

At the same time, our egg donor was coming along. In June, egg donor #932 had just finished her last cycle and was ready to work with us. On July 17, we received thirty-nine eggs. We were thrilled. This was more than we got during the last journey!

Twenty-nine eggs were matched with Bryan's sperm, and ten with mine. We were eagerly awaiting Mother Nature's magic.

Day 1, twenty-five embryos were good. That was really good news.

Day 5, Bryan had fourteen good embryos, and I had two. Not bad, we told ourselves.

Ten days later, we got the PGS results back. Bryan had six normal embryos, while none of mine were good.

How ironic! I once thought it was Bryan's cells that made his embryos not normal. Now I ended up with no normal embryos. Once again life taught me how wrong I could be. I also gained a new understanding of couples fighting over fertility problems. Each party might have healthy sperm and eggs, but for whatever reason, Mother Nature would not weave a fertility spell.

"We could still transfer two," Dr. Kumar said. "One from Bryan's batch this time. One from yours from your last journey."

"But mine has been frozen for over two years and was a BB grade." I remembered my grade very well, that's for sure.

"It won't be a problem at all. The grade was just based on visual inspection. It didn't mean anything about the embryo quality, just how fast it was growing."

"I see." Privately, I still doubted that two years in the freezer hadn't done any harm to the embryos.

"How about sex?" Dr. Kumar continued. "Nick, you only have female embryos left, so no question for you. Bryan, you can choose a little boy or girl. Both AA quality and healthy. What do you think?"

"A girl." Bryan's answer was so fast and was not what I was thinking. I was still dreaming of the dragon and phoenix twins.

"Should we talk about it first?" I asked before Dr. Kumar followed up with the plan.

"Sure," Bryan said.

We hung up the phone with Dr. Kumar. Bryan told me that although there were many great stories about how successful a boy could be growing up with gay dads, he just felt more comfortable with a girl. Neither of us was good at sports, especially popular ones like baseball, basketball, or football. I must admit, I was still trying to understand all the rules of football only because the Seahawks were doing well in the last couple of years. And a boy growing up with two gay dads? Wouldn't that create problems for him in the future?

Bryan's words touched part of my memories that I tried to erase or bury. I thought Bryan must have been thinking about his childhood when he needed to hide his sexuality and battle the bigotry. We knew that girls wouldn't be easy either. We had heard so many stories about girls' troubles in their teenage years. But the idea of a princess growing up with two daddies just seemed more like a fairytale.

"I agreed! Let's have three girls! Two dads and three girls!" I said. We looked at each other and smiled.

* * *

OCTOBER TO DECEMBER 2016

We set the transfer date as October 27. To save every penny possible, and considering the transfer was literally two minutes, we decided not to travel to LA. The most important thing was to give Chelsie lots of support and love. We could do that remotely from Seattle. Chelsie said she understood the situation and was very supportive.

The familiarity made the time go so fast. October 27, the transfer was done. October 31, Chelsie did the home pregnancy test. Yes, we wanted to know from the beginning this time.

In the morning, Chelsie sent us a photo of the testing result and told us a vague line was there. I swore that we couldn't see anything. But another test in six hours definitely put the mark on the tube. We were pregnant, again!

Chelsie continued daily testing until the first blood test on November 3. It was 104. Was it good? Was it good enough to be twins? Three days later, we had another check. It was 825! *That's really high.* "Very likely to be twins!" Kim told us. We were cautiously positive.

November 23, in the first ultrasound, we saw two heartbeats pounding on the screen. Yes! Twins! One was measured six weeks four days, the other six weeks two days. The due date was July 16, 2017.

We could not be happier! We were going to be daddies for two more beautiful girls! Mine would have similar genes to Phoebe's, while Bryan's would be totally different.

Would mine look like a twin to Phoebe? Would she love reading and listening to songs or hate them just like Phoebe? How about Bryan's? Would she look like Bryan with brown hair or like the egg donor with blond hair? How about skin color? Would the Mexican gene dominate again as happened with Phoebe and give the baby dark skin?

We read somewhere that eating dark chocolate could not only help provide energy for pregnant women but also made happy babies. We started sending dark chocolate to Chelsie until one day she told us that she had more than enough to last the entire pregnancy.

Bryan and I also started to talk about names. Well, to be honest, it was all me. "Phoebe, Rachel, Monica sound so good. They are going to be best friends," I told Bryan over dinner on our Pizza Tuesday.

234

"Uh…" Bryan put down his slice of pepperoni pizza and gave me a look of "are you serious?"

"This will become a great tradition to name our kids after TV shows or movies. I've watched *Friends* twelve times already!" I was resisting picking up his cues. "This could land us on *The Ellen Show*!"

I always dream of meeting Ellen. I still remember the first time I saw *The Ellen Show* when I was staying at a hotel preparing for my job interview the next day with McKinsey & Company in early 2008. I had never watched any American reality TV before. I was shocked to see a lesbian could host a TV show and be loved by so many people. It was not like Ross's ex-wife Carol, who was fiction; this was a real person! Since then, watching Ellen became my favorite thing to do.

"We are not going to name them after some TV show. End of story." Bryan was serious. He gave me a smirk when he saw my disappointed frowny face. "Case closed."

In December, Delia was going to spend Christmas with her father in Texas. Chelsie asked me whether she could take the flight and escort Delia to her dad. I was worried and wanted to say no. I wanted to remind her of the clause in the contract that said flying might harm the babies. But I didn't know how to tell her no.

I had been a yes man for my entire life. I wanted to please people, especially the person who was our surrogate, carrying our twin girls. Oh, how I missed Melissa! I asked for a detailed itinerary from Chelsie and gave a "happy" yes.

* * *

JANUARY 2017

The number of text messages I received from Chelsie from this journey was way more than last time. She told us that the twins were testing her limits. She could not sleep well. Headache. Always wanted to throw up.

"There are four different genes in your body now. Bryan's, mine, the first egg donor, and the second egg donor. I think your body doesn't know how to react," I texted.

"ROFL," Chelsie texted back. She was very strong. She always just let us know her situation and quickly told us that she would be fine. I loved the transparency, strength, and consideration.

Her OB visits were also way more frequent than the first pregnancy. That also meant more bills for us. When I left Microsoft in November 2016, I knew we could not just rely on real estate sales income. A $30K one month, $0 for two months kind of income wouldn't be healthy and feasible for our growing family with hopefully three girls. I didn't want to live in fear and at the mercy of the market.

Our investment clients had been asking us to start a property management (PM) business. They weren't happy with the ones we referred them to or the ones they found themselves. "You should start a property management company and manage our properties just like you manage your own. We will buy more properties from you if you manage them."

For so long, we didn't want to do it because PM was the lowest in the value chain of the real estate industry. It also meant being on call 24/7 in case of emergency. However, after hearing it again and again and thinking of the stable income we could get from the business, Bryan and I decided to do it.

We started a property management business called GPS Renting. I wanted to use what I learned from the technology industry to help transform the property management space. We also set up a motto of "Professional, Honest. Kind." as the values to guide our daily decision-making and action.

The feeling of working on a new business was like that of having our baby. I was very excited. I devoted all my energy to it. At the same time, while Phoebe was spending time in a local daycare, I carved out as much time as possible to play with her in the evening and on weekends. In the end, that's the purpose of life.

*　*　*

FEBRUARY TO MAY 2017

Feb. 1 – Chelsie texted me that she had low blood pressure from her routine OB test. "What should we do?" I asked.

"My OB asked me to cut my soda intake, switch to diet," she replied.

Oh, how I missed Melissa. She would have told me that she would deliver the message of no soda at all.

Feb. 10 – "My cervix is still long and closed," another message followed. "They will start checking my cervix every two weeks until twenty-four weeks."

Mar. 27 – "My cervix is only 2.5 cm."

"What does that mean?" I was freaking out. Google told me that when a woman's cervix was 2.2 cm, there is a 20 percent chance of preterm delivery. I was scared. But there was nothing I could do.

Mar. 29 – The OB decided to put Chelsie on modified bedrest, doing less housework, not traveling, staying on the couch, and lying down most of the time. The plan sounded good to me.

Mar. 31 – "Delia has a soccer game I want to go. It's only a ten-minute drive, and the game lasts one hour." I didn't know how to respond. Again, I said yes.

Apr. 11 – Chelsie told me that she kept throwing up and couldn't keep any food or fluid in her stomach. The doctor gave her medicine for nausea and asked her to come to the hospital if the situation was not better in twelve hours.

Apr. 12 – The situation was unchanged. Chelsie went to the hospital. A test was done to see whether she would go into labor in two weeks. Results came back negative. Chelsie went home.

Apr. 13 – Chelsie slept most of the time but told me she was starting to have cramps.

Apr. 14 – The contraction/cramps had lasted for over ten hours, but they were not consistent. Chelsie called the doctor's office, and they scheduled an ultrasound for as soon as possible.

Apr. 16 – The ultrasound was done. Baby A measured twenty-seven weeks, four days; she was two pounds, six ounces. Baby B measured twenty-seven weeks, four days; she was two pounds, seven ounces.

Chelsie's cervix, however, measured 1.4 cm. Chelsie was admitted to Labor & Delivery. The doctors used magnesium to try to stop delivery.

I bought my ticket to fly down to Fresno. Bryan would take care of Phoebe at home.

Apr. 17 – Chelsie's situation was stable. She asked me whether I had any questions to ask the doctor. Totally panicked, I sent her four questions.

1. What could we do to keep the babies in the belly as long as possible?
2. What should we not do during this time?
3. What could we do to increase the survival rate and health of the babies?
4. What would help Chelsie more in this situation? Vodka tonic or tequila shots? :)

Later that day, Chelsie was sent home. "How could the doctor send her home when the cervix was measuring 1.4 cm!" I was so angry, but there was nothing I could do but vent to Bryan.

Apr. 18 – I flew down to Fresno. Chelsie was not delivering. Thank God! I brought her to long overdue In and Out Burger for lunch.

Later that day, we went for another ultrasound. I saw the twenty-seven-week Monica and Rachel on the monitor. "Pudong… pudong…" Their heartbeats were so strong. *Please stay as long as possible.*

We also toured the NICU and met the nurse in charge. She introduced us to a few babies that were born at twenty-seven weeks. "They would be fine," the nurse said. "We will take care of your girls." Her words calmed me down.

Apr. 19 – I flew back to Seattle. Chelsie told me that she liked the Theo Raspberry chocolate the most. I ordered some more on Amazon and sent it to her. Anything I could do, I told myself.

Apr. 20 – The contractions came back. They were very close, about ten minutes apart. Chelsie was admitted to Labor & Delivery again. "They should not have released her in the first place!" I cried to Bryan. Her cervix was also dilated to 1 cm.

Apr. 21 - Chelsie was released to return home with nifedipine to control or hopefully stop the contractions. She needed to take the medication every six hours.

Apr. 22 - "No contraction so far!" I was so excited to receive that message. Chelsie followed up with another one: "I'm thinking we can actually make it to a good date in May! Feeling optimistic now! Grow, baby girls!"

Apr. 25 - People in Chelsie's surrogate group on Facebook all started to deliver babies. One surrogate's water broke at sixteen weeks. She then had a C-section at twenty-four weeks; neither baby made it. Another surrogate delivered twins, a boy and girl, at thirty-eight weeks. Chelsie shared the photos of the babies. How lucky they were! *Monica and Rachel, please hold on.*

May 1 - "Thirty weeks today!" Chelsie texted me. Babies passed stress test. What a relief!

May 2 - "Girls are moving a lot," Chelsie texted me. "Hopefully they will stay longer," I replied. Bryan, Phoebe, and I boarded our flight to Kauai. We wanted to continue the tradition of traveling on Bryan's birthday every year. We also knew what was ahead of us. We wanted to take a last chance to relax before entering the three-girls club.

May 7 - We finished all the pre-birth judgment paperwork and sent it back to the lawyer.

May 8 - Chelsie sent us photos of lots of clothes she bought for the girls. She was simply the best we could ever ask for.

May 9 - I woke up with the text, "Thirty-one weeks today!" I searched online and found that the girls were "coconut" size. Chelsie also had another ultrasound. Baby A was three pounds, thirteen ounces; Baby B was three pounds, twelve ounces.

Bryan and I found a new normal of up and down every day. Reading text messages from Chelsie was the most exciting and scary thing.

We were staying in Hanalei Bay that week, our favorite place in Kauai. The blue water. The rural peace. The greenery. The old buildings that were so different than in the next town, Princeville.

Sitting on the half-moon-shaped beach and enjoying the sunset with rainbow shaved ice, Bryan said, "How about Hanalei for the first twin?"

"That sounds great!" I knew how much travel had changed our lives, and we wished the same for the girls. Besides, the pronunciation was just beautiful.

"So you are okay with no Monica and Rachel?"

"That's fine! Ellen will still want to meet us though." I smiled.

"And the youngest one?" Bryan asked.

"Chelsie. We should name her Chelsie to honor our amazing surrogate. She has completely changed our life," I said.

May 12 – Chelsie was having stronger contractions. The doctor asked her to take the meds every four hours.

May 13 – Contractions were still there, but not consistent.

May 15 – Baby A had a dipping heartbeat during the ultrasound. Baby B was okay. Baby A was on a monitor for four hours. If the situation got worse, they would perform a C-section. Later that day, Chelsie was sent home. Strong heartbeat, girls!

May 22 – Chelsie said she was having painful contractions that were thirty to sixty minutes apart. The ultrasound tech said some were real contractions.

May 28 – "The contractions have been picking up, but nothing painful or consistent," Chelsie texted. "Thirty-four weeks tomorrow!" she followed. I smiled. *How far we had come from twenty-seven weeks!*

* * *

MAY 29 – At 7:00 a.m., I woke up with four missed calls, five text messages. "They want to do a C-section in the next couple of hours." That was the last message.

I frantically called Chelsie. She said she would go into labor soon. I rushed to the airport. Hanalei was born at 8:36 a.m., and Chelsie came at 8:37 a.m. Hanalei was four pounds, eleven ounces, while Chelsie was three pounds, almost sixteen ounces. Both Hanalei and Chelsie needed to be on a breathing support system.

My flight landed at Fresno at noon. When I turned my phone on again, photos started coming in from Chelsie from the delivery. And then, the babies. So many wires and tubes on them. They were also in two plastic cases. I could not see them well.

I dialed Chelsie's number. "Are they okay?"

"I think so." Chelsie sounded tired on the other side; her breathing was deep and slow. "I heard both of them crying. They took the babies to the NICU right after delivery."

My heart was in my throat. I took a deep breath. "How are you?"

"I'm fine. I am sorry I couldn't hold them longer," Chelsie said. "C-section is fast though. I didn't realize it was over. We should have done this before," she joked. She was amazing.

The same lady was at the Hertz counter from when I was here seven weeks ago. "They are here," I told her. Nervous inside, I was trying to be calm. So many scenarios ran through my mind. *Why were they in the cases? What are the tubes for? Are they healthy?*

"Congratulations!" the Hertz lady said.

"Thank you!" I squeezed a smile and grabbed the key and ran to the parking lot.

When I arrived at the hospital, I didn't go to the NICU. I needed to honor Chelsie first. She woke up when I walked into the room. Her mom was at her bedside.

"Congratulations for being a daddy again!" She extended her arms and gave me a hug.

"Thank you!" I didn't know what else to say. We had so much appreciation for what she had done during the last few years. I had a little Seattle souvenir gift for her I bought at SeaTac. I felt bad; I didn't even have time to do any proper shopping this time. She was very happy to open the gift.

"We have decided on the names." I wanted Chelsie to know first. I also wanted to have a name to call the girls before I met them for the first time.

"The first one will be Hanalei. It means 'blue bay.' Our favorite vacation place in Hawaii."

"Beautiful name." She smiled.

"The second one will be Chelsie. Just like you, with the weird spelling of 'sie.'"

We both started crying. We knew how much we had experienced. I was never in the army, but I imagine this was something similar. The feeling of life and death sometimes, but no matter what, we were by each other's side.

"You know how to make a girl cry," Chelsie said, wiping her tears.

* * *

HANALEI AND CHELSIE were sleeping in their clear cases when I arrived at their room in the NICU. I had so many questions for the nurses and doctors, but I just wanted to see the girls close up.

They were so small, barely half of Phoebe's weight when she was born. Their skin was almost transparent. I could see the veins and the heartbeat. Seeing the heartbeat made me shiver yet gave me confidence. I could not see their faces well, as they were half covered by the tubes over their nose and mouth. That was a CPAP to help them breathe, I learned later.

Hanalei carried Bryan's genes. The blond hair, big eyes, and bigger body was a dead giveaway. She was almost one pound heavier than Chelsie. Chelsie didn't have any fat on her. Skins and bones, that's it. My heart hurt looking at her. The ultrasound one week ago said that they were almost the same weight. *How wrong could those ultrasounds be!*

I called Bryan and my parents. I introduced Hanalei and Chelsie to them through FaceTime. Phoebe was busy playing with her puzzles. "She will see her sisters when we visit next week," Bryan said.

The hospital and countless generous donors provided Terry House. Similar to the Ronald McDonald House, it gives patients and their family a place to stay at a minimum cost when they're at the hospital. Terry House was right next to the hospital, so it was very convenient. I was lucky to get the only room available that day.

After settling down, I started to spend more time in the NICU and became a NICU dad. I learned that preemie babies had three things to learn before they could leave the NICU –

breathing on their own, keeping warm on their own, and eating on their own.

How much we took for granted when Hanalei and Chelsie needed to learn all these basic skills to survive! "They are strong, and they will be strong in life." I repeated that to myself every day.

The hospital created a binder that detailed all the information needed for parents of preemie babies. They called it "Kangaroo Care" and made a beautiful checklist in a road format – once the little baby kangaroo finishes all the items on the road, he or she can go home. Checklist! Love it! A journey! Cannot be better!

I started to set up a new routine. Waking up before sunrise, I drove to Woodward Park in north Fresno and did my morning run. A run around the park is about three miles. Just the perfect distance. I showered and then grabbed breakfast from the hospital café. After that, I normally had my morning phone meeting with my teammates in Seattle. This was my first year running our property management business, and there were lots of things to discuss and do. At the same time, we were growing really fast. In six months, we were already managing seventy properties. I couldn't use my personal life as an excuse not to provide great service for my clients. "Professional, honest, and kind" is the motto I set up for our company. I needed to live it myself.

After the meeting, I visited Hanalei and Chelsie. Seeing their faces, their breath, and their heartbeat was my B12 vitamin shot every day. I always liked listening to the nurse talking about what happened in the previous shifts. *Did they poop? Pee? How much did they drink? Were there any incidents, like a dropping oxygen level?* That became one of my nightmares.

The oxygen level was tied to the goal of "breathing on their own." Whenever the oxygen level dropped below ninety, the machine would give out the alert: "Beeeeep... Beeeeep..." That gave notice to the nurse to take action to make sure the baby was doing well.

Hanalei did not have much problem breathing, but Chelsie needed lots of help. The doctor was constantly pushing her to use less support, but every attempt meant that there were more alerts from the system. "Beeeeep... Beeeeep..." Those noises still haunt me in my dreams at night.

Lunch was also in the hospital cafe. It was convenient and affordable, and we needed to save every dime for the girls. I normally did some more work before heading back to the NICU. I would try my best to do the 3:00 p.m. and 6:00 p.m. care for the babies.

The care consisted of changing diapers, feeding, and holding. At first, care was easy because both of them were tube feeding. A tiny orange tube sent the calorie-added milk through their nose to their tiny stomachs. Gravity was doing the job.

But in a week, we switched to half feeding with bottles and half tube feeding. They needed to learn to "eat on their own." That made care extremely complicated and lengthy.

Neither Hanalei nor Chelsie were willing to eat by themselves. They would not suck the nipples. Sometimes they fell asleep eating. Lots of times they threw up when the nurse added too many NeoSure calories.

To make it more complex, we needed to limit the feeding time to less than thirty minutes each, because feeding also used the babies' energy. Too much energy consumption would set back their weight gain.

Oh, weight gain! That's what I looked forward to every evening. At the 9:00 p.m. care time, we would weigh both of them. Hanalei and Chelsie needed to breathe, keep warm, and eat on their own, but the main goal was to make them grow. After each weighing, the care nurse wrote their new weight on the whiteboard on top of their tiny plastic case. An up or down arrow would also be added next to the weight to indicate the changes from yesterday. The goal was simple – weight gain every day.

Easier said than done. When Hanalei and Chelsie were still trying to learn how to breathe and eat, there was so much trial and error. It was a "one-day weight gain followed by two-day loss" process. I was trying to make peace with the reality and know how much the girls were trying.

I went back to the hotel after the 9:00 p.m. care, which normally ran until 10:15–10:30 p.m. Saying goodnight to the girls, I called Bryan to check on his day and talk to Phoebe if she was still up. I missed her terribly. We had been together ever since she was born. I was not used to not seeing her smiles, feeding her, changing her diaper, and even listening to her whining and crying every day.

* * *

JUNE 6–8 – Bryan, Phoebe, and my parents flew down to Fresno. Phoebe didn't run to me or hug me at the airport. She was mad at me for just being gone one day when she woke up.

I said sorry to Phoebe so many times. I told her that it was for her sisters whom she would meet soon. She was just one and a half years old; I wasn't sure that she understood. It broke my heart to see her sad little face, hardly bigger than a sunflower.

Phoebe didn't grasp the concept of sisters yet. She didn't see us with big bellies, and we hadn't talked to her about her sisters over the past nine months – maybe because we didn't have to, not having big bellies, and maybe because we didn't want to jinx the pregnancy. She did know that they were babies, just like her two Live Life Babies. One of her dolls had blond hair, and one had dark hair, just like Hanalei and Chelsie. They were actually the same size as the twins.

Bryan, Phoebe, and Dad only stayed in Fresno for one day. There were still so many things to take care of at home. Not having stable jobs meant that we needed to work hard to make a living for the girls. *How I missed my time at Microsoft and the parental leave!*

To make the most out of the trip and give Phoebe some fun, we went to Island Water Park, recommended by our surrogate, Chelsie.

The next day, after Phoebe realized that I was not traveling home with her, she cried a lot at the airport. She knew she would not see me for a while. It was hard saying goodbye to them, but we did, and Mom and I went back to the hospital. Mom was staying to help me with the next step.

* * *

THE DOCTOR WAS talking about discharging Hanalei. She had been breathing by herself for a week. She graduated to a normal baby care station. She still threw up from time to time and needed to switch to tube feeding, but the doctor said they saw changes coming soon. We were excited but also starting to get worried.

We were scared of taking care of Hanalei and Chelsie by ourselves. Every day, we saw incidents in the NICU. A baby turned blue during feeding; the oxygen level had dropped significantly, and he needed special help from the nurse to stop the choking.

Mom and I signed up for the infant CPR course. We also went to the hospital support group for parents of preemie babies. The room was not big, and it was full. There were fifteen people or so, all moms. The hospital provided food. Panda Express! My favorite! I grabbed a full plate and found seats at the end of the big square table.

It was personal and it was painful. Most people didn't want to talk about these thoughts and feelings publicly, but the social worker encouraged everybody to share their stories. People opened up. Most moms talked about how sorry they felt for their babies. They believed it was all their fault for not being able to keep the baby inside longer. They had feelings of guilt, disappointment and even hatred toward themselves. I knew Chelsie felt the same way. Hopefully she knew how much we appreciated her, and the feeling would pass.

There was a lady sitting at the left corner of the table. She had short hair, wore glasses, and kept her eyes down. She hadn't opened her mouth during the entire meeting.

At the end, when I thought everything was done, the social worker turned to her and said in a kind voice, "Do you want to share something today? Speaking will make you feel better."

She lifted her head a little bit and looked at the social worker. Her face was pale and looked bruised under the eyes. Not enough sleep. I knew what that was like.

"I had my delivery at twenty-seven weeks." She started sobbing.

"Little Lucas made it. Jonathan... the other one, didn't make it..." The room became dead silent. "Lucas needs lots of health help and attention… but I just couldn't…" She started crying aloud. "I just received the death certificate of Jonathan. How can you have a birth certificate and death certificate on the same day!"

My heart sank. I started shaking. I thought about little Bryan, our son, whom we lost at twelve weeks. I thought about Hanalei and Chelsie and the almost delivery at twenty-seven weeks. I knew how lucky we were and was grateful, but my heart hurt for this woman.

* * *

IN THE NEXT few days, we were busy planning the girls' discharge. The doctor said it could be any day now. We were thrilled. But how to transport them was a big question. I asked the doctor in charge of the NICU. I called our pediatrician at home. I posted the question on the Men Having Babies Facebook group. I collected feedback from the Seattle Preemie Parents group.

The consensus? Definitely no airplane. The babies were barely able to breathe on their own. The lower pressure and oxygen in an airplane could cause unpredictable harm.

Driving? A long car ride might not be good for their breathing either. We also would still need to see their performance in the car seat challenge.

We decided to take the train back. We could have a sleep cart. Both Mom and I could take care of the girls.

June 15, 11:30 a.m., Hanalei and Chelsie were discharged from Fresno Community Hospital. I bought a dozen cupcakes for the NICU nurses and another dozen for the staff at Terry House. We were indebted forever to the generosity and kindness of all these strangers.

After a twenty-hour bumpy ride, we arrived at King Station in downtown Seattle. Bryan, Phoebe, and Dad were waiting outside of the station. Phoebe was wearing a yellow dress, her hair clipped back with rainbow barrettes. She didn't look like a baby anymore.

We loaded up everybody in our Honda Pilot. The car that once felt so empty just with Bryan and me, now felt so full. "We may need to buy a school bus soon," Bryan joked and started the engine.

"Let's go home, girls!" I cried out loud as I held tight to Bryan's hand to start our next journey.

Two Dads and Three Girls

"It's not only children who grow. Parents do too. As much as we watch to see what our children do with their lives, they are watching us to see what we do with ours. I can't tell my children to reach for the sun. All I can do is reach for it myself."

—Joyce Maynard

Be careful what you wish for. I should have known this already. When Hanalei and Chelsie were in the NICU, the only thing I wanted was to have the girls come home, even though I knew they were preemies and needed lots of help.

But now I was overwhelmed by the amount of work and the emotional intensity.

When they were in the car, we always needed somebody sitting back with them, and I needed to drive so slowly like an eighty-year-old grandma driving her Prius. I worried any small bumps on the road would cause them to choke. They had barely learned to breathe on their own. Now they needed to live like normal full-term babies. We limited their car rides to going to see Dr. Manfred.

Feeding was also a big problem. Hanalei had a very sensitive stomach. She was still not used to the NeoSure 22, which was thicker than normal formula because of the additional calories. However, we needed to feed her that to ensure she had healthy weight gain.

Hanalei's sensitive stomach pushed all the food out of her tiny body from time to time. Phoebe never had problems like this. The projectile-style throwing up made us worry about her growth. Dr. Manfred did an exam and told us that she should be all right and what we needed was patience, strong wills, and love.

Chelsie had her own feeding problems. Coming into the world almost one pound lighter than Hanalei, everything was one size smaller, including her stomach. She drank slowly and less. She could suck on the nipple for half an hour and not finish the bottle until she was too tired and dozing off. A normal feeding schedule would not get her enough calories.

"Let your dad and I help with the feeding and night duty." Mom saw our struggle. "You just started your business six months ago, and you guys have Phoebe to take care of. Let us help during this tough time. That's why we're here."

I didn't say anything. I knew we were on a journey bigger than Bryan and I could handle alone. After a quick conversation with Bryan, Hanalei and Chelsie moved upstairs to spend time with Mom and Dad in the master loft.

Every morning after getting up, I ran upstairs to see Hanalei and Chelsie and ask how the night went. Feeding five times. Three diaper changes. Throwing up once. Mom and Dad were the best caregivers we could ask for. They understood that the number one thing was to have weight gain for Hanalei and Chelsie. Every two hours, they put a bottle in the babies' mouths, even when they were still sleeping. They sucked and slept at the same time.

"Since they have smaller and sensitive stomachs, they need to eat smaller amounts and more frequently," Dad said. The feeding schedule was definitely not by the book, but I didn't have the energy or desire to challenge their feeding methods.

At the two-week checkup with Dr. Manfred, Hanalei's and Chelsie's weight was still below normal, but at the one-month appointment, their weight was above the fiftieth percentile on a full-term baby scale. The doctor was very surprised and asked what we did. I looked at my parents, who were standing in the small exam room, and said, "With the grandparents' love and patience."

"All kudos to your parents!" Dr. Manfred turned to Mom and Dad and gave a smile. Normally, in a situation like this, Mom and Dad would turn to me for a translation, but today, they could tell the meaning from the big thumbs-up they got. I knew how proud they were, but their faces blushed and they gave out timid and humble smiles. They never thought they did enough and never wanted to take credit even for their best effort.

I always thought there was a correct answer and best solution to any problem. Those answers and solutions could not be from my parents; they would be found in the books, from the modern Western world. My parents' love and patience toward Hanalei and Chelsie, however, made me start to doubt this naive belief.

* * *

THAT SUMMER, STANDING in front of the Stars and Stripes American flag, I vowed to devote myself to the country that gave me freedom and an opportunity to raise my daughters, Phoebe, Hanalei, and Chelsie, with Bryan.

During the ceremony, the officer asked each of us to stand up. He said, "Today we have people from forty-three countries. Now, when you are standing up, you are a citizen of your country, but after the vow and when you sit down, you will be an American citizen."

A few people cheered a little. "Please remember that America is an immigrant country. There is not an American way. Instead, please bring the best of your culture into this country to make us the best country in the world."

Bring the best of each culture to make America the best country in the world. That thought shocked me.

For so long, I had been busy running away from the culture and the country that brought me up. In that culture, being gay was not an option, and raising a gay family was not imaginable. In that culture, studying, getting a good job, and following what everybody else was doing was the norm. In that culture, it was believed that people were cheap, not honest, and would trick their own kind. When I first moved to the US, I heard the advice, "Never go to a car repair service run by a Chinese person. They will trick you."

I had been so busy fleeing Chinese culture, I forgot that it was *my* culture. I forgot all the good things that came from the culture. I forgot that parents sacrificed almost everything for their kids. I forgot that we took pride in hard work. I forgot that the studying I once hated gave me everything I had today, from a great education and great job experiences, to the ability to learn, judge right from wrong, and admit when I wasn't correct. I was so busy crossing the bridge from the Bund to Lujiazui that I forgot to treasure what made me and what's inside of me.

An old Chinese saying is, "Bu zhi lu shan zhen mian mu, zhi yuan shen zai ci shan zhong," which means, "You could not see the real Lu Mountain because you are in the mountain."

Now, I was living in America, a country that allowed me to live my true self, and I saw all the great things about my Chinese culture. The studying hard and never-give-up spirit that got me a job when the economy was melting down in 2009. The traditional family values that pushed me to focus on a relationship instead of just sex when I came out. The courage and willingness to sacrifice for my kids and to leave the stable Microsoft job to start an uncertain career journey. And all the love that my parents had shown toward me and toward Phoebe, Hanalei, and Chelsie.

Growing up, I never heard Mom and Dad mention the word "love." They didn't say that to each other and never to me, although I never doubted their love for me. Now, in America, maybe because they heard Bryan and I saying "love" to each other and to the girls, they started to say, "I love you," to the girls. Mom even said that to me from time to time. I didn't know what to say when I heard that. But I was excited to see Mom and Dad also evolving as they brought their best selves into the American culture.

With all the detailed care from Mom and Dad, Hanalei and Chelsie reached the ninetieth percentile on weight at their three-month checkup. Dr. Manfred didn't doubt the effect of Mom and Dad's love on the weight gain but was still impressed.

"They are bigger than Phoebe when she was three months old." I translated what Dr. Manfred said to Mom and Dad. They gave out bigger smiles of accomplishment and happiness on their faces this time.

* * *

HANALEI AND CHELSIE changed from the transparent-skin babies whose veins we could see, to the normal babies you see in photos. Their features started to develop as well. Hanalei had a big head – a huge head. Her weight was actually in the 99th percentile. We believed most of it was her head. Her hair was blond to light brown. It was short, but we could see some curl happening. I loved touching her short hair. It was just like Bryan's, so fine and soft.

Her forehead was unmistakably Bryan's and Bryan's dad Bill's – wide and long. In China, we always said that people with big foreheads were meant to have great and fortunate lives. I sure hope so for Hanalei. Her eyes were undoubtedly big with long, curly lashes. Love it!

Her two big teeth had a gap between them. Bryan said he and his siblings all grew up with teeth like that. We started calling Chelsie "Sisi." With the gap in her teeth, Hanalei said, "Thii-thii." It was like me, who could not pronounce the difference between "si" and "thi," but for a different reason. I was happy about the similarity I shared with Hanalei.

Hanalei was the best behaved among her sisters. She was independent and could sit in her high chair to eat an entire dinner without any help from us. She grabbed a few pieces of rice or noodle and put them in her mouth and moved onto the next bite. She loved eating all vegetables. Broccoli, green beans, green pepper, and even onion! All of them!

She also loved reading. Unlike Phoebe, who cried when I read, Hanalei loved picking out a book, walking to me, and sitting on my lap to ask me to read it to her. We could sit there for half an hour just reading books.

When she started talking, she pointed at everything in the book. "What's thaaat?" she repeated and repeated until I needed some water.

Hanalei loved listening to our singing and music. Her sisters loved dancing to music, but she usually just tilted her head and soaked herself in the sound. From time to time, she would let out a high-pitched note that none of us could match, including Bryan, who could sing the highest note of Whitney's "I Will Always Love You."

Her high-pitched, short cry sometimes created a little competition among her sisters. They all let out a two-second "Ah..." like a singer warming up her vocal cords for her Grammy performance. Hanalei always won with the highest and most piercing voice.

Hanalei was very sensitive. She was a few inches taller than Chelsie. But she didn't fight for herself. When Chelsie took anything away from her, she would just sit there and give the loudest possible cry.

As with Jack, we couldn't say anything harsh to Hanalei. When it was Hanalei's turn to steal a toy away from her sisters and we said a firm "no" with a frown, she would turn around, not look at us, put her head down on the floor with her butt going back and up like child's pose in yoga, and start sobbing. Comforting her from that "trauma" took at least ten minutes. This not only made us struggle with how to teach Hanalei, but also made us question our assumptions that Jack was abused before.

Chelsie didn't share genes with Hanalei but did with Phoebe. This was clear from the beginning. The long, dark hair, dark eyes, and darker skin. When we took Hanalei and Chelsie out walking, seeing people's responses was simply the best.

When they first spotted two similar-size babies, they always started with, "Twins!" But when they took a closer look, their faces became a little puzzled and their voices turned up with a big question mark: "Twins?"

At first, I always tried to explain the situation of sperm from Bryan and me and different egg donors and a surrogate. After seeing even more confused faces, Bryan and I agreed to just smile and respond, "Yes," to puzzled looks. After having three daughters, I learned to simply accept rather than change the subject or tell the truth.

Chelsie was so little when she was born. Less than four pounds. I could hold her entire body with one hand. Maybe that's why she was the champion of milk drinking and food eating after the first month. She always ate more and more frequently. Soon she weighed more than Hanalei even with her shorter body.

Chelsie was very agile. She started walking when she was eleven months. Taking into account her early birth, that's equivalent to nine months. She had barely been walking for a few days when she started running. We were stunned. She ran with her legs wide, one going in front of the other, not in a synchronized fashion. She fell to the floor, looked up with a big smile, pulled herself up, and started running again. "She is a little Simone Biles," we told ourselves when seeing her start to split her legs on the floor.

Chelsie was an entertainer. She never ceased to amaze us with the stunts or performances she put on. She rolled from the couch to the floor and landed perfectly in a seated position, did downward dog with me side by side, and learned the full dance routine of "Head, Shoulders, Knees, and Toes" even before Phoebe. And she did "Yi Ya Yi Ya Yo" non-stop once she heard "Old MacDonald Had a Farm." She slipped "Yi Ya Yi Ya Yo" perfectly into the grocery checkout line, at a random stranger walking down the road, or during a brief silence at dinner time. We always laughed and started singing the song with her.

"Chelsie is a fighter!" we told ourselves from day one when she was having so much trouble trying to breathe. Now, she was a real fighter, an always giggling fighter. She never stopped smiling except when she was crying. It was like there was no stage between happiness and sadness.

The shortest among her sisters, she was never scared of going for what she wanted. She grabbed whatever she wanted from her sisters. She giggled as she reached out her hand to a stuffed animal that Hanalei was playing with and started pulling it away. Hanalei would not let it go. Chelsie kept pulling, turning her body, and dragging the whole scene from one end of the room to the other. By then, Hanalei was already protesting with her loudest cry possible, but Chelsie was still giggling. Until I went up to give a firm "no" to Chelsie, telling her this was a toy Hanalei was playing with and she could have another toy – then she started crying. The crying soon stopped when she was distracted from the song by the big-eared elephant.

More than fifty percent of the time, Chelsie was the one to start stealing toys from her sisters, but Phoebe and Hanalei had their share of guilt. Since Hanalei was not good at fighting and not very mobile, she used everything possible, including her two big gappy teeth. Those bites made Chelsie cry the most, but they were effective. Hanalei always could hold onto her toys in the end.

Growing up as an only kid, I never understood the full extent of sibling relationships, especially the fighting and competition. What I was told before about siblings fighting was real, especially when they were less than two years apart.

I didn't know how to handle the fighting. "Fight back!" I would say to Hanalei. Bryan always looked at me in disbelief and turned to the girls. "Give your sister a hug! Stop! Give your sister a hug!" His voice was firm and gentle. We could only use love to disarm the fighting situation, he told me.

Phoebe was nineteen months older than the twins. She didn't fully understand the role of a big sister. As Hanalei and Chelsie grew, so did Phoebe's understanding of the situation, and her jealousy and love for her sisters. "No cry... no cry..." she tried to comfort her sisters when they cried, especially when Bryan and I were holding a crying one and Phoebe was on the side. She would pat the baby's head gently and ask her not to cry.

Phoebe also volunteered in the diaper-changing routine. She always insisted on pulling her sister's diaper down and starting to wipe. It was all right when it was pee, but when it was solid, an extra thirty minutes of cleaning was inevitable.

Later, Phoebe understood that she was the older one. She also enjoyed seniority. She loved to call, "Come on, Leilei and Sisi," when she decided to play with the train set in the family room, or when she pushed her sisters into the bouncy house with 1,800 balls in Chelsie's future bedroom, or washed Hanalei's and Chelsie's hair in the tub. But her favorite was yelling at her sisters when they were playing with toilet bowl water. "Oh, no! No, no! Oh, my goodness!" Phoebe's voice turned so dramatic and high-pitched, like she was rehearsing a Broadway musical.

Phoebe also realized that she was getting less attention and love. At first, Phoebe would cry and still insist on me holding her if she saw me holding Hanalei or Chelsie. She later learned running to Bryan or Mom and Dad for love was easier.

She never wanted to share her Oreo cookie or Melissa & Doug's coloring book, but after six months of non-stop asking from us, she finally was all right with occasional sharing. She would get a little bit upset, but she was excited with the other thing we'd give her as she was sharing with her sisters.

Phoebe also learned to take advantage of her sisters. Actually, both she and Hanalei learned that. Somehow, they learned that Chelsie was always the troublemaker. Whenever they did something wrong, Phoebe would say, "Chelsie!" with an up-and-down blaming tone, while Hanalei would squeeze out, "Thiii...Thiii..." pointing at the milk she had just spilled.

* * *

RAISING THE THREE growing girls, Bryan and I were walking a fine line regarding work/life balance. I had quit my secure job at Microsoft to be with the kids more. But the financial pressure of raising them always pushed me to work harder – sell one more house and take on one more management client.

In late summer 2018, one and a half years after starting the property management business, we managed more than 250 properties that were worth a collective $200 million.

The trust from owners and occasional drama from tenants added so much pressure to our mental health and stretched our physical limits so much, I started hot yoga practice at Fusion Hot Yoga at noon every day.

Seeing my own sweat forming puddles on the floor near my Yogitoes towel, I felt relaxed, reflective, and myself. Bryan also started getting up at five o'clock in the morning to do his P90X routine and then go to a 7:00 am AA meeting.

However, spending time with the girls was our true sanctuary. Every morning before going to work, Bryan and I would play with all three girls for at least half an hour. Looking at them running to the blackboard to fight and grab for the letter *A* that I had just yelled out, seeing that Chelsie won – no surprise – and watching them rush back to my arms with a big smile was the best way to start the day.

After dinner, Bryan would announce loudly, "Who wants to go grocery shopping?" All three of them would stop what they were doing and rush to us. Phoebe tried to put her shoes on. Just like how she did it yesterday, left was right, right was left. Hanalei was just standing at the door and pointing at the handle to open it. Chelsie started climbing Bryan's leg.

"Who wants to go in the runner stroller?" Bryan picked up Chelsie and put her in the running stroller. Phoebe and Hanalei were already crawling into the double stroller that Dad bought at Goodwill. "We will be back in two hours," I yelled at the top of my lungs to make sure Mom could hear me.

I fell in love with Seattle and with the Pacific Northwest when I first moved here. But every summer evening, when we were walking with the girls, I fell in love a little more.

At 7:00 p.m. on a summer day, the sun was still high in the sky. Sunshine wandered through the big fir trees and warmed my face. The breeze was always a little bit chilly. I zipped up my Patagonia jacket that Bryan bought for me for Christmas last year. This had been my jacket every single day for a year already. I still never bothered dressing up. Bryan was still in his Good Fellow shorts and tank tops that we got from Target last week. They looked good on him. We looked like one of us was living in summer and one in winter.

"Want to go to the playground?" Bryan asked the girls.

"Yeah!" Phoebe was excited. I was thinking about some work that I need to finish, but I tried to push that thought away. *I will get it done later. For now, playground it is!* I had learned not to make all the decisions in life and let the happiness of my family take precedence. I was pushing the double stroller with Phoebe and Hanalei. The $20 stroller from Goodwill turned out to be a good investment.

"What's thaaat? What's thaaat?" Hanalei was pointing at everything on the road and asking non-stop.

Phoebe was trying her best to answer, "Cowcow. Mooo..."

"That's a horse," I corrected her. Maybe because of the sound of moo, Phoebe loved saying the word cowcow. "What does the horsie say?"

"Neigh... Neigh..."

"Good job!" Bryan gave out a big cheer.

Twenty minutes later, we arrived at the downtown Bothell Park right by the Sammamish River. There were not too many people there today. After seeing some swimming duck families and grass-eating rabbits, we headed straight to the playground. Phoebe jumped out of the stroller and ran directly to the slides. Bryan chased after her.

I took Hanalei and Chelsie to swing. They love swinging. When they were swinging to me, I put my head to theirs and gave out a big "muuuah!" As they swung back, they couldn't stop giggling. Those were the most beautiful sounds in the world. I laughed with them.

On the way home, Bryan and I switched. It was my turn to push our lovely monkey Chelsie.

We loved shopping at QFC just down the hill from our house. They had delicious free cookies every night. Phoebe loved the pink ones with rainbow-colored frosting the most.

People there always made us feel welcome. They never acted surprised or had weird looks in their eyes when they saw two dads with their three girls. They never asked, "Where are they from? Where is their mother?" but just handed out the "future QFC shopper" stickers at the checkout line. I enjoyed the moment of just being able to be me, being able to be us.

Pushing the girls and groceries back home was a challenge. The hill was at least 150 yards long and a thirty-degree angle. Bryan and I tried to rush to see who could push faster and reach the corner of our house first. Since we had two watermelons in the stroller today, we decided to take it easy. *We should buy watermelon every day*, I thought.

It was almost 9:00 p.m. when we got home. It was still bright outside. I sat down in the living room, while Bryan took the girls upstairs to go crazy in the bouncy house. *Where was their – including Bryan's – energy coming from?*

Mom brought me a cup of ginger tea. "There is some brown sugar in it. It's getting chilly in the evening. Drink it. It's good for you." The green cards Mom and Dad received in late 2018 set them free from missing the girls so much and gave them a permanent home here with us.

I took a sip. It was hot, a little bit sweet, a little bit harsh and gingery. Just like what I had after every summer storm in Guangzhou.

"It tastes good!" I gave Mom a compliment, which I should have done much more often. Mom was already devoting so much time to the girls but still seemed to have endless love to spread.

"How was your day?" Mom asked.

My mind quickly scanned the day, the plan for two more properties that we were taking on, the listing plan for an almost new $1.4 million Murray Franklin house, the explosive water heater in a house in north Seattle, and one lease broken because of domestic violence.

"It was good." I hesitated a little bit. "Mom, how do you do all this? Take care of Hanalei and Chelsie during the day, go grocery shopping at 99 Ranch Market, take your English class at the library, cook dinner, and now make this delicious ginger tea?"

Mom blushed a little. She was not expecting this compliment. She gave out a gentle smile. "I don't know..."

"I wish I could be like you." I took one more sip of the tea. "I sometimes worry that I'm not doing enough for the girls. I've been so buried in work recently."

Mom sat down next to me. "The girls are lucky to have you and Bryan as their dads."

I was a little surprised. For so long, I thought we were the lucky ones. In the Men Having Babies Facebook group, people shared every day that they had tried surrogacy so many times but weren't successful. My heart always hurt a little when I read those posts, but also felt fuller and realized how lucky we were. But now, Mom said the girls were the lucky ones?

"The girls have two amazing, imperfect and perfect dads, who have been through so much struggling to realize who they are, who are open-minded, who are strong enough to follow love and courage, who love their girls so much, who give up so much for their daughters." Mom choked up a little bit. "Your dad and I are inspired by you two. We wish we were so ready and mature as you when we had you..."

I extended my arms and held Mom tightly while trying to hold back the tears in my eyes. "Thank you," I said. "Now I am going to join Bryan and the girls in the bouncy house!" Trying to lift up my spirits, I took off and ran upstairs, to my love, trouble, and future.

3:30 P.M., DEC. 2018, SEATTLE

I packed up my MacBook into my REI backpack, the one that Bryan gave me as a gift at our first Christmas together back in 2010. The left shoulder belt had broken four years ago, and I just tied it back together. It was something to keep, not throw away.

Leaving my office, I saw a "Made in Washington" gift basket on the table. "Who is it from?" I had searched inside of the entire box but could not find a card. Secret Santa. "I need to spread the love this year too," I told myself.

Once outside the office, I ran to my car. It was a typical winter day in Seattle – the clouds, the rain, the crisp air, and dark at four o'clock in the afternoon. I started driving to Phoebe's school. On the drive, several phone calls came in. I was busy this week. In two years, we had grown to manage over 250 properties. To thank the property management team for all the great work, Bryan and I asked everybody to take the week off to spend time with their family. That meant Bryan and I were super busy.

My previous manager Jill at Microsoft mentioned to me that every time I took a vacation, she needed to do some of my work. That work grounded her, making her realize my work wasn't easy. This in turn made her appreciate me more. At the time, what she said just made me feel good. But now, I deeply understood it. Working on a detailed application process or a maintenance request for a broken furnace made me realize how much I appreciated my team's work.

* * *

A CRAZY SCHEDULE at work kept me on my toes. What made me excited and fired up was inside. Bryan and I had gone to the Best Year Ever event in San Diego the week before. Jon and Hal had hosted the event. Hal is the *Miracle Morning* guy.

I have been practicing Miracle Morning on and off for over three years now, and it has changed my life. I need to get up super-early, like 5:00 a.m., and practice six rituals – exercise, meditation, reading, visualization, confirmation, and scribing (journaling). Each ritual could be two minutes or ten minutes. The key is to start the day in the best way possible, so the rest of the day will follow on autopilot.

Many mornings, I did not do all six rituals. However, this practice was how I visualized what kind of life I wanted to have, how I saw the problems I have with Dad, and how I decided to quit my secure job at Microsoft when our surrogate was pregnant with twins Hanalei and Chelsie.

On the way down to San Diego, I was in the throes of a horrendous stomach flu, which kept me tethered to the bathroom with stomach pains and frequent vomiting. It had started with Phoebe a week prior then made its way through our family – from Hanalei to Chelsie to Bryan to me. Needless to say, I felt awful at the event. The feeling reminded me of Machu Picchu, right before my four-day hike. Thank God I didn't need to get up at 4:00 a.m. to hike eight thousand feet in altitude in eight hours.

Dr. Stephenson gave the event's keynote address. At forty years old, he was the same height as Phoebe, and his arms and

269

legs were even thinner than hers. He'd been born with a genetic disorder, and doctors had predicted that he'd only live a couple of days.

He proved them wrong and went on to become an internationally famous motivational speaker and coach. His talks were not the touchy-feely kind; they were funny and speedy, and they got people fired up.

"Don't be sorry for me," he often said. "You can't dance as well as me." Then he'd start shaking his diminutive body and continue, "I chose this body. Without this body, I would not be able to stand here in front of you. It is my calling to help each of you become a better version of you."

"I chose this body. I chose this body." That sentence was stuck in my mind for the whole day. What a spirit to take control of life!

In the afternoon, right before the day ended, Jon led the five hundred attendees in a visualization exercise – one of the Miracle Morning rituals. It's about visualizing what we want so vividly, in such detail, that those things become a reality in the future. "Your wish is my command." It's the same premise as Rhonda Byrne's book and DVD *The Secret*.

With everybody else, I closed my eyes and let my thoughts blossom. I saw myself on a train from Paris to Munich with Bryan and the girls, sitting in a street vendor's chair in Penang, Malaysia, and sailing from Sydney Harbor to New Zealand. Ever since we welcomed Phoebe into the world, I'd been pinning destinations on a world map on my office wall. I smiled, envisioning the happy faces of the girls on those imaginary trips.

In my meditative state, I also saw the forty-story glass building that I would own and manage in downtown Seattle; I visited our location in San Diego, listening to their feedback and sharing the latest trends in property management; I saw Bryan working blissfully on the cabin on Camano Island that we just purchased and the girls gleefully picking up shells and starfish on the beach.

Those were familiar scenarios that I captured in my mind again and again every day. But I kept searching – there was something missing.

"I chose this body." Dr. Stephenson's words suddenly popped back into my mind. For so long, I wanted to be straight, wanted to be "normal," and I wanted to fit in. "Did I choose to be gay?" I asked myself.

I thought about the TED video Bryan had sent me two weeks ago. Dr. James O'Keefe drew insights from his own experience with his gay son and used scientific research to show why gayness was not about sex, but a strategy for survival.

He told us why we *need* gays in the world, and why mothers turned on the gay gene during pregnancy. He argued that gays had higher EQ in general and are more understanding and less confrontational. He believed that gay people were put on this planet to make the world a better place. His talk made me smile and feel good about myself.

Ever since I became openly gay, I have been researching the science of being gay and searching my memories related to gayness. I realized that it was not Zhang's hand in middle school that turned me gay. From my earliest childhood, I loved playing with beads and making bracelets. I loved hanging out with girls, not because I was attracted to them, but because I felt more comfortable with them and didn't have the pressure of being with guys for whom I had some interesting feelings. I just used Zhang's hand as an excuse because I was not brave or wise enough to know and accept who I was.

I was sure that I chose to be gay and my mom turned on the gay gene when I was in her belly. These thoughts excited me, fired me up.

I realized that the reason *empathy* is my number one strength, no matter what tests I take, is because being gay empowers me to go through the journey from denial, doubt, fear, and hopelessness to acceptance, courage, and love. I always try to see things from other people's perspectives, to understand their unique challenges and problems, and to give them patience and understanding. Empathy has helped me tremendously in both my personal life and professional career.

I also recalled Andrew Solomon's TED talk: *How the Worst Moments in Our Lives Make Us Who We Are.* I saw myself running in Woodward Park in Fresno in the morning when Hanalei and Chelsie were still staying in the NICU. Listening to Andrew's talk, I was crying with excitement. I listened to the talk again the next day, the next day, and the next day.

The gay activist Harvey Milk was once asked by a younger gay man what he could do to help the movement, and Harvey Milk said, "Go out and tell someone." There's always somebody who wants to confiscate our humanity. And there are always stories that restore it. If we live out loud, we can trounce the hatred, and expand everyone's lives.

He told his story to pass down hope, to infuse inspiration, and to make the world a better place. Although my story was nothing compared to his, maybe I had a story to tell?

I chose to be gay. The thought excited me – fired me up. At dinner that night after the Best Year Ever event, I shared my thoughts with Bryan. We were at a little restaurant on the water in San Diego's downtown park. It was a warm and humid night, but lovely. As excited as I was by the idea of writing a book to tell my story, I knew Bryan was a private person, so I was a bit apprehensive about how he would feel making our personal life public. Much to my relief, Bryan was 150 percent onboard.

"You should totally write a book!" he exclaimed. "Even if it helps just one person, it's worth it." Honestly, I was a bit surprised by his reaction, but I guess I shouldn't have been, given how supportive he always is.

On the way back from San Diego, I started my book-writing adventure. I had never written a book before; English is not my first language. It doesn't matter. I just needed to tell my little story, with the hope that it can help people and encourage somebody else to tell their story. Isn't that how humans have been passing down love and courage through generations for thousands of years?

Every day, I woke up at 5:30 a.m. – yes, the quiet time before girls are up – to collect my thoughts, dig through memories, and put my life puzzles together. I always admired those people who don't need alarm clocks to get up early in the morning. Now I'm one of them. I can't wait to get up every day. Sometimes I even get up at 4:30 a.m. for no reason other than a passionate heart.

One morning, Bryan brought a cup of coffee to my office after his exercise routine. I was sitting in front of my computer and sobbing.

"Are you okay?"

"Yes, I am. These are happy tears. I am so happy and feeling full." I paused and sipped the coffee Bryan just brought in.

"You know that for so long, I hated my childhood, my Chinese education, all the Communist politics that I needed to recite and write down on the exams. The pressure from my parents. The pressure from my peers and from society. I didn't even have a chance to understand I am gay, nor an option to be gay."

I was so excited. "But you know what? It was because of the education system that I developed the habit of working hard. Because there was no option to be gay in China, I traveled all the way across the Pacific Ocean and found you. I remember how much my parents sacrificed for me, and now we are doing the same for our girls."

Bryan leaned over and gave me a kiss. I couldn't stop letting my thoughts out. "I also realized that life isn't linear. You know the Gio Armani cologne that I used to buy and like to wear? For so long, I forgot why I like the smell. It wasn't until I started writing the book and digging through the memories that I realized it was from Tom, the first gay guy I met back in college!"

Life was like connecting dots, as Steve Jobs said. It is also like making wine. When you are mixing the grapes and the yeast, you don't smell or taste the result. It is only after years of seasoning, when you open the bottle, that you enjoy the smell and the taste in a way that wasn't possible before. Sometimes in life, we are not aware that we are making the best wine ever, the wine of our true self, the wine of our life.

* * *

I ARRIVED AT Phoebe's school. It was already dark outside. The Christmas lights on the building were beautiful. Phoebe had been going to this daycare for eight months now.

We very much wanted Phoebe to learn Chinese. At home, Bryan and I talked English to Phoebe, and although she understood Chinese, Phoebe refused to speak it. So we switched her from the local American daycare to this home daycare run by an older Chinese couple.

"Baba... Baba..." Phoebe ran to me after I opened the door. She must have been waiting for me for a while now.

"How's your day, Phoebe?" No response. She just kept smiling at me and holding my neck really tight. "I love you, girl." I smiled back. On the way home, I continued to try to talk to Phoebe. I talked about my day, the troubles at work, the surprising Made in Washington gift basket. Phoebe was not talking at all. I was used to it.

I used to love the image of kids talking about their days to their parents on the way home. That was the Hollywood movie version of childhood. I used to be jealous of my friends' kids who were younger than Phoebe and would have meaningful conversations with their parents. That worry and jealousy disappeared one day when Mom said, "Just let them be; they will be fine. Just love them as they are." She must understand that deeply because having her whole life and belief system shaped by the Communist party, she accepted her only son being gay.

Phoebe opened the front door as we arrived at home. "Wow, Christmas tree!" She yelled in a language that only she and Hanalei and Chelsie could fully understand. Bryan had surprised us with a huge Christmas tree. Because of our busy schedule, we had decided to have a Christmas tree only at the island cabin this year. I knew all of us were regretting the decision because we still spent most of the time at home. We just never said anything so we were not adding too much to our already overflowing plates.

Bryan was the one who always noticed and sacrificed. "Let's decorate the tree tonight! Do you want to help, Phoebe?" He raised Phoebe into the air as she ran toward him.

"Yes!" Phoebe decided when she wanted to talk.

We all crowded around the Christmas tree. Bryan moved the decoration boxes one by one from the garage. "We will go rainbow color this year," Bryan said.

"Rainbow," Phoebe repeated and yelled. Hanalei and Chelsie didn't fully understand what Christmas was about yet. Mom and Dad were keeping them entertained.

"My ex-girlfriend and I made this together in 2005." Bryan brought up a clear ornament with some sparkling stuff inside. I took over and hung it on a branch on the right side of the tree.

"Do you remember this sea turtle one from Cabo? The sex adventure of our egg donors almost made us lose hope." Bryan smiled and handed me the green turtle made of clay.

"This one was when Phoebe was born." I picked up the white cube that we got in December 2015.

"And this one – could you believe how little they were when they were born?" Bryan handed me the one with Hanalei's and Chelsie's photos when they were born.

"What's this one about again?" Bryan unwrapped the glass ornament with a yellow ladybug on it.

"It was from Mom. She gave me it when she visited us in 2011." I thought about that Christmas, my first Christmas with Bryan and my parents, the first Christmas I was honest with them. She surprised me with the yellow ladybug.

Remember you have a piece of the sun in you. Even when it is dark, you can light up yourself and around yourself.

"Let me put it up." I took over the ladybug ornament and put it on the tree.

We never celebrated Christmas in China. But now I liked the holiday. Just like Chinese New Year, it is about family spending time together. Stuffing ourselves with delicious food. Telling stories and re-living memories. Loving each other.

It was Bryan's turn to put Phoebe to sleep while my parents took care of the twins. I made a cup of chrysanthemum tea and sat in front of my desk.

My head was fired up with the thoughts and ideas of my past, and my heart was full of emotion. *I was born gay and I chose to be gay.* I was sure about that. That thought gave me a weird sense of confidence that wiped out my fear and shame.

I was scared of sharing about my deskmate Zhang touching me in middle school, my nights with Tom from Vancouver in college, and my sexual exploration after I moved to Seattle. I used to be so ashamed of most of those experiences. They collided with the values I grew up with. I felt terrible that I hadn't even had the courage to talk to my ex-girlfriend, Meimei, to simply say sorry to her after all these years.

But I also thought about my first ever coming out to Ally in De Kas in Amsterdam. The unconditional support she gave me then, and now. She came to Seattle earlier this year to buy a house from Bryan and me. I thought about my mom and dad changing from never wanting to come to Seattle to being part of our new family here now. I thought about the commitment Bryan and I made to each other and made to the girls the first time we saw them.

I played Andrew's TED talk again. "Go out and tell someone. There's always somebody who wants to confiscate our humanity. And there are always stories that restore it. If we live out loud, we can trounce the hatred, and expand everyone's lives."

Maybe, just maybe my story could help somebody who is struggling with their sexuality because of their parents, or society, or religion. When all pointers are telling them that being gay isn't an option, they need to know there's hope if they have courage and love. Maybe it could help somebody who is giving up hope in finding a life partner because it seems that everybody is just interested in sex. Or somebody who is trying to create a family through creative avenues, such as surrogacy, or has some hiccups in their current journey.

And then I realized that maybe it is for more than the LGBT community. I realized that it is about breaking all the constraints and limits we set for ourselves, no matter what culture, what religion, what sexuality, what age, and what race we are. It's about following your gut and your heart when the whole world seems to doubt you. It is about keeping your head up when everything is going against your plan. It is about stepping out of the bubble of "something is not an option" and telling yourself it is possible.

It made me think about the first time I took off my shirt in hot yoga practice to let go of the insecurity about my belly fat, to let the sweat flow and fully enjoy hot yoga. Since I started practicing hot yoga months ago, I have changed so much. I learned to love who I am. I learned that sometimes you just need to focus on breathing out and the inhale will happen automatically. I learned that happiness is not a what, but a how.

I realized how lucky I am to be gay. It gave me an opportunity to face the limits I set for myself beyond sexuality. It gave me a chance to practice being strong and true to myself. It infused me with courage and love.

I also realized how tiny I am in this universe. As Deepak Chopra said, a lifetime is just a glimpse in the universe. My story is just a drop in the vast ocean of human history.

There is an old Chinese saying: "Pao zhuan yin yu." It means to "throw a stone to attract a jade." I humbly wish that by telling my story of a stone, there might be more people sharing their stories of the jade.

Go out and tell someone. If we live out loud, we can trounce the hatred and expand everyone's lives.

LETTER TO PARENTS (给父母的信)

妈妈爸爸，

你们好。听说湖南家里装了暖气。爷爷奶奶终于能过上个温暖的冬天了。我还记得小时候烧煤的炉子，我总是躲在边上烤火。有时候还会把雪花冰块放到炉子上，听到滋滋的雪融声，那股味道犹如在昨天。

妈妈一直说我是一个只报喜不报忧的人。呵呵，我也一直是这样认为。我们家里的人都是在这样的氛围文化下长大的—让周围你爱和爱你的人开心，分享快乐，痛苦和不好的事情，那就自己承担吧。

我自认为是一个非常听话的孩子。小时候妈妈说学习重要，那么我就认真的学习，放弃其他的事情，专心的投入到学习-考试-**学习**-考试中。记得小时候快乐的事情就是每周五晚上骑车去岛内价买果冻吃。简单的快乐让我度过了很多枯燥的学习日子。现在回想起来，真的非常感谢"认真学习"的**决定，看看周**围的人，我发现教育给我提供的平台是很多人达不到的。每当我在世界各地旅行的途中，我就会想起父母对我的影响。

但是单调的学习生活也让我在很多方面的发展不够成熟。在初三的时候，我非常喜欢一个女生，但是由于感觉到学习的压力，我却一直没有勇气跟她表白。我们每天一起相处，但已"师傅-徒弟"相称。**我知道早恋会影响学习**，就像潘多拉的魔盒一样，**一发不可收拾，我也就完全不敢触碰**。

但是这样的约束也在无形之中慢慢的改变我。不知什么时候起，我在和男生相处的时候感觉非常舒服，没有压力感，没有负罪感。渐渐的，我发现自己开始喜欢男生。这是一种莫名奇妙的感觉，我也无法描述，但是我感觉开心。

在**大学**毕业后，我交了第一个正式的女朋友-美美（化名）。我完全不知道**什么叫**爱一个人，但是找个爱自己的女朋友是一个大家都认为正确的事情。我们在一起也开心了一段时间，但我知道自己并不真正的爱她。我在一个特殊变革时代的中国长大-陈旧的观念和西方开发的思想冲突，加上金钱的无限追求和思想意识落后的鲜明对比。很多时候，做大家认为正确的事情，就是正确的事情。这一直是我的生活准则。

但真的是这样吗？

以前我一直都不敢面对"同性恋"这个词。似乎这是一个罪恶，是一种羞耻，是不可饶恕的事情。但在这几年在海外的生活让我认识到故事的另外一面。

在麦肯锡工作我发现了一个男同事，他在麦肯锡做了很多年，然后和他的男朋友一起在 2010 去哈佛和麻省理工读 MBA。在 Duke，学校有各种支持同性恋，女性，和黑人的组织。在美国，支持同性恋的组织都叫 PRIDE。中文翻译成为"骄傲"。在微软，有同性恋的社团，我们的福利还专门的包涵同性伴侣的福利。当我逐渐了解故事的另外一面后，我发现这没人什么可怕的，我也可以更好的认识自己-到底更喜欢女生还是男生，在追求什么样的生活。

我现在有一个男朋友，他的名字叫 Bryan。我们认识了几个月左右。他是我的第一个男朋友。我想你们来西雅图的时候会想见到他。

我知道这对你们来说肯定是一个打击。你们一直在提我的女朋友，结婚，或者孙子孙女之类的话题。我写这封email 并不想伤害你们。而我更想让你们认识一个真实的何瑜。报喜不报忧，我想在这里停止。

人生追求的是什么，就是让自己快乐，让爱自己的人和自己爱的人开心。爸爸妈妈，你们是我生活当中最重要的人，我希望你们能开心和幸福。但是我不能妥协自己的快乐，而去创造一个虚假的幸福世界。以前的我在同性恋问题上有过很多的挣扎和痛苦，现在的我，无比的清楚和快乐。真正的成功的人，是那些能面对自己，面对现实，并且能从柠檬中挤出柠檬汁，并且笑着品尝的人。我希望成为那样的人。

我在过去的几个月当中，已经将我的故事告诉了最好的朋友邓彦。她都给了我很多无限的支持。这让我觉得非常的开心。可是年龄，文化和教育的背景差异使得将这一切告诉你们成为了我最担心的事情。我知道你们在传统的中国文化中长大，未必能接受这个消息。但我也怀着希望，随着你们对美国认识的不断增强，你们应该能够逐渐接受并且意识到这并不是一个违背道德常规和让人感到羞耻的丑事，而是一个让敢于面对自己的人快乐并且真正发现自己的价值和幸福的旅途。我还是那个我，并没有因为同性恋而改变什么。

我对你们没有任何的要求，只是希望你们不要跟奶奶和爷爷说这件事情。他们年纪大了，不需要受到额外的惊喜。所以，也希望你们不要跟燕子说。她跟爷爷奶奶生活在一起，说漏嘴时很可能的事情。我也理解你们无法将这些倾诉于同事，朋友。所以，张鑫可能能够成为你们的倾诉对象。我和张鑫讨论如何跟你们沟通能最小的降低对你们的打击。张鑫在上学期中接触了很多这类事情的培训，他可以和你们聊聊。

当然，你们的儿子我，更愿意跟你们谈谈。如果你们需要时间，我明白。我只想让你们知道，我永远的爱着你们。

童童

2011 年 1 月 5 号

ACKNOWLEDGMENTS

Growing up, I was never good at writing. My middle school Chinese teacher used to say that my essay writing was too simple and too naive. Writing in English created another level of difficulty. I have only a couple of words for each action, feeling, and object, and I am jealous how a good native writer can use a bag of magic words to make their stories vivid, alive, and sophisticated.

Writing a book like this was my wildest dream. The journey of creating it itself is a journey of love and courage. I owe endless gratitude to everybody who has helped me through the process.

I want to thank Hal and Jon's Best Year Ever event. Going into the event with some doubts, although I had been practicing Miracle Morning for a few years, I left with a heart full and mind on fire. It helped me dig deeper and decide to tell my stories. Digging through memories and reliving episodes of my life that I chose to forget was a shockingly healing process. I felt stronger, more loved, and better connected to my family and to myself afterward.

I want to thank my amazing editor, Margaret Diehl. I am so glad that I got connected to her on Reedsy. The matchmaking process erased some of my painful memories with Match.com :). Seriously, though, she is beyond wonderful. She is always calm, honest, candid, thoughtful, collaborative, and efficient.

She looked over all my grammar problems and helped me identify the holes in the book. Without her advice, the two chapters "Becoming Dads" and "Two Dads and Three Girls" wouldn't even exist. She helped me realize that telling the stories of two young gay dads is as important as sharing the struggles and hard work to get there. Writing down all the little moments with Phoebe, Hanalei, and Chelsie also pushed me to a higher level of gratitude for them, and a realization of how lucky Bryan and I are to call them our daughters.

I really appreciate how much Margaret respected my voice and way of telling stories and edited with so much thoughtfulness. She helped me to build an identity for the book, which is unmistakably my identity that sometimes I lost in the process of finding similarity and harmony with others and the world.

I want to thank everybody at Self-Publishing School. The course provides a thirty-thousand-foot view of the writing-to-publishing process, and more importantly, made it seem doable to my doubtful mind. I want to thank Scott Allen for being my coach and walking me through every step of the process of creating this book.

I want to thank Men Having Babies and CRN (China Rainbow Network) for helping all LGBT people to be themselves and build families. The positive energy you created, the platform you established, and the stories you told are shaping this world into a better place.

I want to thank Chelsie and her family for giving us the joy and purpose of our life. You are a dreamer, a fighter, and an example of the kind of parent Bryan and I dream of being. We are honored to have you in our lives, and you always have a home in Seattle.

I want to thank my manager Jill at Microsoft. She not only taught me how to work productively and effectively, but also demonstrated a true leader who can balance work and life.

I want to thank all my friends Denise, Elynn, Joe, Batu, Lixia, who have been part of my life journey. I want to give especial thanks to Ally and Echo, who have been an inspiration to me and shown me what it means not just to be alive, but living. I am forever indebted to the role model you provided so I can look up and smile when I'm facing my worst moments.

I want to thank my family. Thank you, Mom and Dad, for never giving up on me and all the unconditional love, for teaching me how to be a good husband and a good parent. Thank you, Bryan, for always, *always* being so supportive of what I want to do and helping me find who I am. Thank you for all the countless moments of taking care of the girls while I was trying to relive memories and write down my stories.

Lastly, I want to thank Phoebe, Hanalei, and Chelsie. Although you may not know it yet, you have given me new meaning and purpose in life and enabled me to see through things that don't matter and live life truthfully. My wish for you is that you will have life journeys full of love and courage.

ABOUT THE AUTHOR

100 percent made in China, Nick was shipped to Durham, NC, for his MBA at Duke in 2007. He has over ten years of marketing and strategy experience at SAP, McKinsey, and Microsoft. In 2016, when their first daughter had just turned one and their surrogate was pregnant with twin daughters, Nick quit his job at Microsoft and devoted himself to real estate while raising his family of three girls. He is running two companies today: a real estate sales business (*www.gpsfang.com*) that is the top 1 percent agent in Washington state by sales volume in 2017 and 2018, and a property management business (*www.gpsrenting.com*) that manages over $200 million in assets.

Visit the two dads and three girls' daily life update at www.2dads3girls.com.

ASK AND CONNECT

It is amazing that you are reading this last page of the book! I appreciate your support and hope you enjoy our stories of two dads and three girls.

As mentioned in the last chapter, the best part of human society is passing stories down through the generations. If you think our stories of love and courage help you or could help other people, could you kindly leave a review on Amazon?

Additionally, if you have a story to tell, please go ahead to let the world know! If you want to share your story with me, please email me at hello@2dads3girls.com or connect with me at www.2dads3girls.com.

Thank you and have a wonderful day!

CPSIA information can be obtained
at www.ICGtesting.com
Printed in the USA
FSHW020957150719
60031FS